Black Women against the Land Grab

BLACK WOMEN AGAINST THE LAND GRAB
The Fight for Racial Justice in Brazil

KEISHA-KHAN Y. PERRY

University of Minnesota Press
Minneapolis | London

Portions of chapter 1 and chapter 3 were previously published as "The Black Movement's 'Foot Soldiers': Grassroots Feminism and Neighborhood Struggles in Brazil," in *Comparative Perspectives on Afro-Latin America,* edited by Kwame Dixon and John Burdick, 219–40 (Gainesville: University Press of Florida, 2012); reprinted with permission of the University Press of Florida. Portions of chapter 3 and chapter 6 were previously published as "Politics Is *uma Coisinha de Mulher* (a Woman's Thing)," in *Latin American Social Movements in the Twenty-First Century,* edited by Richard Stahler-Sholk, Harry E. Vanden, and Glen David Kuecker, 197–211 (Lanham, Md.: Rowman and Littlefield, 2008). Portions of chapter 3 were previously published as "Social Memory and Black Resistance: Black Women and Neighborhood Struggles in Salvador, Bahia, Brazil," *Latin Americanist* 49, no. 1 (September 2005): 811–31, and as "The Roots of Black Resistance: Race, Gender, and the Struggle for Urban Land Rights in Salvador, Bahia, Brazil," *Social Identities* 10, no. 6 (2004): 7–38. Portions of chapter 6 were previously published as "'If We Didn't Have Water': Black Women's Struggle for Urban Land Rights in Brazil," *Environmental Justice* 2, no. 1 (March 2009): 9–14.

Excerpt from the Gamboa de Baixo neighborhood political hymn republished with permission of Ana Cristina da Silva Caminha. Excerpt from "o muro" by Oliveira Silveira republished with permission of Naira Rodrigues Silveira. Excerpt from Medea Benjamin and Maisa Mendonça, *Benedita da Silva: An Afro-Brazilian Woman's Story of Politics and Love* (Oakland, Calif.: Food First Books, 1997); republished with permission.

Published by the University of Minnesota Press
111 Third Avenue South, Suite 290
Minneapolis, MN 55401-2520
http://www.upress.umn.edu

Library of Congress Cataloging-in-Publication Data
Perry, Keisha-Khan Y.
Black women against the land grab : the fight for racial justice in Brazil /
Keisha Khan Y. Perry.
Includes bibliographical references and index.
ISBN 978-0-8166-8323-9 (hc)
ISBN 978-0-8166-8324-6 (pb)
1. Women, Black—Political activity—Brazil—Salvador. 2. Urban poor—Political activity—
Brazil—Salvador. 3. Blacks—Brazil—Salvador—Social conditions. 4. Urban renewal—
Brazil—Salvador. 5. Salvador (Brazil)—Politics and government. I. Title.
HQ1236.5.B6P47 2013
305.896'081—dc23   2013029575

Printed in the United States of America on acid-free paper

The University of Minnesota is an equal-opportunity educator and employer.

25 24 23 22 21 20 19   10 9 8 7 6

CONTENTS

Acknowledgments   vii

INTRODUCTION Diasporic Blackness and Afro-Brazilian Agency   xi

1. Engendering the Grassroots   1

2. The Gendered Racial Logic of Spatial Exclusion   27

3. The Black Movement's Foot Soldiers   55

4. Violent Policing and Disposing of Urban Landscapes   87

5. "Picking Up the Pieces": Everyday Violence and Community   117

6. Politics Is a Women's Thing   139

CONCLUSION Above the Asphalt: From the Margins to the
Center of Black Diaspora Politics   169

References   179

Index   197

ACKNOWLEDGMENTS

In some ways the inspiration for this book began when I took Kim Hall's Introduction to Women's Studies at Georgetown University as an undergraduate. I express heartfelt gratitude to her. She ignited my initial interest in black women's thought and political practice, introducing me to the scholarship of Patricia Hill Collins, Audre Lorde, Barbara Smith, and many other black feminist theorists who have influenced my personal politics and the framing of this book. Over the years she has contributed her time by reading my work, applauding as well as critiquing, and giving me crucial advice on how to be a serious scholar and survive the academy.

As the saying goes, it takes a village to raise a child. A village, led by the village chief herself, my mother, Joy Anderson, has nurtured my aspirations as an academic and my intellectual desires. She raised me to be strong like her and the other women in our family. She has taught, by example, how to persevere in the never-ending pursuit of knowledge. She has raised my brothers, "teen prodigy" Kofi and "artiste extraordinaire" Emeka, to shower me with an abundance of love. I also thank my father, Paul Perry, for instilling in me the meaning of a proverb popular in Jamaica: "Labor for learning before you grow old, for learning is better than silver or gold. Silver and gold will vanish away, but a good education will never decay."

Without Ana Cristina, one of the most important leaders of the housing and land rights struggle in Salvador da Bahia, Brazil, the research for this book could not have been completed. Ana Cristina's assistance was priceless. The level of her political commitment to collective social change and the breadth of her political influence in Salvador's grassroots networks are remarkable. I would be an exceptional woman, activist, and scholar if I had only a spoonful of her courage. Because of her, I decided to name the neighborhood and the activists in this book rather than leaving them anonymous. I thank the members of the Gamboa de Baixo neighborhood association who welcomed me into their homes and hearts: Rita, Angela, Adriano, Lu, Lia, Boa Morte, Nice, Lula, Joelma, Dona Iraci, Dona Lenilda, Dona Detinha, Dona Marinalva, Ivani, and Maria José. I hope I have adequately told the stories of their struggle to maintain peace in their community and the city of Salvador. Special thanks go to Ritinha and my friends Simone, Nicelia, and Luciana, who continue to ensure my trips to Salvador are filled with good food, conversation, and laughter.

I am also beholden to Elizete da Silva, João Rocha, and Elizete's niece Janmile Cerqueira, who have been a constant source of encouragement over the years. I am grateful for the friendship of Lazaro Cunha and his family (Silvio, Ana Paula, Dona Silvia, and Marcia), who have been good to me and the many other diasporic visitors I sent to them. Ari Lima, Sales Augusto dos Santos, Vilma Reis, Isabelle Pereira, and Lisa Earl Castillo have been great friends and colleagues in Brazil, and their scholarship and intellectual exchanges shaped and benefited this work.

This book would not have been possible without the intellectual and personal support of the following people at the University of Texas at Austin: Edmund T. Gordon, for his consistent generosity and intellectual insights over more than a decade; Asale Angel-Ajani, who deeply influenced my decision to foreground black women's voices; João Costa Vargas, who guided the development of my ideas on urban space and politics; and Charlie Hale and Angela Gilliam, who encouraged me to think of Brazilians' material reality as not so different from those of black people globally. I thank Paula V. Saunders, my closest friend and colleague while at the University of Texas at Austin. She diligently read every page of my dissertation and taught me the true meaning of friendship and sisterhood.

I credit Sônia Beatriz dos Santos with broadening my thinking about Afro-Brazilian women and black Brazilian feminist thought. Jennifer, Lisa, Miguel, Amanda, and the late Vincent Woodard gave me the necessary community space to thrive as a scholar. Kahlil Hart, the older brother we all should have, introduced me to the diverse Caribbean community in Austin that offered a necessary respite from campus life. I am grateful for his friendship and profoundly appreciate his willingness to try to "reason" with me.

Christen Smith, Erica Williams, Cheryl Sterling, Kim Butler, and Kia Lilly Caldwell are African American Brazilianist scholars who have shared the journey of conducting research in Salvador. Trimiko Melancon, Carol Bailey, and Jonathan Fenderson have supported me in completing this book and in being successful as a young teacher and scholar. Lamonte Aidoo, Ebony Bridgewell-Mitchell, Edizon León, Michelle McKenzie, Lindah Mhando, Karen Flynn, Kamille Gentles-Peart, Luis Ramos, Jermain McCalpin, Silvia Rodrigues, and Robyn Spencer have been wonderful friends who have counseled me through the rough times and helped me move forward.

This project has been supported by numerous research grants and fellowships: the National Science Foundation (NSF) Graduate Research Fellowship, the NSF Dissertation Improvement Grant, the J. William Fulbright Foreign Scholarship (Brazil), the Mendenhall Dissertation Fellowship, the Andrew W. Mellon Postdoctoral Fellowship at Smith College, and the Africana Research Center Postdoctoral Fellowship at Pennsylvania State University. I have received funding from the African and African American Studies Center, the Center for Latin American Studies, and the Department of Anthropology at the University of Texas at Austin and from the Africana Studies Department, the Humanities Fund, the Center for Latin American and Caribbean Studies, the Faculty Development Fund, and the Office of International Affairs at Brown University.

I thank my colleagues in the Africana Studies Department at Brown University: Anani Dzidzienyo, who read every page of the manuscript draft and offered keen insights; Corey D. B. Walker, who has been crucial in my understanding of theoretical contributions to black political thought and Africana women's studies; Deborah Bowen, a cherished friend; and all of my colleagues (Chinua Achebe, Geri Augusto, Karen Baxter, Anthony Bogues, Lundy Braun, Matthew Guterl, Françoise Hamlin, Paget Henry, Alonzo Jones, Michael Ruo, Tricia Rose, Ruth Simmons, Elmo Terry-Morgan, and John Edgar Wideman), who deeply inspired this work. It is hard to imagine my dear sister, Dr. Aaronette White, is not here to share this important achievement with me. This book is just one small example of Aaronette's enormous influence during her short life.

Special thanks go to Margaret Copeley, Rhoda Flaxman, and Tatiana

Nascimento Santos, who encouraged me to stay focused and keep my passion for global justice, and to Javier Escudero in Salvador, who secured the permissions for photographs from *A Tarde* newspaper and allowed me to use some of his own striking images.

Special thanks go to my editor, Jason Weidemann, and to the professional editorial, marketing, and production team at the University of Minnesota Press for bringing this book to press in a beautiful form.

My greatest motivation to finish this book came from my son, Jai, who teaches me so much about everyday joy and love. I extend my appreciation to his father, Jailton, and his grandmother, Dona Iraci, a remarkable woman warrior who led a movement and gave me and many others the courage to carry on political work.

To those important people whom I have forgotten, I hope this opportunity is not the last I will have to thank you in a public forum. I expect my memory will serve me better in the future. Thank you, *gracias, obrigada,* and *merci beaucoup* for your love, generosity, and patience.

Introduction

DIASPORIC BLACKNESS AND AFRO-BRAZILIAN AGENCY

Racial Encounters

One afternoon in August 2000, during a short research visit to Salvador, I accompanied my friends Ana Cristina and Luciana to the Bank of Brazil in Salvador's commercial center. In Salvador to get beyond the ATM lobby and access the tellers, you must first pass through a security door and be scanned by a metal detector. Ana Cristina and Luciana—black women considerably lighter skinned than I—passed through the door. When I attempted to pass, the door locked, and the armed security guard asked me to remove all metal objects from my bag. I removed an umbrella and a key and tried to pass again, but the door locked a second time. I removed a small spiral notebook, but the door locked a third time as a long line formed behind me. Left with an empty bag, a small pair of gold earrings in my ears, and a few miniscule chips of silver fillings in my mouth, I was furious when the female guard demanded that I open my bag a fourth time. Ana Cristina and Luciana protested, but I complied. Finding the bag was empty, she finally allowed me to enter the bank.

As we were leaving the bank, I stopped to ask the guard why I had been singled out for a prolonged security check. Luciana pointed out that she had not removed her cell phone and keys and had walked through the door without setting off the metal detector. I asked the guard whether being detained had anything to do with my being a black woman. As the guard defended the racial and gender objectivity of the metal detector, I noticed that she held a remote control button behind her back that she pressed to open and close the revolving doors. When the manager, a light-skinned male, approached to inquire about my complaints, I said that the security guards were in fact using this manually controlled button to profile bank customers and refuse entry to black people, especially those who were darker skinned. By this time the bank was crowded, and almost all eyes and ears were focused on our fierce discussion about the explicit racism of the bank's security practices. A second armed security guard—a dark-skinned black man—approached us and said, "That's why you all should stay on the streets." The conversation became louder as we denounced racial profiling and the idea that our rightful place was on the streets and not inside the Bank of Brazil. After leaving the bank, we registered a formal criminal complaint of racial discrimination against the bank with the police (Figure 1) and, later on, with the government agency charged with investigating cases of racism.

Later that afternoon, we boarded a city bus to head home, and I gave the bus conductor a five-*real* bill (worth approximately $1.50 at the time). I told Ana Cristina and Luciana that I would pay their fares because I had taken up so much of their time with what should have been a simple visit to the local bank. The conductor held the bill up to the light to check if it was counterfeit. The three of us looked at each other and burst out laughing.

Ana Cristina exclaimed, "Oh man, you too? You're checking a five-*real* bill?" I was speechless. When we sat down, Ana Cristina said to me, "I am a black woman, but spending one day with you in this city makes me realize just how bad things are for black women, especially those who are darker skinned."

I retorted, "Well, that's why I'm glad you're here, so you can be a witness."

She replied, "Right, because otherwise people would think you make this stuff up."

This account of my personal experience with racial profiling at the Bank of Brazil and on the bus illustrates that racism is part of the everyday experiences of Afro-Brazilians and African Americans who conduct research in Brazil. I try to avoid going to banks in Salvador, but if I must, I give my bag to a lighter-skinned friend and walk through the security door empty-handed. We do what we must to avoid the everyday social indignities that black women experience in Brazil. These examples show the reality of how gendered racism, racial consciousness, and antiracism resistance operate. It is especially noteworthy that the players involved in reinforcing racism in these two incidents were both male and female and both black and white. This complexity of antiblack racism is not unlike what has been observed in other majority-black contexts, such as apartheid in South Africa or postcolonial Jamaica.

MINISTÉRIO PÚBLICO DA BAHIA
PROCURADORIA GERAL DE JUSTIÇA

2ª PROMOTORIA DE JUSTIÇA DA CIDADANIA – COMBATE AO RACISMO

TERMO DE DEPOIMENTO

Aos trinta dias do mês de agosto do ano de dois mil, às 18:50 horas, no Centro de Apoio Operacional às Promotorias de Justiça da Cidadania, localizado na rua Arquimedes Gonçalves, nº 400, Jardim Baiano, nesta Capital, perante o Promotor de Justiça infrafirmado, compareceu a Sra. LUCIANA DOS SANTOS, brasileira, solteira, baiana de acarajé, natural de Salvador (BA), nascida em 19/02/1975, RG 06412523 82 SSP/BA, filiação Jaciara dos Santos, residente e domiciliada na Rua Manoel Velho, Casa 01, Fazenda Garcia, nesta Capital, telefone para contato 245-5390, e, compromissada, declarou o seguinte: que no dia 11/08/00, logo após o almoço, a depoente acompanhou sua amiga Ana Cristina e Keisha-Khan, uma norte americana, até Agência Centro do Banco do Brasil, localizada no Comércio; que a depoente e Ana Cristina tiveram acesso sem problemas ao interior da agência bancária, porém quando Keisha-Khan foi passar pela porta giratória, esta foi travada; que Keisha-Khan colocou vários pertences de metal na bandeja e mesmo assim a segurança não destravava a porta; que a segurança queria ver o que continha a bolsa de Keisha-Khan, porém Ana Cristina e a depoente protestaram; que Keisha-Khan estava muito assustada, mesmo porque, ela é estrangeira; que só após muitos protestos, a segurança resolveu destravar a porta para Keisha-Khan Ter acesso ao banco; que após Ana Cristina Ter sido atendida, na saída, mais uma vez a depoente e Ana Cristina protestaram junto a segurança que havia tentado revistar a bolsa de Keisha-Khan, quando um segurança se aproximou e disse que se dependesse dele Keisha-Khan permanecia ainda do lado de fora do banco; que a segurança, no momento em que Keisha-Khan tentava entrar na agência bancária, solicitou que esta abrisse a sua bolsa; que ao saírem da agência, a depoente, Ana Cristina e Keisha-Khan comentaram que havia tido discriminação racial pelo fato de Keisha-Khan ser negra; que Keisha-Khan ficou bastante abalada emocionalmente. E nada mais disse nem lhe foi perguntado razão por que manda esta autoridade encerrar o presente termo, que depois de lido e achado conforme vai assinado por todos.

Luciana dos Santos
Luciana dos Santos

Lidivaldo Raimundo Britto
Lidivaldo Raimundo Britto
PROMOTOR DE JUSTIÇA

FIGURE 1. Racism complaint filed with the Brazilian court, 2000.

Social science research is never a neutral undertaking. My experiences working and living as an ethnographer in Brazil confirm that it is simply impossible for me as a Jamaican-born African American to exclude a discussion of racism and sexism in my ethnographic analyses when I confront these issues in my fieldwork.

Over the past few years, there has been a significant movement into Brazilian studies of African American women like myself who have had to grapple with these issues in their work (for example, Kim Butler, Kia Lilly Caldwell, Rachel Harding, Gladys Mitchell, Melissa Nobles, Tianna Paschel, Christen Smith, Cheryl Sterling, France Winddance Twine, and Erica Williams). The development of U.S. black women's social thought reflects a significant shift in representations of black Brazilian subjectivity, with an increased focus on social justice and women's experiences, albeit from distinct theoretical and analytical perspectives. Like all foreign social scientists, we come from a social context in which notions of race and gender differ from those in Brazil. Our presumed predisposition as black women to systems of discrimination and inequality in the U.S. context brings into question, however, the way we experience and interpret black Brazilian culture and race relations. Critiques of ethnocentrism against analyses of race, racial discrimination, and antiracism struggles (Bourdieu and Wacquant 1999; Camara 1998; Corrêa 2008) almost always target the works of black American scholars (French 2000; Hanchard 2003). This supposed antiethnocentric critique of the positioning of U.S. blacks in social science research represents an ethnocentric perspective insofar as these critics assume that Brazil's black radical tradition is both foreign and geographically isolated from the historical evolution of pan-diaspora politics (Butler 1998, 2011; Hanchard 2003; Vargas 2008). These critiques also reflect a lack of knowledge of the social and economic realities of African-descendant peoples globally, as well as how a narrow research lens obfuscates the similarities of gendered racialized experiences and social justice movements.

Despite critiques maintaining that American black scholars can understand the reality of race and racism from only a U.S. perspective, this book defends the possibility of discussing gendered race and racism within a diasporic continuum, attuned to commonalities and distinctions. As Ana Cristina and Luciana demonstrated when they came to my defense in the Bank of Brazil, "Rather than assuming an enforced commonality of oppression, the practice of solidarity foregrounds communities of people who have chosen to work together" (Mohanty 2003, 3).

Structural Racism and Black Resistance

This book deals explicitly with structural and global power relationships and explores the various articulations of racism throughout the African diaspora. As is evident from my friends' protests against racism at the bank, black women's activism at the community level should not be perceived as a political anomaly. Contrary to popular myth, racial democracy does not exist in Brazil. This book explores a concrete example of state-sponsored racism and violence toward blacks in the forced demolition of urban neighborhoods and the relocation of blacks to the periphery of the city.

Spatial exclusion is at the core of gendered racial stratification in Brazilian cities, and this exclusion produces mass black political organization, as is occurring in the neighborhood of Gamboa de Baixo in the city of Salvador. The racial logic of modernization and urban renewal informed by European models of development nurtures a nostalgic desire for the colonial past on the part of white Brazilians. The threat of the displacement of Gamboa de Baixo began in the 1960s with the construction of Contorno Avenue, which cut off black residents from the affluent neighborhoods, and continued in the 1990s with the mass revitalization of the city center. These events have shaped the political formation of the neighborhood and influenced local activists' need to articulate a politics of land permanence and ownership.

The Gamboa de Baixo neighborhood is representative of a widespread violent struggle for land rights in the city of Salvador. Local activists use their political knowledge to build community and forge group solidarity at the neighborhood level. These are the conditions that create black women's grassroots leadership, although they are often not recognized as political leaders. Definitions of race and culture are integral to this struggle and must include material resources, such as land, that are at the core of the everyday experience of blacks in Salvador. The nexus of political solidarity between neighborhood struggles and black movement activism in Salvador advances the claim that it is black women who lead neighborhood movements and constitute the foot soldiers of Brazil's black movement. Neighborhood struggles are vital to the black movement, specifically for the mass mobilization of black people around issues of material resources such as housing and land rights. Black movement ideas are practiced in the everyday life of Salvador's most marginalized neighborhoods, particularly the positive affirmation of blackness and black womanhood that informs the collective ability to challenge and redefine urbanization policies.

Police violence plays a large role in urban renewal practices in the form of arbitrary demolition, forced expulsion, and displacement, and that violence shapes political activism at the neighborhood level. The act of policing is central to constructing, maintaining, and disposing of black marginalized landscapes and the people who occupy them. Black women of Gamboa de Baixo, such as Iracema Isabel da Silva (Dona Iraci), a former leader of the neighborhood movement who died while fighting the police, have unique experiences with these interrelated forms of urban violence and have historically organized against them.

Examining systematic and structural forms of violence demonstrates how people organize politically for land rights amid rampant police and drug-related violence. In addition to police enforcement and linked to state-sponsored urban renewal practices, the media plays a consequential role in misrepresenting poor black urban spaces like Gamboa de Baixo as dangerous and criminal. Community leaders in Gamboa de Baixo have had to not only contest this distorted view but also struggle—sometimes, to the death—against police abuse. This then brings attention to the nexus of racism and sexism—embedded in the fear of their neighborhood—as well as the marginalization and violence inflicted on the residents of these communities.

Neighborhood movements also highlight the relationship between the racialization and feminization of poverty and the emergence of class-based antiracism activism led by black women. Understanding the complexities and particularities of black women's participation in Brazil's antiblack racism struggles first requires knowing their experiences in that country, specifically their predominant participation in domestic work. Neighborhood-based social movements have become a crucial political site for these black women workers, who are not generally expected to reshape policy or to engage in the global transformation of ideologies and practices of modern urban development.

Hence, the experiences of the female-led Gamboa de Baixo political organization are crucial to understanding the significance of race and gender identity in forging political cohesion and nurturing grassroots feminist struggles. Black women's politics in community organizations support the theoretical link between experience and politics framed within emergent debates around the question of identity politics. Furthermore, neighborhood movements also mark the changing landscape of black politics in Brazil, which includes broader definitions of black culture and forms of black group solidarity informed by gender consciousness. This in turn shows how the knowledge that black women gain from the built environment and their social conditions informs their creative strategies in building more democratic urban landscapes.

Black women's leadership in black grassroots organizations is not limited to a focus on their subjectivities. Black women activists are attuned to the discursive and everyday institutional aspects of racial and gender identity and space as blacks, women, poor people, and residents of the coast. Their views of self and identity are important aspects of waging the struggle for liberation (Gore 2011; McDuffie 2011; Santos 2008; Sudbury 1998). Black neighborhood associations place emphasis, however, on social action that contributes to urban policy reform. They affirm black womanhood as well as the right to coastal lands. An analysis of the political economy of black diaspora communities is crucial for understanding the urgency of black women's political struggle and their demands for the improvement of black communities' everyday material existence (Davies 2006; Fikes 2009; Harrison 2005, 2008; Ulysse 2008; Wekker 2006). My focus on the gendered dimension of black women's activism forces us to rethink black resistance, as well as reconsider how blacks offer alternative views on how African diasporic communities operate and should operate.

Neighborhood movements are at the heart of the black movement in Brazil, a political space in which black women's mass participation and leadership are key. Black neighborhoods such as Gamboa de Baixo in Salvador are where we find vibrant examples of black political thought in action.

From Identity Fetishism to Material Transformation

Although my theoretical grounding in black feminist thought, critical race and diaspora theories, and urban studies crosses several borders, my analysis of black women's activism emphasizes black Brazilian agency, particularly its understandings of race and articulations of antiracism politics. I argue that the complex racial politics of identification are linked to gender and class consciousness and identification as blacks, women, and poor people. For example, neighborhood activists are far from confused about the validity of blackness as a social category, which is often debated among Brazilian and Brazilianist scholars alike. In an informal conversation with Luiza Bairros (now the minister of Brazil's Secretariat for Policies of Promotion of Racial Equality) several years ago, she affirmed that the ambiguity of race and racism in Brazil is an academic problem, not the problem of women, like some in her family, who have been domestic workers for elite white families. Black women who live the very real material nature of the intersections of gendered, racial, and class inequalities hardly debate the need for radical social change in Brazil, nor are they passively waiting for that change to take place.

Given the political saliency of blackness and the struggles that have emerged against racial inequality, why are scholars fascinated with the supposed Brazilian plurality of racial identities when it is not key to how black women in Brazil see themselves? I share many scholars' discomfort with the statistical emphasis on how people identify themselves in Brazil (*Revista Caros Amigos* 2000; Sales Augusto dos Santos 2006; Smith 2008; Vargas 2004). In response to the question of whether the racial perspective is adequate to deal with racial problems, Sueli Carneiro states:

> Look: I am black, and I have absolute consciousness of all the inequalities that my community, that my population suffers, and these inequalities manifest themselves within the reality that we already put forth here: there is a white world and a black world. *How can we assure that policies that promote equality reach the black population without referring to race?* (*Revista Caros Amigos* 2000, 27; emphasis mine)

Carneiro affirms that racial problems are hardly rhetorical, something that she understands as a black woman in her community. Racial problems in Brazil are the result of several generations of systemic social and economic exclusion negatively impacting black people throughout Brazil in both urban and rural contexts. Despite this recognition, the social science focus on identification prevents serious academic attention to racial dysfunction in Brazilian society (Sales Augusto dos Santos 2006). The argument persists that racial identity in Brazil is ambiguous and that there are at least 135 categories of self-identification that have produced a vast color gradient unlike any other nation in the Americas (34). Santos highlights the absurdity of this ambiguity:

> Brazilian intellectuals declare themselves unable to decipher who is black in Brazil, even though the police, the justice system, public and private employers, the media (especially television), and other social groups and institutions can instantly identify blacks when physically and symbolically attacking them, denying them jobs for which they are qualified, and punishing them more severely than their white counterparts for committing crimes of equal or comparable gravity. (37)

When Gamboa de Baixo neighborhood activists began to analyze urban renewal trends in Salvador in the early to mid-1990s, there was a clear racial and class pattern among targets of demolition squads and displacement. Race and class have been the strongest variables in determining which neighborhoods should be completely removed from the new modern spaces of the city center. It has not been difficult for poor black people in Brazil to decipher who is black in Brazil, since they see and feel race and class structures in their everyday lives *na pele* (in the skin). Nor do policy makers, development agents, and the police have much difficulty deciding who is black.

This book does not use the multiracial self-classification model to understand black land rights struggles in Brazil. I believe, as Santos writes, that "through these sociopolitical lenses it is quite possible to identify blacks in Brazil" (40) and to see the tangible effects of the vast racial inequalities permeating black communities (Johnson 1998; Mitchell and Wood 1998; Nobles 2000; Paixão and Carvano 2008; Santos 2008; Smith 2009; Telles 2006).

African Diaspora Anthropology as Solidarity Work

This theoretical stance is the direct result of my participation in the Gamboa de Baixo political organization. Initially, my research in Salvador focused on the popular Afro-Brazilian cultural group Ilê Aiyê. But as I learned more about the issues that impacted the people of Gamboa de Baixo, I came to see the importance, overlooked in current analyses, of grassroots politics against land expulsion in black urban neighborhoods. I saw an opportunity to contribute my time and skills directly to the cause of land rights in Gamboa de Baixo. I attended activist meetings, helped members write and edit manifestos, offered my computer and photography skills, and cleaned sewers. At times I was just one more person to fill a room or to stop traffic in a protest.

This level of activist and scholarly engagement in grassroots social movements in Brazil and throughout Latin America is expected and encouraged among anthropologists (French 2009; Perry and Rappaport 2013; Rappaport 2008). Yet this approach does not mean that I have omitted critiques of movements' ideas and actions or that I have not received my fair share of critiques of my theoretical and practical interventions. After a major rally in front of a government office, for instance, a member of the neighborhood association brought up my participation at the weekly meeting. She said that although my actions were brave, I could have been arrested, which could have led to my immediate deportation from the country. I was embarrassed by my own naïveté but heartened by the group's expression that they would have something to lose if I were unable to return to Brazil.

This book and my ongoing work examine the need for international solidarity with grassroots movements throughout the black diaspora. Research and writing on social movements are crucial aspects of waging struggle, particularly by contributing to the production of knowledge on urbanization policies in Brazil and elsewhere. Kamala Visweswaran's notion of homework, as opposed to fieldwork, is useful for understanding my approach to describing the mobilization of Salvador's poorest residents.

> "Homework" is, I contend, the actualization of what some writers have termed "anthropology in reverse." David Scott has noted that the ethnographic project is characterized by the anthropological journey, which entails a recursive movement between departure and return. It is this "going and returning that organizes the epistemological and geographical disposition of the anthropological gaze." (1994, 102)

Furthermore, Visweswaran claims, "'Anthropology in reverse' then means speaking from the place one is located, to specify our sites of enunciation as 'home'" (104). This book narrates this anthropological journey across black diaspora communities. I represent that journey as being intertwined with the everyday happenings of a social movement currently under way. I want to convey an in-depth sense of the women who drive the community movement in Gamboa de Baixo from the perspective of someone who knew them and shared their friendship and their ideals. This approach to ethnographic writing on black women's politics exemplifies "persistent re-membering and re-connecting" (Davies 1994, 1) as a participant within the spaces I describe. Yet community leaders in Gamboa de Baixo and other neighborhoods on Salvador's socioeconomic and spatial margins are the primary voices we hear throughout. Without the theoretical and ethnographic insights of scholar–activist collaborators such as Ana Cristina and Ritinha, this book would not have been possible. Only these black women can fully describe how land evictions and displacement work in the racist, sexist, and classist urban contexts of Brazil and how the complex process of galvanizing resistance against land expulsion operates.

1

ENGENDERING THE GRASSROOTS

> Our greatest asset in Kenya is our land. This is the heritage we
> received from our forefathers. In land lies our salvation and
> survival. It was in this knowledge that we fought for the freedom
> of our country.
>
> Jomo Kenyatta, 1964 speech in *Suffering without Bitterness*

> I saw in Chicago, on the street where I was visiting my sister-
> in-law, this "Urban Renewal" and it means one thing: "Negro
> removal." But they want to tear the homes down and put a park-
> ing lot there. Where are those people going? Where will they
> go? And as soon as the Negroes take to the street demonstrating,
> one hears people say, "they shouldn't have done it."
>
> Fannie Lou Hamer, 1965 interview in
> "Life in Mississippi: An Interview with Fannie Lou Hamer"

Uma Mulher (One Woman)

On Saturday, May 3, 2003, the front cover of the Brazilian newspaper
A Tarde showed a photo of fifty-three-year-old Amilton dos Santos sitting on top of a yellow bulldozer. His left hand covered his face, which
was hidden by a blue Firestone baseball cap that matched his uniform,
and Senhor Amilton was crying. The headline read, "Um Homem"
(One Man), and the accompanying caption described the dramatic
scene as follows: "The screams of revolt and pain were stronger than
the 20 policemen armed even with rifles."

The day before, in Palestina, a predominantly poor black neighborhood located on the periphery of Brazil's northeastern city of Salvador
in the state of Bahia, six police cars with more than twenty fully armed
military policemen, some with machine guns and rifles, stopped in
front of the two adjoining homes of Telma Sueli dos Santos Sena and
Ana Célia Gomes Conceição. Accompanying a bulldozer and a moving

1

truck, the military police had arrived in Palestina to carry out orders to remove the residents and their belongings from their homes, demolish the houses, and clear the land where Dona Telma lived with her husband, seven children, two grandchildren, and a daughter-in-law. Ana Célia lived with her husband, Edmilson Neves (Dona Telma's brother-in-law); daughter; mother-in-law; and brother. The two families were home when the police and demolition squad arrived, and their neighbors immediately reacted with alarm.

Upon seeing the families inside the houses, the three men who were in charge of moving the residents refused to follow through with the job. The police told the movers that if they did not carry out their duties, they would be arrested. The men then reluctantly worked to load the families' belongings into the truck parked in front of the houses, where a crowd of neighborhood residents, primarily women, had begun to gather and vocalize their indignation. Dona Telma cried uncontrollably as she pleaded with the police and the driver of the bulldozer.

Dona Antônia, Telma's aunt, showed the police officers legal documents certifying that the land had passed from the original owner, already deceased, to Telma's grandmother almost two decades earlier. According to the family, they had always lived on the land. After Dona Telma's grandmother died, the land was bequeathed to her children and grandchildren. Before Dona Telma built her house on the property, the land was undeveloped, and other families occupied adjacent plots, where they built their houses and raised their children. Recently, a Bahian engineer, Adolfo Stelmach, had claimed ownership of the land, saying that he had inherited it. With the support of the courts, he ordered the families to buy the land from him or vacate immediately. Even with documents supporting Dona Telma's claims to ownership, the two families lost all legal battles to secure the land.

Since they had no resources to buy the land and they refused to move, Stelmach ordered that both houses be demolished. The families were unable to meet his demand that they pay more than R$25,000 (approximately $15,000) for the land. They not only did not want to pay the exorbitant amount but simply could not afford it on their meager salaries. Dona Telma asked, "But how am I going to pay if I only earn R$200 per month and the money is not even enough to eat on?" In addition, Dona Telma asserted that they were the rightful owners of the land and that the man who ordered their eviction was a speculator and a thief. The president of the neighborhood association supported the families' claims, and as the crowd gathered around the bulldozer, he said to the media, "[Stelmach] is a land grabber and wants to take possession of everything here. You have to get to the bottom of this." He continued, referencing both the specific families and the general nature of land loss among the *povão* (masses), "The family is poor. We don't have the legal information we need to fight back. The result is what we're seeing—the shark wanting to gobble up us little fish" (*A Tarde,* May 3, 2003).

"He has no heart, but God will not let this happen!" a woman shouted from the crowd. Stelmach, described as heartless and shameless by the families and their neighbors, arrived to oversee the progress of the demolition. Demonstrating the truth of these judgments of his character, he refused to get out of his car when he saw the crowd. He informed the police and the demolition company that they were obligated to follow through with the legal order to destroy the houses and clear what he now considered his land. When Dona Telma's children approached him to show proof of their great-grandmother's ownership, he sped away. As Edmilson Neves later stated to the media, "I hope that later on tonight, with a calm head, Adolfo can think a little and look at our situation" (*A Tarde,* May 3, 2003).

By late afternoon the crowd of protestors in front of the house had grown. Senhor Amilton, the bulldozer operator, turned the key in the ignition. Dona Telma (Figure 2), kneeling in the dirt road with her hands on her head in a gesture of desperation, led the crowd in pleading with him to stop: "Pare, pare, pare!" The screams to save the houses became louder. Overwhelmed by the pressure of the crowd, Amilton sat paralyzed in the bulldozer, unable to put the machine in gear. "For the love of God!" pleaded the women who stood in front of the bulldozer. The police threatened to arrest the driver if he did not carry out the demolition. The police's pressure intensified, and the journalists focused their cameras on the face of the conflicted man.

An employee of the demolition company for more than a decade, Senhor Amilton was there to do his job. Visibly distraught, he remained motionless in his bulldozer as tears trickled down his face. He appeared to be sick, as if about to faint. The police repeated that he

FIGURE 2. Telma Sueli dos Santos reacts as Senhor Amilton turns the key in the ignition to demolish her home in Palestina neighborhood on May 2, 2003. Photograph by Gildo Lima. Courtesy of Agência A Tarde.

needed to carry out the orders to demolish the houses. He mumbled that he suffered from high blood pressure and had a bad heart. "I can't do this. I am a family man and I have nine children," he said, refusing to climb down from the bulldozer to be arrested (*A Tarde,* May 3, 2003). The police surrounded him and continued to threaten him. Shaking, he whispered that he was sick and wanted to be taken to a local health center. Applauded by those at the scene, Senhor Amilton later became known as a hero for standing up to the military police and refusing to carry out the order to demolish the home, even though he faced the threat of being fired as well as incarcerated.

Meanwhile, another woman in the crowd fainted, and Telma's aunt, a recent breast cancer survivor, entered a state of epileptic shock and was also taken to a local health center. The police stayed at the location until another driver arrived to finish the job Senhor Amilton was unwilling to do. Though the second driver was more than willing to demolish the house, facing the tension of the crowd the owner of the demolition company ordered him to turn off the bulldozer and leave the cabin. The owner accused Stelmach of failing to inform him that there were families living inside the houses. He was met with applause from the crowd as he drove away from the swarming media. The two homes and land were safe, at least for the moment.

Salvador, Mecca of the Black Diaspora

Salvador is located on the southeastern shore of the Bay of All Saints (Map 1). With 3 million people in the city itself and another 3.5 million in the surrounding area, it is the third most populous city in Brazil and one of the 120 largest cities in the world. Founded in 1549 by the Portuguese colonialist Tomé de Souza, Salvador was Brazil's first capital until 1763, when the capital was moved to Rio de Janeiro. It was the wealthiest and most populous city in Brazil during the colonial period (1500–1822). Salvador's population was second only to that of Lisbon in the Portuguese empire. It served as the economic center and major port of entry for trade between Europe and Africa, particularly for the importation of African slaves, who were brought to work on the sugar and tobacco plantations in the interior of the state of Bahia. Gold mining became an important economic activity in the early eighteenth century. It is customary to hear Salvador referred to as Bahia, as it is also the state capital.

The city boasts a unique design because of its hills overlooking the bay. It is divided into two levels: the Cidade Alta (Upper City) and the Cidade Baixa (Lower City). The Cidade Alta prided itself on its private residences, institutions of colonial government, and even the first medical school in Latin America. The Cidade Baixa is closer to the city's waterfront and served as the center of commerce and military defense during the colonial period.

Salvador's economy saw a rapid decline after the colonial capital relocated to Rio de Janeiro, and further decline resulted from the reduction of profits in the sugar- and gold-mining industries. Once considered the wealthiest state in Brazil, Bahia has witnessed a steady increase in poverty during the past century. The focus on economic development in the southern regions of Brazil led to uneven urban development in northeastern cities like Salvador, negatively affecting public services such as transportation, housing, water, and sewers (Greenfield 1994, 99).

MAP 1. Salvador, Bahia, Brazil. Map by Lynn Carlson, Brown University, 2012.

In addition to its historic importance and natural beauty as a coastal city, Salvador boasts a vibrant African heritage. Brazil has more than 90 million black people. The population of the state of Bahia and the city of Salvador is 77 percent black (Instituto Brasileiro de Geografia e Estatística 2012). With 2.3 million black residents, Salvador has the largest black population outside Africa, second only to Lagos, Nigeria. Popular Brazilian social thought reflects the beliefs of Bahian anthropologist Ordep Serra and others who refer to Salvador as "the great Black Rome of [French anthropologist of Afro-Brazilian culture] Roger Bastide, mythical Africa of African ancestry, passed on for almost five centuries and making up the cultural quilt of Bahianess" (2002, 25). Bahia and Salvador are widely recognized as the African mecca of the black diaspora, and the Africanity of the region has been overstudied (Capone 2010; Lima 2011; Matory 2005; Pinho 2010). Salvador is the center of Afro-Brazilian culture and has greatly influenced the formation of a global black identity.

European traveler Robert Avé-Lallemant chronicled his visit to Salvador in 1859 and noted the strong African character of the city:

> In fact, there can be few cities with such an original settlement as Bahia. If you didn't know that this city was located in Brazil, you could take it, without much imagination, for an African capital, residence of powerful black princes, in which a population of pure white foreigners goes entirely unnoticed. Everything seems black: blacks on the beach, blacks in the city, blacks in the lower part, blacks in the upper neighborhoods. Everything that runs, shouts, works, everything that transports and carries is black; even the horses of the carriages in Bahia are black. (Avé-Lallemant 1961, 20)

This vibrant imagery of Salvador's blackness, which the writer compares to some African cities where the white population is relatively small, is not surprising. Today, visitors to Salvador are similarly struck by the omnipresence of blackness, black people, and African symbolism on the streets and on the beaches (Pinho 2010).

The observation that blacks carry out the most labor-intensive and often dangerous jobs in the city still resonates. Missing in Avé-Lallemant's account, however, is the recognition of a white-dominated colonial society that subordinated the majority black population. For almost four centuries prior to his visit, Salvador was the largest and most important port for the trafficking of Africans and other goods on the transatlantic trade route. Most enslaved Africans who were forcibly transported to other regions of the Americas and Europe passed through the Bay of All Saints. For Africans worldwide the waters of the bay are an important part of black heritage in the Americas, especially because the Atlantic Ocean was a burial ground for many Africans who died during the crossing. This city, while perhaps the blackest city in all of Brazil and indeed almost the world, has a violent history—evidence of the racial violence of enslavement and colonialism that has shaped racial, gender, and class relations in Salvador to the present day.

Land Rights and Urban Development

State-sponsored reurbanization practices in Salvador have fostered a practice of demolition and removal that has negatively impacted black communities on a mass scale, including neighborhoods located on the coast and in the city center. I began this chapter with the story of Dona Telma and her neighbors in Palestina to illustrate the pervasiveness of the violent expulsion of black families from urban land in Brazil in the name of urban development and the resulting displacement they experience, as well as the methods that residents, often led by women, use to resist these events. The story conveys how intense and traumatic the daily struggle between state and private urban developers— aggressively reinforced by the police—and poor black families can be. In response neighbors mobilize, at the risk of being killed by the police or the bulldozers.

Urban redevelopment is a global problem (Dávila 2004; Davis 2007; Fikes 2009; Gandolfo 2009; Murray 2008; Patillo 2007; Smith 2012). Facing a shortage of unoccupied land for new development, as well as decaying urban neighborhoods on prime city center and waterfront land, governments, land speculators, and commercial enterprises seek to transform these areas for the construction of homes and businesses, for cultural heritage projects, and for tourism. Homes, buildings, and neighborhoods that are considered substandard or crime ridden stand in the way of profit-motivated redevelopment and are targeted for demolition in a process that government agencies refer to as "slum clearance."

Urban spaces are the marked manifestations of racial, gender, and class marginality (Dávila 2004; Gregory 1999; Jackson 2003; Samara 2011; Sugrue 1996; Winant 2001). In Brazil and other areas of the world, these privately owned land parcels and neighborhoods are typically occupied by poor people who oftentimes are established there and have cultivated the land for several generations. Because of racial patterns of poverty and forced segregation, in Brazil these are black neighborhoods. Mass land eviction and relocation during urban renewal is motivated by underlying state-sanctioned racial, class, and gender bias. Cloaked in the language of cleansing the city center or making the city more aesthetically appealing or safer, so-called slum clearance is in essence black clearance, reflecting deeply embedded institutional racism in Brazilian society. The stated official objective may be enhancement of local culture derived from black residents—such as the martial art capoeira, the Candomblé religion, music, dance such as the samba, arts and crafts, and traditional Afro-Bahian foods like *feijoada*—but it is clear that the black people themselves are not. The usurpation of land in the Palestina neighborhood was not an arbitrary act by a few elite white businessmen and urban developers but part of the systemic destruction of black settlements and the pervasive negation of black citizenship that marks Brazilian cities. Salvador's urban redevelopment process, entailing widespread demolition of poor neighborhoods, is a manifestation of the racial, gender, and class differentials that have defined power relations between the majority black and the minority white populations of Brazil since the colonial period (Andrews 1991; Dávila 2003; Garcia 2006; Meade 1997; McCallum 2007).

Urban revitalization in the city center of Salvador during recent decades has consisted of the violent demolition of homes and the mass expulsion and displacement from urban land to the city's periphery. In these inner-city neighborhoods poor blacks maintain social and political networks, as well as contributing to the economic viability of their families. Black women work as domestics in the high-rise buildings nearby; their children attend schools and access hospitals within walking distance; and families buy all the goods they need in markets and shops in the city center. Being forced to relocate to the distant periphery leads to the destruction of their livelihoods, reduced access to vital material resources and services such as hospitals, and the disruption of family and community relationships.

Forced displacement is aided by the lack of legal recourse of residents in poor neighborhoods. In Salvador land grabbing has been a common practice among wealthy white Bahians, who have the financial resources to back up their land claims with the support of the courts. Without an understanding of the legal system or financial means, families like Dona Telma's are often left with no legal remedy. The *povão,* the blacks who occupy Salvador's poorest neighborhoods, are unable to prove their legal right to the land they have lived on for generations.

Signifying more than just the physical space where families live, work, and build social and political networks, urban land represents the ability of poor blacks to pass resources from one generation to the next. As blacks migrate to Brazilian cities in increasing numbers and form neighborhoods, they rearticulate their sense of belonging to and owning these urban spaces. But institutional roadblocks to winning state recognition of land ownership mean that poor blacks throughout Salvador suffer the threat of eviction and violent displacement.

Some black urban communities can trace their origins back to *quilombos,* settlements established by escaped enslaved Africans living as free people in sovereign territories during the colonial period. Those free people (called *quilombolas*), like modern-day blacks, imagined and practiced freedom on land that was not given to them but that they claimed as their own (French 2009; A. Nascimento 1980; M. B. Nascimento 1981, 1985; O'Dwyer 2002; Ratts 2007; Reis and Gomes 1996). Today, the quilombolo identity symbolizes the historical black struggle for "full freedom" in Brazil (Butler 1998). With Brazilian constitutional reform in 1998, the quilombos were granted territorial rights. But gaining legal recognition as a quilombo in order to earn land rights is a complicated process (French 2009), and it may not always be an option or advantage for vast numbers of urban communities.

As rural quilombos gain territorial rights, the majority of black people living in Brazilian cities see the possibility of obtaining land rights as a key means of securing socioeconomic freedom in a racially unjust society. But activists assert that land rights should not predicate on being a descendant of quilombolos. Blacks who have occupied and cultivated Brazilian land throughout the various periods of development and urbanization should also be entitled to land as a basic right. Brazilians can legally claim ownership to land based on *usucapião,* equivalent to the English common-law term *adverse possession,* meaning "acquired by use." According to constitutional law, poor families can acquire property rights after uninterrupted use of the land for at least five years. James Holston writes:

> In Brazilian law (as in American), usucapiao is considered a fundamental guarantee of property rights because, in the last analysis, it supersedes all other claims of ownership, ending doubts and conflicts over tenure. Indeed, in many circumstances of settlement, where proof of ownership may have been lost, nonexistent, or erroneously recorded, it is the only means to do so. (2008, 140)

Black Women as Grassroots Leaders

As a result of the forced demolition of urban neighborhoods and the displacement of residents, urban spaces are terrains of constant struggle for blacks, women, and poor people. Lacking the legal and financial means of countering urban redevelopment, residents of poor black neighborhoods have mounted a significant grassroots resistance against the threat of loss of their land and homes. Organizations such as the Articulação de Comunidades em Luta Por Moradia (Voices for Communities Fighting for Housing Rights), a collective of neighborhood organizations, document state-supported actions like unequal urbanization practices, land evictions, and forced displacement. They attempt to engage local politicians and representatives of nongovernmental organizations in a dialogue with poor black communities struggling for adequate housing and land ownership. They work to counter representations of black urban residents as squatters or invaders who occupy the city's social and geographic periphery without any rights to ownership (Gay 1993; Holston 2008; Perlman 2010; Silva 2012). When all else fails, they develop strategies for resisting demolition when the bulldozers arrive.

In Brazil there is a lack of awareness of the existence and importance of neighborhood political organizations that have emerged alongside formal social movement organizations. Activism by these neighborhood organizations is made to appear spontaneous by the media, as if arising in response to a single incident, but in fact, they are part of a broad movement of organized resistance. Political labor at the neighborhood level is central to the mass mobilization of black people against institutional racism and for citizenship rights and resources in Brazil. Organized community movements for land rights are an important facet of the historical struggle for social and territorial belonging as black citizens in Brazil.

A salient aspect of neighborhood activist organizations is that they are frequently led by black women, yet the important role of women as activist leaders generally goes unacknowledged in the media, while the light is shined on male actors. Many can still remember exactly where they were almost a decade ago when the emotional scene in Palestina unfolded on live television and was repeated on the local and national news for several days afterward. They watched through the glass windows of electronics stores, from the stoops of their neighbors' houses, or from the living rooms of their employers as they cleaned. They watched Senhor Amilton step down from the bulldozer and collectively sighed in relief that he had done the right thing. Many asked themselves if they would have done the same. In a recent news update, Senhor Amilton was asked if he would do the same again today. He replied, "It was a day that changed everything for me and I would do exactly the same again. I have a home, I have a family, and what right do I have to come and pass a tractor over another person's house, leaving everyone with no place to sleep? Without shelter? I have never done this kind of work; I have never been asked to do it" (*iBahia*, November 13, 2011).

The media focus on Senhor Amilton's decision to spare the houses—admittedly, an act of good conscience that merited public recognition—speaks to the general invisibility of poor black women and families who arduously work to mobilize urban communities in defiance of the demolition of homes and the usurpation of land. More than a decade later, in popular memory the incident remains a story about

Senhor Amilton, not about the courageous homeowner who defied the police, Dona Telma.

This invisibility reflects a general lack of knowledge about the lives of black women in Brazil, the brutality of their experiences with systems of oppression, and their painful political trajectories. While black women are at the heart of the struggle for urban housing and land rights in Salvador, they are virtually ignored. From the news media the public learned of the courage of *one man* in the Palestina incident, a notoriety that led to national and international invitations to Senhor Amilton to give lectures and massive support for a political post for him in the municipal government. Yet very little was heard and little is still known about Dona Telma, her neighbors in Palestina, and the numerous other poor black families and peripheral neighborhoods facing similar land disputes.

I met Dona Telma in Salvador during a forum on housing and land rights organized by the Articulação de Comunidades em Luta Por Moradia a few months after the government's attempt to forcibly evict her family. The forum was attended by community leaders from geographically dispersed neighborhoods. Politicians and officials were invited to attend to hear the residents' experiences and speak with them.

At the forum black community activists from around Salvador, the majority of them women, expressed their solidarity with Dona Telma and the Palestina neighborhood. They were in agreement that there was a need to highlight black women's central political role in urban communities. I had been documenting the black-women-led Gamboa de Baixo neighborhood organization and its participation in a city-wide movement for housing and land rights since 1998. Like these activists, I was intrigued by the story of one woman who represented the collective experience of black Brazilian women's violent reality as well as their long history of resistance.

When Dona Telma delivered her speech at the forum, the struggle to keep her home and land had not yet been resolved, and she urgently called for collective action across the city to support her legal claims, as well as those of families unable to formally legalize their land. She described the ongoing fight against displacement and the anger and anguish she felt as a target of the structural violence that black women endure in their efforts to claim rights to land throughout Brazil. She related a brief history of the Palestina neighborhood, aptly named to symbolize the connection between black urban settlements in Salvador that are fighting for territorial rights and the settlements of the Palestinians.

Dona Telma recounted that on the day of the scheduled demolition of her home, she had used peaceful tactics to organize family members and neighbors to defend her. The decision to gather her family, including elderly relatives and children, inside her home was a strategic technique used by neighborhood activists throughout the city. Media coverage of the event had told the public little of her ongoing conflict with the wealthy white businessmen who claimed to own her land, which had begun several years before the military police and demolition squad appeared on her doorstep. The political organization of her neighborhood was presented as a spontaneous incident, when in fact the female-led grassroots movement had long been preparing for the violent confrontation.

While journalists focused on one man and the one moment of the bulldozer driver's bold decision to stop the demolition, not much was said of this calculated, female-led strategic resistance and the politically savvy local population that collectively fought to prevent the demolition. More important, Dona Telma affirmed in her speech, the bulldozer driver's actions should be understood within the context of poor and black people's solidarity with an ongoing urban movement against land evictions. He was also a poor black worker who lived in one of Salvador's peripheral neighborhoods. It happened to be Telma's house and land in Palestina that were targeted, but it could just as well have been his family's house and land under siege elsewhere.

After Dona Telma spoke, Ana Cristina, an activist from the Gamboa de Baixo neighborhood association, boldly asked the audience, "What kind of city do we live in that prepares architects and engineers to demolish homes and expel local populations in order to implement their urban development projects?" The audience nodded in agreement and applauded when she firmly asserted, "The land belongs to the people."

Black women throughout the city fight to preserve the land where they have built their homes, forged social networks, and generated material resources necessary to sustain their families. As a female homeless-movement activist affirmed during an Articulação planning meeting, "I want the right to my own backyard."

Claiming the right to urban land means challenging gendered, racial, and class dominance rooted in colonialism and the legacy of the unequal distribution of material resources. The central focus on black women in these discussions—since to speak of *terra de preto* (black land) is necessarily to speak of *terra de mulheres negras* (black women's land)—remains relevant today (Gusmão 1995; Harding 2003; Castillo 2011), as the story of Dona Telma illustrates.

In Brazil black women are often uniquely positioned because they have both collective memory of residence and, in some cases, legal documentation of ownership of ancestral land. They also serve as the primary mediators of familial and social relations within their communities, influencing political decisions and how important resources such as land are distributed. Historically, in Brazil land has been perceived as *o lugar da mulher* (the woman's place; Gusmão 1995, 109), which helps in understanding black women's political force in land struggles in urban areas.

In Salvador it is mainly women who are interpreting the racial, gender, and class dynamics of urban development policies (Garcia 2006, 2012). This focus on black women's engagement with public policy highlights how their views on development have radicalized local communities to demand justice and social change. They are key political interlocutors between local communities and the Brazilian state for greater access to material resources. They are the foot soldiers of the historical struggle for social and territorial belonging, participatory urbanization policies, and improved living conditions for black citizens in Brazil.

Yet in Brazil and throughout the African diaspora, rarely are black women, especially poor black women, considered leaders of social movements, much less political theorists (Caldwell 2007; Davies 2008; Hamlin 2012; Holsaert et al. 2012; Ransby 2003, 2012; Ratts and Rios 2010; Robnett 1997; Santos 2009, 2012; Silva, Benjamin, and Mendonça 1997; Theoharis 2013). The public image of black women, particularly those who live in poor neighborhoods, is that they lack the political sophistication needed to organize social movements. This image, so different from the reality of black women's actual leadership, stems from women's visible social and economic roles. Black women are celebrated for their role in maintaining Afro-Brazilian culture and religious traditions. The vast majority of black women in Salvador are domestic workers whose work is greatly undervalued (Figueiredo 2011; González 2004; McCallum 2007). In Salvador 96.7 percent of domestic workers are black women (Figueiredo 2011), and most of the black women activists in Gamboa de Baixo do domestic work. Most of the government officials that these activists confront have interacted with black women only as babysitters, housekeepers, and washerwomen in their homes or as janitors in their workplaces. As Cecilia McCallum writes, "Some five million women worked as *empregadas domésticas* (domestic employees) in Brazil in 2001. Their symbolic place is in the kitchen, a stereotype reinforced on a daily basis in the mass media. . . . Many women spend much of their lives in these spaces, thereby reinforcing the symbolic ties of black female gender and domestic work" (2007, 56).

The stereotypical gendered, racist ideas of black women as passive and undereducated servants have been historically tied to the image of them as sexually available (Gilliam 2001; McCallum 1999; Williams 2013). These controlling images of black women are key aspects of the discourses of collective pathology and criminality that are used to police and destroy entire black urban neighborhoods.

The end result of these limited images of black women is that although people are accustomed to seeing them occupy the support bases of social movements—those masses who participate in community assemblies and street protests—they are not envisioned as leaders. And yet the political organization of black urban neighborhoods has depended largely on the leadership and mass participation of women, who use their local wisdom and social networks within their communities to galvanize political support when their homes and lands are under siege.

The Gamboa de Baixo Neighborhood

I first became aware of Dona Telma's story and numerous similar stories while conducting ethnographic research on the female-led grassroots movement in the neighborhood of Gamboa de Baixo in Salvador's city center (Map 2). About 350 families, or 2,000 people, live

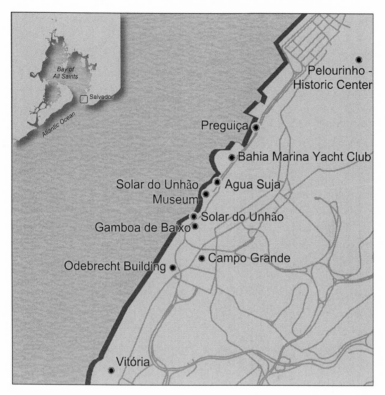

MAP 2. Gamboa de Baixo in Salvador's city center. Map by Lynn Carlson, Brown University, 2012.

in Gamboa de Baixo. The best panoramic view of the neighborhood is from a boat in the Baía de Todos os Santos (Bay of All Saints; Figure 3). Red brick houses with ceramic-tiled roofs spread across the area located between the upper-class neighborhood of Vitória and the Solar do Unhão mansion that houses the Museum of Modern Art. Gamboa de Baixo residents live inside and around the historic São Paulo Fort. All the houses have a view of the bay, Itaparica Island, the small fishing boats anchored near the beach, and the cargo and cruise ships that pass by on their way to Salvador's main port.

The title of this book, *Black Women against the Land Grab,* highlights the Gamboa de Baixo neighborhood's ongoing struggle against land grabbers and for legalized ownership. The neighborhood is located

FIGURE 3. Gamboa de Baixo, as seen from a boat on the Bay of All Saints. Photograph by the author.

underneath Contorno Avenue, along the bay, with *de baixo* meaning "below" or "lower," and popularly described as situated "below the asphalt." The construction of the avenue in the 1960s, a history explained in greater detail later in this book, dramatically shaped the neighborhood's identity within the city and solidified sociospatial hierarchies. The asphalt street displaced the neighborhood and its residents spatially and socially.

This neighborhood exists in stark contrast to the nearby middle-class neighborhood of Gamboa de Cima, with *de cima* meaning "above." The location of this land "below the asphalt street" also conveys the popular representation of the neighborhood as a separate urban subworld, marked by the immoral and illegal activities of black men and women that are obscured from public view by busy Contorno Avenue.

This coastal land is considered prime real estate in the city center, and urban developers have long suggested that it could be revitalized to resemble coastal development along the Mediterranean coast. Traditionally perceived as an undesirable coastal space where black people have lived since slavery times, since the mid-1990s the neighborhood has been targeted for modernization and redevelopment to transform Gamboa de Baixo into a historical and cultural site for domestic and international tourism and leisure. Expulsion of local residents is a key part of the redevelopment process. Under this plan the local population would be relocated to the distant periphery of Salvador.

The Gamboa de Baixo neighborhood is located on the geographic as well as the socioeconomic margins of the city. Its sociospatial uniqueness—a poor black fishing colony squeezed in among the wealth of luxury residences, museums, and yacht clubs—is the primary reason that local residents, led by women activists, are currently caught up in the struggle against displacement and for land rights. Whereas the periphery is oftentimes understood as distant from the city center in neighborhoods like Palestina, the urban periphery represents more than a geographic experience—it represents racial and socioeconomic marginalization. Small brick houses inhabited by fishermen and fisherwomen who anchor small boats in the bay do not belong amid the old and emergent wealth in a revived city center. Paradoxically, although they are far from being privileged, they live in a coveted paradise, *um paraíso cobiçado.*

Many Bahians I talked to claimed to not know where Gamboa de Baixo was located while simultaneously saying that the neighborhood was dangerously violent and drug ridden—a place where *marginais* (criminals) live. Women who work as domestics or store clerks say they have trouble finding work and gaining their employers' trust when they reveal that they live "below" the street. Mothers from the neighborhood have had to fight with school administrators who refuse to admit their children, who they perceive as predisposed to criminality, violence, and an inability to learn.

Thus, in the public imagination Gamboa de Baixo is both visible and invisible, in plain view and out of view, a critical sociospatial relationship that troubles naturalized categories of the periphery and the center. The political meaning of those images is not lost on the black women activists who lead the community movement in Gamboa de Baixo. The asphalt street represents a crucial dimension of the invisibility, marginalization, and abandonment that the neighborhood experiences.

Gamboa de Baixo's location "below the asphalt" focuses critical attention on black women's social location on the periphery of Bahian and Brazilian society. As in Gamboa de Baixo, the majority of black women in Salvador work as domestic servants for middle- and upper-class white families throughout the city. The men and, increasingly, the women earn their living by fishing, by selling their fish to markets, in hotels, and in restaurants *lá em cima* (up above). The fact that neighborhoods across the city have mobilized as the Gamboa de Baixo neighborhood illustrates how widespread efforts are to displace black residents in Salvador. Within this context of widespread violence, Gamboa de Baixo struggles to remain intact as a community.

Gamboa de Baixo women residents such as Ana Cristina are among the key leaders in the Articulação who are fighting for land rights for poor blacks. As Ana Cristina says of the root of their frustration with institutional roadblocks to the legalization of land ownership, "Urban planners, engineers and architects have stated, 'Gamboa is the face of Bahia, but it's not a place for blacks and poor people to live'" (personal communication, 2007). Black women shape the everyday and structural conditions of those living "below the asphalt." The gendered racial and class hierarchies created by the spatial demarcations of the city streets are the very conditions that create a black female–led social movement to combat those inequalities. Thus, black women's politics emerge on the urban margins—specifically, on spatial margins developed underneath an asphalt street.

Rethinking Black Political Culture

Scholarly interest in Brazil, the country with the largest black majority in the African diaspora, in recent decades has brought attention to the complexities of racial, gender, and class politics, specifically the interrogation of the myth of a racial paradise and the historical development of antiracism struggles (Caldwell 2007; French 2009; Goldstein 2003; Hanchard 1994; Sheriff 2001; Twine 1997). The foregoing authors have critiqued the canonical work of Gilberto Freyre (1933) and others who have maintained that neither blackness as a social category nor racism against blacks exists in Brazil. These Brazilianist scholars have documented institutionalized racial discrimination and oppression in Brazilian society in areas such as education and employment.

Their analyses call into question the hegemonic ideology of Brazil's racial democracy, a notion central in Freyre's work.

In the past two decades, much of the scholarship has focused on the supposed paucity of effective political mobilization by Afro-Brazilians against racism. This literature tends to overemphasize the importance of formal black movement organizations (Bailey 2009; Covin 2006; Pereira and Silva 2009; Seigel 2009), often making the claims that no mass social movements exist and that these organizations do not impact the politicization of the broader black population (Hanchard 1994; Twine 1997). France Winddance Twine claims that Afro-Brazilian movements have been unsuccessful because most Afro-Brazilians tend to reject a bipolar racial model and continue to accept the ideology of racial democracy (1997, 9). According to Twine, commonly accepted notions of race and race relations among ordinary people undermine the organization of an antiblack racism movement. The racial order, she concludes, is one of absolute white supremacy in which "Afro-Brazilians are noticeably absent from all positions of power" (1997, 27). While Twine identifies multiple acts of racism in her research, she was surprised to find that Afro-Brazilians fail to recognize aesthetic, semiotic, socioeconomic, and institutional forms of racism. The underlying assumption in her study is that the racial "false consciousness" among Afro-Brazilians should be attributed to their "narrowly defined conceptualizations of racism" (1997, 63). Thus, Twine's central thesis is that nonelite Afro-Brazilians' acceptance of the hegemonic ideology of racial democracy explains their participation in and their lack of resistance to white supremacist structures.

In challenging Twine's assumptions, there has been a tendency to focus on the cultural dimensions of black politics that include identity formation and consciousness, especially the importance of positive affirmations of blackness and African-derived cultural practices and aesthetics (Butler 1998; Harding 2003; Sterling 2007, 2012; Williamson 2012). Diverging from Twine's thesis, the central thesis of Michael Hanchard's foundational text on the Brazilian black movement, *Orpheus and Power: The Movimento Negro of Rio de Janeiro and São Paulo, 1945–1988* (1994), remains unchallenged more than two decades after its publication. He asserts that it simply is not the case that Afro-Brazilians accept the racial democracy myth and have racial "false consciousness." Moreover, he observes that black activists, because of their focus on the politics of Afro-Brazilian cultural practices, have been unable to organize a mass political movement aimed at transforming institutionalized forms of racial inequality. A process in black activism, culturalism is an approach to Afro-Brazilian resistance that hypervalorizes Afro-Brazilian cultural practices as national cultural symbols, but as removed from "the cultural and political contexts from which they originated" (21). Black movements in Brazil are unsuccessful at dismantling racial hegemony, Hanchard writes, because these culturalist political practices commodify and reproduce the very cultural tendencies that sustain the Brazilian ideology of racial democracy. Hanchard believes that whites and nonwhites alike use the culturalist argument—that Afro-Brazilian culture permeates the fabric of the nation—in contradictory ways that end up supporting racist claims of Brazil as a racial paradise.

Folkloric aspects of black culture are suitable for public consumption at all levels of society, but actual black people are not as easily welcomed in those spaces (Collins 2008; Lima 2011; Pinho 2010; Sodré 2010). A national focus on black culture in political movements does not necessarily dismantle racial hegemony nor conceive of notions of citizenship that affect concrete black subjects. In addition, when black activists do make some attempt to shed light on the histories and processes of consciousness that produce Afro-Brazilian culture, they are overlooked as contributing to the hegemonic values of Brazilian racial democracy that they fight against (Hanchard 1994, 21).

Both of these scholarly trends offer a limited definition of Brazilian blackness, which points to a need to grapple with identity issues as well as the material concerns at the heart of black antiracism struggles in Brazil. Grassroots activism against displacement and for land rights is an example of the kinds of black politics that have emerged alongside formal social movement organizations such as the Movimento Negro Unificado (MNU; United Black Movement) and União de Negros pela Igualdade (UNEGRO; the Black Union for Equality). Recognizing the existence and central role of community-based movements in black politics, Hanchard (1994, 2006) argues, is critical for advancing the racial, gender, and class interests of entire black communities. Race is very apparent in the neighborhood movements and the central role of black women's political participation further illustrates how black women have always organized through these grassroots political networks, oftentimes as leaders, to address the everyday and institutional concerns of their material existence (Garcia 2006, 2012; Hautzinger 2007; Santos 2008). Mobilizing around resources such as housing, land, clean water, women's police stations, and health care—key demands made by black women activists—shows that the grassroots base and leadership of the Brazilian black movement work to broaden the definition of citizenship to include not just culture but also concrete material resources. The widespread existence of neighborhood activism debunks the notion that there are no mass black social movements of any consequence or that if there are, they are culturalist movements. Hanchard asks black Brazilian activists to do the political work that already actually exists (Bairros 1996; Garcia 2006, 2012; Smith 2008; Vargas 2010).

Grassroots activists' fight against institutionalized forms of racism does not suggest that black culture is not a central concern for them. In fact, for black women activists—oftentimes hypersexualized as potential prostitutes or rendered invisible as always-available domestic workers—the material aspects of the gendered racism that determines their class status is intricately tied to representational aspects of gendered racism (Gomes 1995; McCallum 1999; Santos 2008; Williams 2013). Black women activists do express explicit interest in maintaining positive aspects of black womanhood such as natural hair, oftentimes a key marker of blackness and a source of discrimination and low self-esteem (Caldwell 2007; Gomes 2008). Neighborhood activists promote, however, a definition of black culture that belies the scholarly and cultural nationalist definition of culture as devoid of political attention to the acquisition of resources such as land and housing. This is quite distinct from the cultural artifacts such as music, dance, religion, and food that have been widely accepted as part of the repertoire of black consciousness or even Brazilian national plurality.

Black culture, for black women who lead neighborhood associations in the Gamboa de Baixo coastal community in Salvador, for instance, means being century-old land owners, fishermen and fisherwomen, divers and seamen. Black culture is understood as deeply tied to coastal lands and the sea where African-descendant traditions have flourished. More important, living, working, attending school, and playing in the city center are significant to how they understand themselves as black men, women, and children. Black culture is the community formed in blackness, place, occupation, livelihood, and everyday life and structured around race, class, and gender. This is the black culture under attack by the redevelopment agencies, the police, and the demolition squads, and this is the black culture neighborhood activists fight to preserve.

The tendency to see black politics as legible only when formed around cultural citizenship renders invisible the neighborhood associations and domestic-worker unions that comprise the black political masses, and it demonstrates a complex relationship of legitimacy deeply tied to racial hegemony. Scholars of black social movements do not read these issue-based struggles as part of the black movement, because they have been able to understand political movements only as cultural or identity movements for recognition. Major black organizations do focus on cultural recognition and do represent the kinds of cultural movements that have efficacy on a mass scale (Agier 2000; Pinho 2011; Williamson 2012). For instance, Ilê Aiyê was founded in 1974 in the Liberdade neighborhood of Salvador to preserve and valorize Afro-Brazilian culture. It is best known for its carnival group, formed in response to racial exclusion at festivals, which promotes unique African rhythms and dances.

As a result of this cultural purpose of major organizations, scholars may not be aware of what is taking place in local communities, because they are looking only at certain kinds of cultural movements. If, as the opening conflict illustrates, urban land and territorial rights struggles represent a major problem for black people in Brazilian cities, then why are they unrecognized as struggles around race and culture? Why has so much of the scholarship on Afro-Brazilians focused on cultural politics when forced land expulsion and displacement constitute a violent aspect of the everyday black experience in cities such as Salvador? To fully understand antiblack racism, a deeper understanding is needed of the exclusion of blacks from the spaces that form the core of their everyday lives.

The invisibility of local black political activism is evident in the scholarship on black Brazilian social movements, but the hypervisibility of cultural movements is also the consequence of how racial hegemony operates in Latin America. Black social movements focus on cultural recognition in order to confront racial invisibility and whitening ideals promoted as part of the national culture. The state recognizes black social movements as black movements only when they are framed in terms of cultural citizenship. Consequently, blacks organize around cultural recognition to meet state requirements and to garner state resources such as land rights (French 2009; Ratts 2007).

In Salvador this is evident in cultural organizations such as Ilê Aiyê and Olodum. Like Ilê Aiyê, Olodum was established in the 1970s to offer African-centered alternatives to Afro-Brazilians during the racially segregated carnival festivities. They are best known for their percussion courses and became world renowned when they performed in the Michael Jackson video for the song "They Don't Care about Us." Those organizations receive much more state financial support than does the Steve Biko Cultural Institute, founded in Salvador in 1992, which prepares Afro-Brazilian students for university entrance exams and raises awareness of the antiracism struggle.

Thus, black politics are legible only when they take a cultural form. The state recognizes these movements precisely because they fit into the kinds of cultural categories that are used to exclude blacks in the first place. Land rights struggles go unrecognized as struggles around race, reinforcing a tacit agreement that racism is about a lack of cultural recognition or a politics of national belonging rather than citizenship rights and access to material resources. Nations such as Brazil recognize blacks and Afro-Brazilian culture as part of the national fabric, but only certain aspects of black culture—not including blacks as urban land owners or consideration for the spaces where black culture is produced.

Exploring black activism, gender identity, and grassroots activism allows us to recognize the existence and central role of community-based movements in black identity politics. Foregrounding the political identity of black women in Salvador illustrates the ways in which grassroots organizations have advanced the racial, gender, and class interests of entire black communities. Racial consciousness in the Gamboa de Baixo community movement is the unquestionable result of the central role of black women's activism. Studies on black politics must include in their analyses social movements that have significant participation and leadership on the part of women and blacks, as in neighborhood associations.

Black Brazilian feminist scholar and activist Sueli Carneiro asks, "Why did black women reach the conclusion that they had to organize themselves politically in order to face the triple discrimination as women, poor people, and blacks?" (*Revista Caros Amigos* 2000, 27). Black women in Brazilian black social movements recognize the importance not only of racial and gender inequality but also of class-based struggles over material resources in their urban communities. In partial contrast with culturally oriented politics, black women activists in Gamboa de Baixo focus on issues of basic survival for black communities. They perceive housing and land as vital material resources, and through community networks they expand their grassroots political organization to mobilize against the racist practices of urban renewal. The next chapter outlines the exclusionary practices of urban redevelopment that have been the impetus of black mobilization.

2

THE GENDERED RACIAL LOGIC OF SPATIAL EXCLUSION

The dissemination of a culture of exclusion . . . principally towards the black and poor population, distances it farther and farther from the so-called "privileged" areas of our city.

Gamboa de Baixo neighborhood association flyer

Brazil as a nation proclaims herself the only racial democracy in the world, and much of the world views and accepts her as such. But an examination of the historical development of my country reveals the true nature of her social, cultural, political and economic autonomy: it is essentially racist and vitally threatening to Black people.

Abdias do Nascimento, *Brazil: Mixture or Massacre? Essays in the Genocide of a Black People*

"How Salvador Is Made"

In December 2002 I joined activists of the Articulação por Moradia on a tour of the city of Salvador to see *como Salvador se faz* (how Salvador is made), the title of the document they produced a few months later at the forum described in the previous chapter. The group was primarily made up of community leaders belonging to a newly formed citywide coalition of neighborhood associations. This was no ordinary tour: their neighborhoods—Ribeira, Mangueira da Ribeira, Marechal Rondon, Dique do Cabrito, São Marcos, Pau da Lima, Gamboa de Baixo, and Alto de Ondina (Map 3)—are not included on traditional tour routes for national and international visitors to the city. These grassroots activists had joined forces to fight against the arbitrary and violent actions of the state development agencies. The tour was part of the political training for both experienced and inexperienced activists in the group. This united effort to expand their knowledge of the city would help them understand the lived experiences of poor black

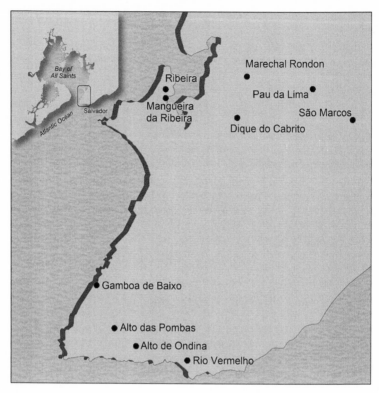

MAP 3. Neighborhoods involved in the city tour and the citywide movement for housing rights. Map by Lynn Carlson, Brown University, 2012.

neighborhoods facing demolition, land expulsion, and displacement. The knowledge gained on the tour changed these activists' view of the city and strengthened the coalition against the racial politics of spatial exclusion.

Rita de Cássia Pereira Santa Rita (nicknamed Ritinha), who held two jobs as both a social worker at the Center for Social Action Studies (CEAS) and a public school teacher, an activist of Alto das Pombas, picked up Gamboa de Baixo activists on Contorno Avenue. Ana Cristina, Lu, and her infant son squeezed themselves into the station wagon and headed to Ribeira to join the others. They thought they might have missed the tour bus, but most of the activists did not live near the city center and public transportation from their neighborhoods wasn't always reliable, especially on the weekend.

Luciana, the president of the neighborhood association in Alto de Ondina, exclaimed when she arrived that though she lived relatively close to Ribeira, she and her neighbors had walked several kilometers to reach the bus stop. Alto de Ondina is one of the largest neighborhoods in the city, but there is no public transportation that provides direct service to Ribeira. Luciana also said that mobilizing other members of her neighborhood association to participate in an all-day activity on a Saturday had been an arduous task. Some struggled with leaving their household responsibilities on one of the few days they had off from work. The other women listened and nodded in agreement, as they knew the sacrifice of leaving home, and a few of the women, like Lu, had brought their young children.

Two hours after the scheduled departure time, we settled into an old bus to begin the tour. This bus was nothing like the new shuttle buses that transported tourists and the local elites between the Historic Center, the coastal neighborhoods, and the international airport. The group was embarking on an important political lesson in unequal urban development and racial stratification in the city of Salvador. These Articulação members had named the tour Knowing the Communities, but they all agreed that a better name would have been Knowing the Ill Effects of Revitalization and Gentrification.

We started our tour in Ribeira. The bus pulled up at the main beach, which was undergoing revitalization by the state development agency, Companhia de Desenvolvimento Urbano do Estado da Bahia (CONDER; the Urban Development Company of the State of Bahia). A Ribeira community representative described the neighborhood's conflict with the state over the revitalization project. He explained that Ribeira was a beach area that attracted blacks and people from the *bairros populares* ("popular neighborhoods," meaning where poor people lived). The revitalization plan for the area involved drastic physical restructuring of the beach front and the adjoining ocean floor. These changes threatened to destroy the ecosystem and artisanal fishing and other professional and leisure activities on which surrounding communities depended. Ritinha observed, "We must understand the implications of these projects to be interrelated in terms of race, gender, and class." She said that black communities throughout the city faced the loss of public spaces for work and leisure. In the past few years, the renewal of public spaces like beaches and parks in Salvador had displaced poor blacks and denied them free access to spaces near their homes.

Ritinha reminded the group that as community leaders they needed to be attentive to the question of gender during this all-day political-formation workshop. She pointed out that although women worked in these community organizations, the men usually represented and spoke for the communities in public forums. She asked, "Will we hear the women speak throughout this day?"

The tour next stopped in the neighborhood of Rua Mangueira da Ribeira (also known as Ribeira LeBlanc). A male community representative introduced the neighborhood by saying, "Here in Mangueira we have true apartheid." This area of the city is known for its *palafitas,* wooden houses built on stilts, some above piles of garbage and polluted seawater. Often the feature of newspaper articles, especially related to fatal fires, the palafitas are considered Salvador's poorest form of housing. They are also notorious because of the governments' multiple attempts to restore the area and relocate the residents inland. The activists expressed shock when they realized that the apartheid in this case was literal: there was an actual rope in the water that marked the separation between the palafitas and the local shipyard. This neighborhood was chosen as part of the government's projected "cleanup" plans for the area, which included the removal and relocation of families, as well as a shopping center for marine supply stores to be built adjacent the shipyard. Previous attempts at relocation to the distant periphery of the city failed because some residents returned shortly after to reconstruct their homes on wooden stilts.

This visit to the palafitas sparked a discussion among the activists on the meaning of "housing" and the struggle for housing rights. They saw the houses built on stilts and the everyday lives of people there, including a *terreiro* (a sacred place of worship for Candomblé practitioners) and a reggae bar, but they asked if this was adequate housing for their communities. Was this what they were fighting for? According to development agencies, living on wooden stilts was altogether unacceptable, but was it possible to imagine palafitas as dignified housing?

While they acknowledged the problems with poor infrastructure, pollution, and trash, land expulsion was not the only alternative for appropriate urbanization in Mangueira da Ribeira. One activist asked, when they waged their struggle for housing, did they have the defense of the palafitas in mind? In the ensuing discussion, it was acknowledged that these kinds of houses were common in the Amazon region, Central America, and Asia and that with proper infrastructure this form of architecture was a viable option for urban living.

Although all of the activists were from poor neighborhoods throughout Salvador, as one activist admitted openly, the sight of "other people's poverty" was very sobering and seemed more distressing than their own.

The bus left Mangueira da Ribeira for the neighborhoods of Marechal Rondon and Dique do Cabrito. The debate about a more expansive definition of housing rights again emerged when they arrived. Marechal Rondon, in stark contrast with Ribeira and Mangueira da Ribeira, is massive in physical size and population. Located approximately thirty minutes by bus from the city center, this hilly area has a more rural landscape. The houses had extensive yard space with lush vegetation such as mango and coconut trees. The socioeconomic differences among the communities visited throughout the day were visible here. Unlike the palafitas of Ribeira, many of the houses in Marechal Rondon were large, and almost all were made of concrete. The level of education and employment among the activists, some of whom had college degrees and owned their own businesses, was reflected in their homes and in how they presented their political project. Still, this neighborhood was diverse and had some of the same problems with inadequate housing and sewer systems, poor schools, and high unemployment and crime rates. The struggle for the right to own the land these families had occupied for generations was a common struggle.

The Articulação members stopped in the yard of tour member Angela's family, where her mother told them about her life in Marechal Rondon and how the development projects were going to affect her family and her neighbors. She stressed the freedom her grandchildren had to play in the yard and climb trees, and she asked some of the children running around to pick some jambo, a dark red fruit similar to an apple, for the visitors to eat.

The municipal government planned to "revitalize" the dike, a water-way that runs though the neighborhoods of Marechal Rondon and Dique do Cabrito, by filling it in and creating leisure spaces like playgrounds and bike paths in its place. Meant to imitate the newly restored Dique dos Orixás, located near the city center, the project also promised sanitation and transportation, and a "revived" local history and culture. The government also planned to build a highway linking the dike to federal highways and future metro stations.

Not completely opposed to the betterment of their community, the activists questioned the urgency of the project and the lack of local participation in the planning. Residents wanted to know why the revitalization of their dike and the displacement of hundreds of families was important at that particular moment in time. For community activists the project was arbitrary and unnecessary for both the beautification and the technical improvement of the area. Claudia and Angela, two of the neighborhood's leading activists, said that the prospect of losing the houses and land in which they had invested over several generations provoked fear and would continue to motivate political action. They wanted to defend the pleasant aspects of their daily lives and rally the residents to fight against demolition and relocation.

The next stops on our tour were the rural periphery neighborhoods of São Marcos and Pau da Lima. Here, a national highway was built that blocked the drainage of rainwater and caused flooding, displacing families. Residents were also concerned about a prison that had been constructed in their neighborhood. The situation in these areas summed up the conflict between the residents' desire for better living conditions and the government's perspective that redevelopment could be achieved only by displacing residents and that it was not necessary to involve them in planning.

As spokespersons for Pau da Lima talked about the failed development projects, they emphasized that residents were not opposed to improved housing and sanitation. The government ignored the specific needs that they voiced, however, and the construction caused further damage to an already deteriorating sewer system, resulting in rising floodwaters during the rainy season.

Seeing the political tourists, resident Dona Rosa came out of her house to share her story. She showed us the contaminated well water and the damage that floodwaters had caused to her home. A partially constructed sewer system, low payments for demolished houses, displacement to an even more distant periphery, and social abandonment exemplified the problems these neighborhoods faced during urban revitalization in Salvador.

The next stop on the tour, Gamboa de Baixo, was a crucial introduction to the aftereffects of state interventions in community development, particularly the exclusionary practices of the state development agencies. Tour participants learned about the initial lack of community involvement in the plans to revitalize the oceanfront, threats to move the population to the fringes of the city, the battle that followed to gain access to information on the project, and political mobilization against land expulsion. The community demanded an urbanization plan that included land ownership and the right to live in their homes permanently, as well as the construction and improvement of housing and sanitation.

Only five years after the beginning of the neighborhood improvement project, however, the Articulação witnessed for themselves the deterioration of poorly built houses, some of which were no longer fit for habitation. Ana Cristina spoke about difficulties mobilizing residents to participate in community politics, negotiating with arrogant and racist state representatives, and convincing the development agency to return to fix the problems they caused or left unresolved. After the somewhat abridged lesson on the ongoing struggle for permanence and improved living conditions in a poor black neighborhood located in the economically booming city center, Ana Cristina made the activists promise to return for a swim and a *moqueca,* a typical Bahian fish dish made in palm oil and coconut milk. She boasted that fish was abundant in Gamboa de Baixo, before they left for their final neighborhood, Alto de Ondina, where a feast of *feijoada* and *mocotó,* typical Bahian meat dishes, awaited them.

The last neighborhood on the tour, Alto de Ondina, reminded the group of Gamboa de Baixo because its residents had confronted some of the same invasive state interventions. Alto de Ondina is much larger in physical size and population than Gamboa de Baixo and most of the neighborhoods on the tour. Alto de Ondina is located on top of a hill above the upper- and middle-class neighborhoods of Ondina and Rio

Vermelho and Oceanic Avenue, a main tourist street lined with hotels, restaurants, night clubs, and stores. Luciana, the neighborhood association president, led the community tour. She highlighted the physical beauty of the area overlooking the bay and its proximity to the governor's mansion and the state zoo. It is this coveted ocean view that has made the area a target for land speculation and state claims to ownership. Of all the areas the Articulação visited that day, Alto de Ondina had suffered the most instances of arbitrary and violent demolitions by the state over the years. After many generations of living on the land, residents had expanded their houses to accommodate their growing families. Many times, hooded police officers invaded their community, accusing homeowners of trespassing on government property and demolishing their houses. Like Palestina, Alto de Ondina organized to fight against the violent demolitions and for the right to land ownership. They used similar political tactics, such as mobilizing members of the media to film demolitions and occupying the houses under siege.

The real intentions of the state in Alto de Ondina were evident in its recent project, called Cores da Cidade (City Colors). To beautify the coastline, the government painted the brick houses a variety of pastel colors while leaving the interiors without basic infrastructure such as running water and toilets. This attempt to revitalize the poor community located amid the wealth of luxury apartment buildings exemplified the government's sole preoccupation with the appearance of the coast for the elite and tourists. Luciana exclaimed, "This is a mask so that everyone below can see everything as beautiful." Residents struggled to participate in the implementation of projects like these, demanding more than a superficial improvement of the neighborhood.

At the top of the hill of Alto de Ondina, the Articulação ended its city tour and engaged in a wrap-up discussion about common problems with urbanization plans throughout the city and strategies to organize a collective movement for greater participation in those projects. Getting to know their communities meant knowing the realities of the impact of state actions. The activists declared CONDER the main culprit. In all the communities, it had planned to destroy or had already destroyed homes, vital aspects of local culture, and means of economic survival for their populations. As community activists, they declared that they were willing to collectively take on the struggle for equal and participatory development in the face of racist and violent practices in Salvador.

The Articulação's tour of Salvador marked the emergence of a citywide struggle that transformed community activists and neighborhood politics throughout the city. The revitalization of Gamboa de Baixo and the threat of losing land rights represent only one experience in a city with destructive urbanization practices that exclude by race and class. These activists' experiences illustrate the multiple facets of Brazilian racism as manifested in urbanization programs in Salvador's black neighborhoods on the coastline, in the city center, and on the periphery.

The Visibility and Invisibility of Blackness

While many writers have portrayed Salvador as a happy and naturally beautiful black city in the African diaspora, urbanization reveals that it also is a city saddened by disparities in wealth, the intrinsic segregationist policies that govern the region, and the racialized and gendered implications of social and economic development. Salvador is a city of contrasts: "The city of Bahia is unequal and contradictory. Happy and sad, rich, poor, and miserable. Beautiful and ugly" (Serra 2002, 25). The leader of the carnival group Ilê Aiyê, Antonio Carlos Vovô, reminds us, "It is important to have a voice of happiness, of festivity, of animation, but we need to have a voice of citizenship with equal rights" (Vovô 2002, 92).

Although blacks are everywhere in this majority-black city, it is difficult to find blacks in positions of political and economic power, such as public office, executive positions in banks, or even store clerks in shopping malls (Dzidzienyo 1979; Mitchell 2003; Oliveira 1999; Reis 2008a; Santos and Silva 2006). In many respects the massive black population still carries the burden of centuries of enslavement and social marginalization. In a city where blacks predominate and where Afro-descendant cultural forms define Bahian identity, how can these vast inequalities between blacks and whites be explained? In 1999 a group of professors from the Federal University of Bahia (UFBA), along with community leaders and laypeople, met to tackle this question in relation to contemporary urban politics, specifically the challenges of social exclusion for poor black communities. The rapid transformation in urban development is designed to enhance the interests of traditional elite groups and the nouveaux riches, while the poor black majority of the population is forgotten. This process of forgetting is essential to the social construction of the city, creating in essence two cities, a "visible city as much as an invisible city" (Serra 2002, 17). The two cities of Salvador—created by elite white architects, engineers, developers, and builders and marked by race and class—struggle to coexist.

The invisible city is the product of constructed concealment (*ocultação construída*). On the one hand, Salvador is known for its extreme visibility, attracting visitors to its natural and cultural beauty, including its beaches and hillsides, as well as Afro-Bahian performances and street festivals that create a "visible spectacle" for all to enjoy (Cordiviola 2002, 35). On the other hand, in describing Salvador, Chango Cordiviola cites Angel Rama's key text *La ciudad letrada* (The lettered city; 2002), in which he argues that an invisible city can exist within that sociospatial order of hypervisibility:

> It is impossible not to refer to the power of concealing the visible as customary. And, in this sense, the extreme visibility of Salvador makes it so that, as a matter of habit, its contrasts end up becoming invisible in the eyes of the everyday. For this reason, the exercise of estrangement becomes fundamental in urban praxis. (quoted in Cordiviola 2002, 35)

Invisibility is the direct result of extreme visibility—a dual construction formalized by the legal system and the local bureaucracy that determines what the city is, what the city should be like, while hiding the things, places, and people that do not belong in the new social order.

The extreme visibility of the city depends on the invisibility of unwanted elements. In Salvador and in most Brazilian cities, urban planning is a chief political instrument of cultural order. These projects make black communities visible because they stand in the way of urban renewal, and removing them maintains a racialized, gendered, and class-based social order that keeps the city tidy. The expulsion of blacks from urban neighborhoods simultaneously recognizes the visibility of blackness and attempts to make that blackness invisible.

The interplay of visibility and invisibility in the city of Salvador explains the logic of urbanization ideologies and practices as well as the experiences of poor black communities confronting expulsion. Gamboa de Baixo represents one example of how a predominant black population can simultaneously be visible and invisible, included and excluded, a majority and a minority. It is a neighborhood that is socially and geographically visible in many regards but that is also ignored and abandoned in key historical moments that render the space and its residents invisible.

Contorno Avenue Divides a Community

The construction of Contorno Avenue by the technocratic military regime in the 1950s and 1960s was crucial in making Gamboa de Baixo and its residents invisible both spatially and socially. Connecting the commercial zone of Cidade Baixa and the affluent neighborhoods of Canela and Campo Grande in Cidade Alta, it has become one of Salvador's most important roadways (Leme and Fernandes 1999). At the time of its construction, newspapers reported that the new road was one of the most beautiful of all Bahian urban streets because of its picturesque view of the Bay of All Saints, which defines the city of Salvador. Contorno Avenue represented the state of Bahia's most "modern dimension" and was the ideal model for other roads in Salvador (Leme and Fernandes 1999, 353).

The construction of Contorno Avenue exemplified two essential processes for achieving the goals of urbanization in Salvador: "the technical, displayed in the search for fluidity and healthfulness of physical and social environments," and "the aesthetic, instrumentalized in a perspective of formation of a new city and a new sociability" (Leme and Fernandes 1999, 167). A journalist for the local newspaper *A Tarde* wrote in 1959, during the road's construction, "This avenue, besides serving to decongest traffic and preventing Salvador from being just a 'one-road city,' will be more than a tourist attraction to contribute to our capital, endowed with so many natural resources waiting to be enjoyed and valued." As a technical and aesthetic improvement to the capital city, Contorno Avenue expanded the commercial center and established the social and environmental aspects necessary for increasing tourism in Salvador.

Most reports presented Contorno Avenue in terms of natural and technical beauty, progress, and economic prosperity. Few mentioned the impact its construction had on the black population that lived in this coastal region. As older Gamboa de Baixo residents remember, the government did not consider them in either the planning or the construction phases of the avenue. Homes were demolished, and the government undercompensated owners for the huge amounts of land appropriated. The construction of the road laid the groundwork for further problems that communities located along the avenue faced in the 1990s with urbanization programs. A reporter for *A Tarde* mentioned briefly in 1961 that near the beginning of the road "a house stands intact in the middle of the street, though in precarious situation due to the demolitions of the neighboring houses." The article also reported that the engineer directing the construction project informed government officials that "the proprietor asked for a very elevated price for compensation."

In 1969 *A Tarde* presented a disparaging report that described the population living literally below the street after the completion of Contorno Avenue. The journalist depicted the community as primarily comprising thieves, prostitutes, and the "feeble-minded" who lived in dilapidated and overcrowded housing structures without basic sewer systems, running water, or electricity. The more dangerous, he claimed, lived under the street's concrete arches. In contrast, he wrote of hundreds of other families (including civil servants and students) who lived on small streets closer to the beach front and in the ruins of the old navy fort. Though his piece displayed dismay at the lack of sanitary conditions, he did recognize the existence of a small fishing settlement that actively contributed to the economy of Salvador. In general, the article expressed disapproval of what he called a "*favela* [shanty town] of marginality" existing in plain view in the center of a reviving city. Gamboa de Baixo's social and geographic location, he communicated clearly, was a "challenge to a civilized city." The journalist's portrayal of Gamboa de Baixo is only one example of misinformation and a negative stereotype that the print media has generated since the construction of Contorno Avenue. Disparaging public opinions have lingered since that time.

As this newspaper report suggests, on the surface decayed urban communities such as Gamboa de Baixo remind the rest of Salvador of its undesirable past. Pejorative descriptions of Gamboa de Baixo as an uncivilized element of the city holding back a thriving and continually urbanizing Salvador have had material consequences for local residents. "Gamboa was one community before the construction of Contorno Avenue in the sixties and seventies," one elderly woman who has lived there since birth explains. Gamboa "was marginalized by the passage of Contorno Avenue, bringing to the residents oblivion and even discrimination in relationship to the rest of the city," residents wrote in a 1996 communiqué. The division of Gamboa into two sectors, lower and upper, has served to uphold hierarchies of racial, social, and economic differences between the two neighborhoods. The construction of the street constrained the previously unrestricted movement of communication, labor, and goods. Only in the mid-1990s did the government construct a staircase that provided access from Gamboa de Baixo to the rest of the city. Most residents can still remember the difficulty of climbing the shaky wooden stairs to reach Contorno Avenue and the rest of the city. Infrastructural changes within the city separated and isolated them as those below. Elena, a woman in her midthirties who has always lived below, points out that some women work as domestics in Gamboa de Cima and nearby neighborhoods, such as Vitória, that literally look down on their homes in Gamboa de Baixo. Even today, identifying Gamboa de Baixo as one's place of residence might prevent a person from getting a job because, as she states, some employers "still think we're all thieves."

Sentiments of inferiority and superiority have run deep since the separation of Gamboa de Baixo from Gamboa de Cima by Contorno Avenue, demonstrating that the project had tremendous symbolic significance. In stark contrast to the flourishing city center above the street, the public relegated the community below to a cluster of undesirables who lingered behind in both space and time. The construction of Contorno Avenue made Gamboa de Baixo invisible underneath, making the neighborhood vulnerable to displacement in the decades that followed.

Changing the Face (Race) of the City Center

De-Africanizing the Street

Throughout the history of Salvador, both the city center and the areas along the Bay of All Saints have been strategically important for the development of leisure and cultural sites, as well as the target of modern urban reform. The idea and the function of the street tell a remarkable story about the salience of race in the organization of social space in the city. Scholars of race and urban space such as Talmadge Wright have drawn upon this idea of spatial consciousness—thinking about how space, knowledge, and power intersect—which was the central message of Henri Lefebvre's major work *The Production of Space*, first published in 1974 and translated in 1991: "Space is not a scientific object removed from ideology or politics, it has always been political and strategic" (quoted in Wright 1997, 39).

The term *rua* (street) in Brazil has undergone various ideological shifts throughout history, reflecting the changed urban landscape and racial restructuring over time. The idea of the street, as understood in cities—specifically, its shifting interpretations, functions, and regulations—speaks to the sociability of urban public spaces. Who has the right to inhabit the street and to regulate it? Urbanization practices have intended, in many ways, to regulate the uses of the street and all public spaces, for that matter.

Until the end of the nineteenth and the beginning of the twentieth centuries, in Brazilian society there was a strict oppositional relationship between the notions of house and street, as well as between those of private and public (Butler 1998; Cortés 2008; Graham 1992; Reis 1995). Initially, the street was considered the place of the excluded—enslaved Africans, free blacks, the poor, beggars, thieves, and prostitutes—while the white elite converted their homes into private fortresses to protect themselves from the supposed immoral and unhygienic ways of life on the street. In these instances the street posed a threat to the morality and health of wealthier segments of the society, particularly for white wives of slave owners. But for poor black women the street was a place of freedom and autonomy (Farias, Xavier, and Gomes 2012; Graham 1992). One primary activity for black women was selling food in the streets, an activity they had previously dominated in their African countries of origin. The presence of women in the open markets of the eighteenth century characterized small businesses on Salvador's streets (Filho 1999, 245). At the beginning of the twentieth century, urban reform focused on transforming the street into a hygienic space for public sociability for white elites. This subsequently also transformed the activities of the "public women," as black women who occupied the streets for work and leisure were called. Regulations of these kinds of activities, such as the sale of cow intestines (the main ingredient of *mocotó*) and other kinds of raw meat, were set to crack down on the unsanitary conditions of the streets. The rapid de-Africanization of the city streets in Salvador under the guise of modernization was one example of the belief among the elite that the social and aesthetic Europeanization of this black city was possible through urban reform (Ferreira Filho 1999).

Exorcising Candomblé

Describing the de-Africanization and Europeanization of Salvador is important because present-day social actions reflect this urban history. Black women, specifically, challenged the Europeanization of Salvador's city streets and public spaces. The description by traveler Robert Avé-Lallemant of Salvador as a "black city" illustrates the general sentiments about the strong African presence in the city at the time. Black women's active participation in public spaces sustained this image of a black city, particularly in the *terreiros*. The city of Salvador has been likened to a woman, specifically *uma mocinha negra* (a young black lady; Serra 2002). In her famous 1947 ethnography, *The City of Women*, Ruth Landes centralized the experiences of black women in the leadership base of Bahian Candomblé to illustrate the relationship between race and gender in Brazil and the formation of Afro-Brazilian group identity. Serving as spiritual spaces of racial and gender solidarity, the female-centered terreiros were crucial for the maintenance of an African cultural identity and black community formation in Salvador. Though Landes makes the bold claim that Salvador was a "city of women" and, more specifically, a city of black women who maintained a racialized cultural order in Brazil, she failed to examine the role that antiblack racism and sexism played in the perseverance of the terreiros in Bahia. This does not take away, however, from her ethnographic example of the institutionalization of black women's leadership in the most important black cultural organizations in Salvador, the terreiros.

The terreiros as sociopolitical spaces are understudied (Butler 1998; Harding 2003; Hautzinger 2007; Matory 2005; Sterling 2010), but the importance of black women's spirituality and African cultural expression is intricately tied to an understanding of how social and physical space is determined. The racialized feminization of Salvador is relevant to the impact that urban restructuring has had on black women specifically. In colonial times Candomblé was one aspect of black public culture that most bothered the Bahian elite, who complained of the "primitive African religion" (Ferreira Filho 1999, 251). The terreiros of Salvador were the focus of the government's effort to clean up the city. As Ferreira Filho affirms, the government "customarily [spread] the image that Candomblé disturbed public peace with its 'hellish noise from the drums,' jeopardizing the cleanliness and hygiene with its 'filthy and degrading' [religious] offerings" (249). In addition to supposedly disturbing the public order, the loud drumming and singing of the terreiros disrupted a certain moral order. Religious ceremonies were considered to be orgies in which the women participants, almost always black, were viewed as prostitutes who promoted sexual promiscuity among young women and men.

The black female–led religious community of Candomblé challenged the Catholic Church's promotion of "feminine virginity, the nuclear family, and the cultural whitening attempts of the Bahian population" (Ferreira Filho 1999, 252). For these reasons the terreiros, which were central to local neighborhood life, became the target of morally driven efforts to reform the city and control the activities of black women and the spaces where they practiced their religion. Police repression and violence against the terreiros and practitioners were intense, as the state sought to protect the public and distance white families of the gentry from the supposed promiscuity and dangerous actions of black women. These state actions continued until recent decades, after the last military dictatorship, exemplifying that the destruction of the terreiros and black women's leadership had long been an urban development tactic to achieve racial amalgamation. The early attack on women-led terreiros allows us to understand the struggle against land eviction in Salvador as an antiblack racism movement.

Whitening the City

De-Africanizing Salvador's streets and public spaces and making them hygienic is a key aspect of the ongoing cultural project of the white elite of Salvador. Whereas Jerry Dávila (2003) makes the case that education was a crucial tool of whitening the Brazilian population, I understand urban development as the spatial dimension of that whitening project. Brazilian elites have always preferred European urban models of the late nineteenth and early twentieth centuries, as illustrated in the architectural and cultural construction of major cities like Rio de Janeiro and Belo Horizonte (Meade 1997; Pinheiro 2002). The necessity of dealing with Salvador's colonial heritage, including its slave past and African ancestry, which deeply influences housing patterns and other aspects of urban design, deeply impacted whites' imagination of the city:

> The elite idealizes a "white" Europeanized city, but they confront limitations in its materialization, for Salvador being a city comprised of approximately 75% blacks and mixed-raced people. As an alternative, the bourgeoisie creates spaces where it can fabricate this idealized Europeanized city—Barra e Ondina, besides Vitória and Graça. The middle class settles predominantly on the second row of the hills, in neighborhoods like Nazaré, Barris, and Barbalho, etc. The poorest gather in the unreformed central areas, or they are displaced towards neighborhoods to the North of the center, like Liberdade and São Caetano. (Pinheiro 2002, 257)

To materialize whiteness in a city where blacks are the majority, neighborhood segregation represented a key way to distance white Brazilians from the savagery of their slave-based colonial past, which was characterized by the residential proximity of people of different social and racial classes. Urban planning had a civilizing and modernizing mission that required the institutionalization of cultural racism.

Ironically, spatial separation by the elite was not always desirable, especially during colonial times, when enslaved Africans lived close to their white owners or to the places where they worked. The new spatial distance between social classes that formerly lived together is part of a new plan for social and class separation, as well as subsequent racial separation. The Parisian model of urban planning, characterized by sociospatial segregation, was one way for the elite to restructure the city in a way that consolidated its power (Pinheiro 2002).

Salvador is a product of French urbanization practices as also implemented in Rio de Janeiro, but a U.S. model of urban reform influenced by the Chicago school of human ecology would later take ideological and physical shape after the 1930s. Those practices (physical extension of the city, zoning to organize new political and social regions, and the preoccupation with cultural heritage), as outlined by urban planners during Urbanization Week in Salvador in October 1935 (Pinheiro 2002, 277), illustrate the similar ways in which the former capitals of Brazil, Salvador and Rio de Janeiro, transformed their cities to reflect a move toward the future by incorporating modernist models like Buenos Aires and Montevideo while distancing themselves from the backwardness of the colonial period. As Brandão writes, "The cities are, like all social processes, as much a fruit of the past as they are projections of the future" (2002, 151). These urbanization techniques had devastating effects on poor and black communities in these Brazilian cities, as has also occurred in other Latin American and even North American cities. In cities like Rio de Janeiro and Salvador there has always existed a conflicting relationship between urban restructuring, such as in the construction of modern highways and residential communities, and the destruction of existing residences deemed unacceptable in the modern city (Kowarick 1994; Meade 1997; Rolnik 1994). These transformations affected the future of infrastructural changes, particularly housing standards, and popular residential communities located in the center of the city and along the coast of Salvador.

The Cleansing of the Historic Center

Every city has a plan, and the city center or downtown becomes the focus of developers. The Historic Center of Salvador (also known as the Pelourinho, meaning "whipping post," referring to the whipping posts that were used to publicly punish slaves), during previous centuries was the site of administrative offices and home to middle-class merchants and government officials—"operations of the highest social classes constituting the cultural center of the city of Salvador" (Espinheira 1989). After the flight of the middle classes toward the coastal areas of the city and nobler neighborhoods (such as Vitória, Graça, Barra, and Rio Vermelho), the poorest segments of the population began to occupy the former mansions, converting them into tenements.

The inability of residents to care for the old buildings, exacerbated by social abandonment by the bourgeois property owners and political leaders who no longer valued the city center, led to their physical and social degradation. This new population was responsible for preserving the area, but they lacked the economic resources to do so.

According to an official report produced by the municipal government in the 1960s, 57.6 percent of the women, almost all black, residing in the Pelourinho were prostitutes, who constituted 36.6 percent of the neighborhood's population (Nobre 1995, 7). Black women became prostitutes because, like domestic work, it was one of few options for work. Like the gendered racial stereotypes of black women being readily available servants, so are their bodies hypersexualized as easily accessible or consumed (Caldwell 2007; Gilliam 1998; Gilliam and Gilliam 1999; McCallum 1999). In the slavery period black women not only suffered from sexual exploitation at the hands of their masters but also were bought and sold as sexual servants (Williams 2013).

Since prostitution was concentrated in the historic part of the city, men went to the Pelourinho for these services (Bacelar 1982; Kulick 1998; Williams 2013). This created an environment in which prostitution could be permitted and controlled by the police. As Gey Espinheira describes in his 1989 essay "Pelourinho: A hora e a vez do Centro Histórico" (Pelourinho: The hour and the time of the Historic Center):

> The prostitutes converged upon the Pelourinho, on the one hand, attracted to the social and economic conditions of the locale, while on the other hand, there they established themselves constrained by police actions of the entities in charge of these practices. . . . Localized prostitution allows control and

effective inspection and at the same time impedes the *"trot-toir"* [street] from extending to the rest of the city. (quoted in Nobre 1995, 8)

Government officials blamed these black sex workers for the degradation of the urban center during the earlier part of the twentieth century. Prostitutes tended to live in poor housing conditions and suffered intense police repression. Moreover, a general preoccupation with hygiene was linked to the beautification of the city because old, decayed houses did not complement the natural and historic beauty of the city. A plan for the city had to include the ordered and hygienic construction of residential areas, with adequate water pipes and sewer systems. Dilapidated residential buildings were neither aesthetically acceptable nor healthy forms of habitation. The destruction of these kinds of residences in the city center, usually buildings occupied by poor and black workers, was a key phase of urbanization plans based on aesthetic transformations. The forced expulsion and displacement of these populations to standardized housing projects located on the outskirts of the city characterized subsequent phases of the rebuilding. This later resulted in distant residences from the city center for poor people, whereas bourgeois residential communities emerged in the interior regions of Salvador.

The process of transforming the Historic Center of Salvador into a tourist attraction as well as a financial and cultural center and disposing of its bad elements began during the 1950s after extensive social science research had been conducted on the activities and housing conditions there. Social science research on urban conditions until the 1960s almost always focused on the population of the Historic Center. The process of cleansing began with the mass displacement of the prostitutes to the lower city in 1959 and later extended to sanitation efforts and other public health campaigns.

Officially known as Operation Cleanup, the mass cleansing of these women involved violent police action that rapidly eradicated prostitution from the area. These actions demonstrated that the government did not intend to improve living conditions for residents in the Historic Center. Rather, these cleanup programs were implemented to recuperate the area to benefit local merchants and tourists. Part of a citywide focus on urbanization for greater capital accumulation, the Pelourinho returned to its historic function as a financial and political district. The difference this time around was that the primary capital was cultural, a history embedded in the restored buildings and monuments—but without the local population of black female prostitutes who occupied the area for many years. The expulsion of the prostitutes during the 1950s and 1960s exemplified mass expulsion during urban renewal processes in Salvador and the systemic disappearance of black female bodies in the process. The cleansing of the physical aspects of Salvador was accompanied by the racial and gendered moral reordering of the city. Although it is commonly told that the expulsion of residents from the Pelourinho began in the 1990s, the cleansing of prostitutes had actually taken place several decades earlier, setting a pattern of displacement in the years that followed.

Revitalizing the Past, Erasing the Present

In 1984 the Brazilian government declared the Pelourinho a part of the national patrimony, and in 1985 UNESCO added the Historic Center to its list of world heritage sites (Collins 2008; Dunn 1994; Pinho 2010; Romo 2010; Sansi-Roca 2007). In the early 1990s the city began to spend millions of dollars, supported by international funders like the World Bank, on revitalization projects such as the restoration of historic buildings, fountains, and squares in the Pelourinho. In the process the government expanded the expulsion and relocation of the so-called dangerous and criminal local black population that lingered to other neighborhoods throughout the city's periphery. It has transformed their homes into museums, restaurants, hotels, performance stages, and shops to serve the flourishing tourism industry. The Pelourinho became an important global landmark visited by national and international tourists every day.

From a cultural heritage standpoint, the restoration and marketing of the Pelourinho was successful in that it became a renewed space for celebrating the colonial past—as seen in the restoration of historic monuments like the São Marcelo Fort—and for tourism and leisure.

The gentrification of the Pelourinho is also, however, a symbolic marker of black experiences with mass displacement and the repressive regimes of urban restructuring (Pinho 1999).

The revitalization of areas along Contorno Avenue in the city center constitutes a central objective of subsequent stages of Salvador's urban renewal program. As in the case of the Pelourinho, the people of Gamboa de Baixo do not fit into the government's plans for the area. Less than a five-minute walk from Gamboa de Baixo, the Bahia Marina Yacht Club and the Museum of Modern Art Park of Sculptures replaced the local black community of Preguiça in 1995. Today, visitors can sit on benches in the waterfront park, admiring displays of modernity in the form of abstract art, without any remnants of the more than seventy-five families that were relocated to a neighborhood on the outskirts of the city. In addition to the restoration of the São Paulo Fort in Gamboa de Baixo, the revitalization plans for Contorno Avenue included the installation of upscale marine supply stores and a park with restaurants, bars, and kiosks under the arches of the street where visitors will be able to enjoy the view and the seafood of the Bay of All Saints. Just as in the Pelourinho and Preguiça, however, the government does not envision the presence of the people of Gamboa de Baixo in the new environment. In fact, very few traditional poor black fishing communities continue to exist along the bay (Figure 4).

On the shores of Gamboa de Baixo lies the São Paulo da Gamboa Fort, built in 1722 and declared a national heritage site in 1937. Some residents of the neighborhood still live inside its ruins (Figure 5). The Bahian Navy used the base during the eighteenth century for military reinforcement and protection of the city (Rebouças and Filho 1985). The navy abandoned the São Paulo Fort and the surrounding area around the end of the nineteenth century. Then, during the mid-1990s, the navy reclaimed ownership of the fort as public land, declaring it an aspect of the city's history in need of immediate revitalization and preservation.

The memory of a powerful capital of Portuguese America, specifically the history of economic, military, and economic might, drives the recent restoration of the forts of Salvador. The forts were constructed to protect one of the most important financial and cultural centers in Brazil's history and became the symbol of Portuguese expansion in

FIGURE 4. Gamboa de Baixo, Banco dos Ingleses, Campo Grande, and Vitória neighborhoods. Photograph by Javier Escudero.

the Americas. For instance, the São Marcelo Fort, built more than 350 years ago in the middle of the ocean near Salvador's commercial district and Historic Center, was restored during the late 1990s. Antônio Imbassahy, the mayor of Salvador at the time of its restoration, stated:

> What more can one say, besides our certainty of completing our duty, of our commitment that we have with our history and with our future. In a city like Salvador, where new and old mix with such harmony . . . the races form an ethnicity and that peculiar personality of being Bahian. . . . We share with everyone, Bahians, Brazilians and citizens of the world, more happiness, to see our São Marcelo Fort restored, joining the Mercado Modelo and the Elevador Lacerda as one of our well-known postcards. (Imbassahy 2000, 4)

A civic duty that shows the government's commitment to preserving Bahian and Brazilian history, the restoration of forts in Salvador also created new spaces for tourists to enjoy. As Imbassahy's statement shows, this image of Bahia, living in harmony with the old and new, the colonial and the modern, stems from the idea of racial mixture and harmony in Bahia. Nevertheless, Imbassahy fails to mention the violence involved in acquiring the land on which the forts were built or the forced enslavement of Africans and indigenous peoples whose labor created these present-day monuments.

The restoration of the São Marcelo and São Paulo da Gamboa forts is part of a broader municipal government initiative called Via Náutica, which will be developed along the coastal zone of the city over the next few years. Beginning from the Ponta de Humaitá, the project proposes to create a maritime tour through the Bay of All Saints linking various historical sites, including the restored forts, the Museum of Modern Art, the Historic Center, and the famous former slave marketplace, the Mercado Modelo. Each fort, including São Marcelo and São Paulo da Gamboa, will include a museum for tourists. Other restored forts in Barra and Monte Serrat already have similar museum tours. The restoration of the São Paulo da Gamboa Fort poses a problem because of the population that inhabits the area and the local community's resistance to relocation during and after the restoration process.

Urban renewal in Salvador has focused on preserving physical and cultural aspects of Bahia and Brazil, including present-day spatial memories of colonialism and slavery such as São Paulo Fort in Gamboa de Baixo. History has become a commodity for public consumption and tourism in Salvador. These revitalized historic buildings and their modern imitations, however, "symbolize the era of black slavery and white domination," representing a new form of socioeconomic subjugation for black Brazilians (Fagence 1995, 99). Places where black people once lived have become commercial sites for the consumption of black experiences and cultures, but without the people who have produced that culture. Imported notions of black culture like art and music displace undesirables, those who embody the violent, deviant, and menacing meanings of blackness that previously characterized Salvador's urban landscape (Collins 2008; Pinho 2010). Thus, tourism in Salvador commodifies and consumes black culture as folkloric representations of local and national identities distant from the everyday concerns of material survival such as employment, housing, and food. Bahia and Bahians have become "living museums" in the tour-

FIGURE 5. Dona Rosa, who lives inside the ruins of the São Paulo da Gamboa Fort, 2000. Photograph by the author.

ism industry, a form of racial inclusion that "has often worked to limit economic and social reform" (Romo 2010, 8).

The situation in Salvador characterizes global urban reconstruction practices throughout almost all Brazilian cities, as well as cities such as New York and Paris. A modernist vision of the city tends to include the aesthetic revival of "ugly, dirty, and mistreated" historical sites into "clean, pure, and distinct" remnants of the past. History becomes a viable product for public consumption in modern cities (Lacarrieu 2000, ii; see also Espinheira 2008; Pinheiro 2002; Pinho 1999; Romo 2010; Sansi-Roca 2007). The underlying logic is that appropriating these urban spaces gives new hygienic meanings to the past, representing the city as healthier, less dangerous, and more desirable for those living in it (Lacarrieu 2000, iii). Revalorizing the past translates into urban nostalgic desire in the local and national imaginary. It reconstructs the essential "good old days" as a means of "rescuing the identity of the city of Salvador—the city which generated the nation of Brazil, the culture of Brazil"—as Luciano Borges said of the Instituto do Patrimônio Artístico e Cultural de Bahia (IPAC; Institute of Artistic and Cultural

Heritage of Bahia) at the beginning of the Pelourinho restoration project in 1994 (quoted in Dunn 1994, 28).

From this perspective Salvador is an ideal site for the revitalization of history. The Bahian municipal Secretary of Planning, Science, and Technology (SEPLANTEC; Secretaria do Planejamento, Ciência, e Technologia), during the peak of the urban revitalization programs of the mid-1990s, writes the following in a 1996 brochure:

> The vision of tourism for Salvador is centered on leisure tourism with the extraordinary content of culture and history, involving beaches, ecology, festivals, music, and an exceptional architectonic patrimony. . . . Having been the first capital of Brazil and center of the beginning of Portuguese colonization, with their political and economic displays, and more markedly, the installation of the slave regime, Salvador is developing the richest historic and cultural values sui generis of the country, preserved in the form of an exceptional physical patrimony and customs.

The government of Bahia wants to recapture local and national history in Salvador to boost the tourism industry, including significant investments in sites such as the Pelourinho and the São Paulo Fort. Once considered dangerous, the Pelourinho, for example, is now one of Brazil's best examples of a revived neighborhood. More important, it is a renewed space in the national identity.

Renowned Brazilian geographer Milton Santos predicted the mass displacement of the Pelourinho population before it occurred (1959, 1987a). Urban memory, as Santos posits, compromises the valorization of a political economy that privileges the market value of property such as old mansions formally occupied by a white colonial elite. This reinvention of colonial history displaces the recent urban memory of local residents, usually poor black people who inhabit and use the deteriorating old buildings. The restoration of the urban center is driven only by the symbolic valorization and preservation of the historical product distant from present-day reality, erasing the memory of slavery and racial and gender violence, such as the violence associated with the whipping post. The modernizing project, Santos asserts, involves deliberate social abandonment by the city government and the subsequent deterioration of historic buildings, followed by the forced displacement of local residents during and after renovations (1987b, 26).

Nevertheless, as Michel-Rolph Trouillot states, "The value of the historical product cannot be debated without taking into account both the context of its production and the context of its consumption" (1995, 146). Urban development around the celebration of a colonial heritage excludes descendants of enslaved Africans whose labor, traditions, and customs constitute essential elements of that colonial past. Development in Bahia represents the renewal of a colonial past for both the colonialist visitor and the colonized host, reflecting the physical and spatial forms of racial and gender oppression. For example, Olodum, one of Bahia's most celebrated Afrocentric cultural organizations, moved its central offices to the Historic Center in 1990. Even today, black cultural artifacts such as Olodum are the primary products that merchants market to tourists who visit the Historic Center. Another example is the way black people participate in this urban economy of tourism and leisure as living artifacts or representations of the colonial past, such as capoeira martial arts practitioners on the streets. The tourism industry sells black men and women's bodies and sexuality, creating what some scholars have identified as a sort of Afro-Disney or living museum in Brazil (Pinho 2010; Romo 2010). Other examples include preparing and serving traditional Afro-Bahian food and performing sensual Afro-Brazilian dances for white audiences and, with increasing frequency, black audiences (Pinho 2010).

This chapter illustrates that the urbanization of Gamboa de Baixo does not occur in isolation but rather as part of a broader institutional process in Salvador intended to modernize old spaces and create new ones. This modernizing project has a detrimental impact on poor neighborhoods caught between their own desires for improved living conditions and permanent residence and the bulldozing private and public enterprises that seek to remove them. The challenge for these black urban communities is to collectively participate in the planning and implementation processes and to offer new ideas on how urbanization should operate. Black communities throughout the African diaspora confront these issues of unequal urban development and organize struggles for adequate housing and sanitation, as well as for

Due 26th

employment and public safety in the cities where they live. Gamboa de
Baixo in the city of Salvador is only one such instance.

Spatialized racial restructuring within the city of Salvador fuels the
political process of fighting for permanent residency and land rights.
The next chapter details the specific nature of the Gamboa de Baixo
political organization that emerged in this context. Strategies of resistance at the neighborhood level amid the threat of expulsion and relocation involve articulating a counter historical narrative of belonging
on the coastal lands of the city center, as well as direct-action protest.

3

THE BLACK MOVEMENT'S FOOT SOLDIERS

> *The right to the city* is like a cry and a demand. This right slowly meanders through the surprising detours of nostalgia and tourism, the return to the heart of the traditional city, and the call of existent or recently developed centralities. . . . The *right to the city* cannot be conceived of as a single visiting right or as a return to traditional cities. It can only be formulated as a transformed and renewed *right to urban life.*
>
> Henri Lefèbvre, Eleonore Kofman, and Elizabeth Lebas, *Writings on Cities*

> The only activity that has ever altered oppression and transformed disenfranchised people's powerlessness is collective grassroots organizing.
>
> Barbara Smith, *The Truth That Never Hurts: Writings on Race, Gender, and Freedom*

Social Protest on the Margins

On March 20, 1997, the women of Gamboa de Baixo prepared in the darkness and silence of early morning. Late the night before, residents had received the shocking news that fourteen-year-old Cristiane Conceição Santos had died from head injuries after being struck by a car on her way to school. The fatal accident was one of three violent incidents at the beginning of that year alone involving Gamboa residents crossing busy Contorno Avenue. One person had died, and another was paralyzed. The week before, women from the neighborhood association, Associação Amigos de Gegê Dos Moradores da Gamboa de Baixo (Gamboa de Baixo Friends of Gegê Neighborhood Association), had met with the mayor of Salvador and requested that he install traffic lights and a crosswalk. They had insisted on the control of traffic for the safety of pedestrians, including women and young children, who risked their lives every day just to go to school or work. "No one respects those of us who try to cross the street," one woman told a newspaper reporter during the protest. The death of Cristiane was a brutal reminder that they had received no official assurance that safety conditions on the road would change.

As dawn approached, the women hurried together with their children into the street, determined to walk without fear on Contorno Avenue. As Gamboa de Baixo activist Maria remembers, "Before [the closing of the street] we fought with fear, but the day we closed the [avenue], full of courage to confront the police, I felt that I had a space in this society that's mine" (personal communication, 2000). The women's anger intensified as the sun rose. They quickly moved to get the word out to other neighborhoods, black movement activists, NGOs, and supporters in the local archdiocese. Between six and eight o'clock in the morning, Contorno Avenue was the site of one of Gamboa de Baixo's and the city of Salvador's largest and most significant acts of public defiance of the late 1990s. Residents carried a banner that read, "Gamboa de Baixo Coveted Paradise Demands Help." The demonstration disrupted traffic throughout the entire city. They blocked the street with burning tires, wood, and other debris. The main actors in this manifestation were black women, young and old, who shouted in defense of their families and their communities. The fire department extinguished the fires and removed the debris to open the congested avenue. The military police in their riot gear stayed the entire morning to prevent the outbreak of new demonstrations.

For activists in Gamboa de Baixo, this Contorno Avenue protest represented one early memory of the neighborhood's grassroots struggle for permanence, land rights, and social and economic change in the area. I first heard this story from local activists in 2000 while researching how black women led social movements. I was living in Salvador, and I marched alongside these women on November 20, the National Day of Black Consciousness, in the center of Salvador. As I continued my research during that decade, neighborhood activists participated in several such protests on Contorno Avenue and throughout the city (Figures 6 and 7). Some of the protests were promoted by larger black organizations like Movimento Negro Unificado and União de Negros pela Igualdade.

FIGURE 6. Contorno Avenue Protest, circa 1997. Courtesy of Gamboa de Baixo neighborhood association archives.

FIGURE 7. Municipal government building protest, 2004. Photograph by the author.

Public demonstrations, oftentimes spontaneous and disruptive to the urban social order, have focused on black concerns with increased police violence and the unemployment and poverty that occurs disproportionately in black communities. Gamboa de Baixo street protests have been a way for poor black people to claim power and space when urban renewal projects are forcibly removing them from these central areas of the city. Gamboa de Baixo's participation in the November 20 events every year has been an expression of a shared understanding of the connection between the social conditions of poor blacks and the structural racism in Salvador and throughout Brazil. Social actions organized by black women at the neighborhood level should be understood as the everyday political manifestations of the broader Brazilian black movement.

This chapter recounts the history of the Gamboa de Baixo community movement against urban renewal programs and for access to material resources such as urban land and housing. Collective memory of how these urban renewal projects have rapidly transformed Salvador and the everyday lives of black neighborhoods is significant for understanding the political formation of black women throughout the city. This movement emerged because, as Gamboa de Baixo residents understood it, they were almost certain to become the next Pelourinho, as expressed in a 1995 neighborhood communiqué: "We do not want to be a second edition of the Pelourinho." Their narratives and methods of resistance show that discourses and practices of urban renewal are prime examples of antiblack racism in Brazil. Political mobilization against urban renewal in Salvador illustrates the racial consciousness of Brazilian blacks: black communities do actively organize around race and gender in political struggles over material resources. Political scientist Elizabeth Perry's following comment on social protest in post-Maoist China encourages a rethinking of how oppressive state policies in Salvador affect the emergence of neighborhood activism: "State-society relations are a two-way street: it is not only that popular protests are influenced by State initiatives; a regime's policies, in turn, are shaped by the perceived protest potential of its social base" (2002, xxviii). This chapter explains how the foundation of urban renewal policies in poor urban communities relates to the perceived knowledge of these communities and the anticipated level of political response to state practices.

Formation of the Neighborhood Struggle

A crucial characteristic of the urban development plans that led to the construction of Contorno Avenue and the expulsion of prostitutes from the Pelourinho in the 1960s and 1970s was that poor communities were considered by the authoritarian government to be incapable of making decisions and taking action and therefore were excluded from the planning process (Associação Amigos de Gegê dos Moradores da Gamboa de Baixo et al. 2001).

The *abertura democrática* (democratic opening) of the military regime in the mid-1970s and the transitional democratic government of the early 1980s created conditions that allowed the emergence of political organization in urban communities such as Gamboa de Baixo. Neighborhood associations became a new political arena for black communities to engage in struggles for citizenship rights and make demands for material resources such as better schooling, housing, and working conditions. Moreover, the growth in grassroots-based political parties such as the Partido dos Trabalhadores (PT; Workers' Party) established what Ruth Corrêa Leite Cardoso identifies as a set of "new relations between excluded citizens and the state apparatus" (1992, 291), which not only reinvigorated broader political participation but also heightened class-based expectations in the developing social democracy project. She writes, furthermore, "Building autonomous associations endowed with a new role, local neighborhood groups made their demands in ways that revealed their ability to bypass traditional mechanisms of political co-optation" (292).

Benedita da Silva, formerly the Brazilian minister of social assistance and a neighborhood and women's rights activist in Rio de Janeiro, affirms that many women leaders in neighborhood movements emerged during these years of military rule, when the persecution of male organizers was widespread. For women who had previously "played a backstage role within the neighborhood associations," political leadership became increasingly possible (Silva, Benjamin, and Mendonça 1997, 45).

The Women's Association in Gamboa de Baixo, organized in the 1980s, was one such example of women's efforts to mobilize local residents to demand social programs for women in Salvador's impoverished neighborhoods. When the municipal government terminated the free milk programs at the end of the 1980s, the Women's Association stopped functioning as a political representative for the neighborhood. After the outbreak of cholera in 1992, however, which caused several deaths in Gamboa de Baixo, the women began to organize again. With the direct assistance of the mayor's office, they founded the organization Associação Amigos de Gegê dos Moradores da Gamboa de Baixo on October 7 of that year to institute collective governance and legal representation for the community. The organization was named after the first president's father, Gegê, one of the cholera victims. The neighborhood association in Gamboa de Baixo began with a focus on issues of life and death. The association struggled to counter the public image of Gamboa de Baixo as a spatial container of cholera. In general the media portrayed black urban and rural communities throughout the state of Bahia as being the loci of the disease, which presented a health threat to nearby affluent neighborhoods such as Vitória and Campo Grande.

Led by the women of the neighborhood association, Gamboa residents made frequent trips to local newspapers and radio stations to bring attention to the cholera outbreak and the contamination of their tap water. Neighborhood residents looked to the women's association for governance and political leadership in the struggle for social improvement. This is confirmed by former community leader Valquíria Boa Morte:

> I was the first person who went to the radio. By the time I got home, EMBASA [the Bahia Water and Sanitation Company] was already researching putting in a fountain. The death of Mr. Geraldo, Lueci's father, reinforced the struggle, and I was mobilized at this time because I knew the family—father and mother, and all the little ones. I was at home when I heard he was going to the hospital with cholera and other residents had already gone. Another boy had died so I called two women, Tônia and Mel, and went to the radio. After that other women arrived—Tinda, Solange, Hilda, and later Lueci. We took steps

and they began bringing water [to Gamboa]. So it was we who started the struggle to organize Gamboa, which was only a marginalized community before then. (personal communication, 2000)

The association demanded that the state test the neighborhood's natural water sources and water pipes in order to dispel the image of their community as unhealthy and dangerous to the public. Testing proved that the cholera victims had died from contaminated water provided by the city and not from the neighborhood's natural water fountains. After these actions the community received some social service interventions, such as the construction of the *chafariz,* a central water fountain in the area. Pioneer activist Dona Lenilda, Sr. Geraldo's widow, remembers:

What led me to participate in the movement was that I wanted a better life for my family, for my children. We had just seen their father die, and other people as well, right? So we wanted a more dignified life, with potable water, toilets so as not throw our waste just anywhere. That's why [cholera] surfaced here, and that was what led me to the movement. If we're going to live in a place, we should treat it properly. (personal communication, 2003)

During this same period, Dona Juana, an elderly Italian nun, worked with women in the neighborhood, teaching them sewing and adult and child literacy. She noted the necessity of buying land and constructing a permanent space in the community for these activities, a space that was later named the Elementary School and Community Center of Gamboa de Baixo. For poor black women in Gamboa de Baixo, these training courses offered the practical skills necessary to seek employment and advance their education. More important, the school became a regular meeting place where the women shared knowledge of everyday happenings in the neighborhood and articulated social and political concerns about the city, the nation, and the world. Dona Juana's work typified the social work of elderly nuns such as Sister Dorothy Stang—killed in 2005 as a result of her advocacy work in the

Amazon—who have used their roles as "external agents" (Assies 1994) to foster ongoing local discussions of global social justice issues.

With the main issue of water resolved during the early 1990s, the neighborhood association was politically dormant for a few years after the cholera outbreak. A resurgence of the association occurred in 1995 when news of the Contorno Avenue Revitalization Project reached Gamboa de Baixo residents. The Bahian press announced that the revitalization project would involve the relocation of the families of Gamboa de Baixo to a new housing development on the outskirts of the city. As the project received more media attention, the Bahian State Development Agency started to collect demographic information on the homes in Gamboa de Baixo. The residents feared that their relocation was imminent. Hence, the community movement against expulsion started out of fear of leaving the homes most of them had known all of their lives.

That fear led to anger, and residents reported to the newspapers that government social workers were conducting surveys in Gamboa de Baixo without any explanation. Residents suspected that social workers were documenting the conditions of the population for probable expulsion from the urban center. At the end of 1995, the government expelled seventy-five families from a coastal community situated on Contorno Avenue, approximately one kilometer away from Gamboa de Baixo. Residents watched as the government advanced the plan to displace all the poor black communities along Contorno Avenue. The city government had already conducted a rapid and thorough cleansing of the city center and displaced residents from the restored historic buildings and monuments of the Pelourinho. From 1995 to 1997, community activism focused on getting detailed information about the Contorno Avenue project, mobilizing Gamboa de Baixo residents to participate in street protests, and developing alternative urbanization projects to improve their community.

Like the Women's Association during the previous decade, the neighborhood association found its leadership and support firmly based in the women of Gamboa de Baixo. Their fear was a crucial factor in pushing forward the grassroots struggle against expulsion from coastal lands of the city center. As Dona Nice recounts, "There were women, a dozen or so women, who began to cause alarm, to shout, 'Hey, look at what's happening.'" A 1997 neighborhood communiqué they handed to residents to recruit them to participate in the political organization read:

> Residents, we need to stay mobilized and alert against the violent and arbitrary actions that are being taken by the mayor and the state government. . . . When they announced the cleansing, before the elections, it was not just trash that they want to remove from the center of the city, but also the blacks, the poor people, the beggars, the street vendors, the street children and everything that they think dirties the city. We are not going to let them treat us like trash. We are working people and we have rights.

Women activists focused on mobilizing their neighbors in defense of permanent residency, land ownership, and adequate housing. As one of the most vocal activists in the early neighborhood, the late Dona Iraci stated, "When we saw them taking [the inhabitants of the Preguiça and Pelourinho neighborhoods] out, that's when we became even stronger" as a movement.

Dona Lenilda, who appropriated a 1950s carnaval march song to create a political anthem for the activists, confirms the reasons that led her to participate in the community movement:

> The government wanted to take all of us away from here, and we didn't want to leave. We don't need to ask people for anything, right? For so many years we had been living in wooden shacks, but it was ours. They wanted to remove us, but we didn't give up. . . . I thought, we have to do something to strike against the government. I began to work on that song. That's when I started to sing this anthem, and we won.

The lyrics of her anthem express her determination:

> I will not leave here
> No one will take me away from here
> The Lord must have the patience to wait!
> I am the mother of so many children
> Where will I live?

In their public street protests, the community was able to garner support from nongovernmental organizations and black movement activist groups. The women worked with NGOs such as the Comissão de Justiça e Paz da Arquidiocese de Salvador (CJP; Commission of Justice and Peace of the Archdiocese of Salvador), the Centro de Estudos e Ação Social (CEAS; Center for Social Action Studies), the MNU, and UNEGRO to mobilize the community and discuss the global, neoliberal roots of citywide revitalization projects. These organizations significantly contributed to the intellectual and political empowerment of black women in Gamboa de Baixo and shifted class-centered debates on social inequality to include racial and gender oppression. This shift implied alterations in black women's definition of themselves as leading political actors in urban social movements and contributors to the democratization of Brazilian society. Moreover, the women maintained local autonomy while calling on leftist NGOs and politicians as resources to decipher their rights as citizens and communities (Cardoso 1992, 301).

This relationship between neighborhood associations and NGOs and political parties was crucial for building activists' knowledge of and fight against the destructive and exclusionary practices of urbanization in Salvador. Gianpaolo Baiocchi describes this form of civic engagement as "government-induced activism," seen in other Brazilian cities such as Porto Alegre (2005, 51), and Willem Assies explains that the increasing numbers of middle-class left-wing militants, church activists, and NGOs who understood themselves to be "at the service of the movements" and as "social articulators" played key roles in the formation of popular organizations (1994, 93). Neighborhood associations have been, however, autonomous organizations that extend from existing political and social networks in local communities.

The 1996 Habitat II Conference organized by the United Nations was also crucial for Brazilian social movements organized around issues of urbanization and housing rights. Political groups like neighborhood associations, the landless movement, and the homeless movement used the Habitat Agenda as a tool for demanding national and state commitment to infrastructural improvement and fair land and housing distribution. Conference discussions centered on marginalized groups—specifically, racial minorities, women, and children—and the

Habitat Agenda held particular meaning for the future development of Brazilian cities. The United Nations Educational, Scientific, and Cultural Organization presented a disparaging report on Brazilian cities in which they confirmed the rapid ghettoization of poor neighborhoods, where the majority of residents were black and brown (*Folha de São Paulo,* June 8, 1996). The report claimed that these actions resulted in the creation of "new frontiers" in the city, reflecting the disparity between the spaces where the poor and the rich, blacks and whites lived. In Salvador the government's plan to expand housing on the periphery for families like those from Gamboa de Baixo provoked debates among activists about the systemic elimination of blacks and poor people from the better areas of the city and generated critiques of Brazil's supposed commitment to poverty alleviation, gender justice, and housing and land reform.

Gamboa de Baixo activists used their knowledge of these international debates to advocate for the intervention of Viver Melhor (Better Living), a federal program of the Projeto Habitar Brasil (Brazil Habitat Project) designed after the Habitat II Conference and responsible for the urbanization of poor communities in the state of Bahia in the late 1990s. They were able to incorporate some of their needs into the project and secure promises for the construction of eighty new homes, the exclusion of the construction of a road within the neighborhood, the restoration of homes that already existed, and the permanence of all families in their place of origin. A 1997 neighborhood association meeting pamphlet states:

> *The time has come!*
> We have achieved urbanization [of the infrastructure] in our community. But we are going to be careful with the unknown persons who enter and leave our Gamboa. The enemy is present! We cannot be fooled by the government's household survey. All caution is not enough! We cannot forget: in the beginning, the government wanted to take everyone away from here. First, they were going to take the 120 families from under the arches; after, with the reconstruction of the fortress and the restoration of the old mansions, they want to take away all the families from the area below. It was through our struggle

and resistance that we got this far. The participation of everyone together with the association has been important to guarantee the permanence of our community. If we are not careful, this government (FHC, ACM, Paulo Souto, Imbassahy) will expel us from here like dogs. But we have only one tune: I will not leave here. No one will take me away from here.

In the process of confronting the threat of expulsion, the activists developed a project proposal to fit the reality of Gamboa de Baixo community residents that envisioned a better quality of life. They teamed up with professors and students from the School of Architecture at the Federal University of Bahia (UFBA). Armed with technical knowledge and the experience and wisdom of local residents, the activists were able to force urban developers to take note of the activists and include their ideas for the construction of new houses instead of relocation away from the city center. This not only challenged how urban planners interacted with communities during negotiations over urban development but also changed the extent to which women participated in these kinds of policy debates that impact entire black communities. As a result the community won participation in a national housing program that guaranteed the construction of better houses for families in the community.

Despite these gains, the late 1990s and 2000s were marked by tense debates about the poor quality of the houses that were eventually constructed and ongoing statements by government officials to the effect that this coastal land was not an area for black and poor people to live, demonstrating that the racial dynamics of the sociospatial order of Salvador's city center had changed little. As the following statement by activist Dona Iraci illustrates, however, Gamboa de Baixo's inclusion in the urbanization programs strengthened the movement even more:

Although you live for thirty years in a wooden shack and you love that shack, . . . the government comes and says, "No, I'll give you a brick house in another place." . . . They call them "shanties"—"Leave these shanties and stop living with rats." And when you are in a brick house, again the government says it will give you a better one in another place. You say, "No,

mine is also made of stone and I like it here, here is where
I want to stay." Then, if before you had feelings of love for
that place, that house, now you're even more attached to it,
because you live in a place that you like and that has a certain
comfort that works for you. . . . Then, it's going to get more
complex. A lot more. The struggle is going to be much more
difficult, and I hope that we are well prepared because that
nautical [development] project makes promises, and it promises a lot. The government does not plan to give up because of
Gamboa. And Gamboa does not plan to give up because of the
nautical project. (personal communication, 2000)

The Grassroots Politics of Community

Organizing the Gamboa de Baixo neighborhood in a collective struggle
against expulsion also involved confronting images of the neighborhood as socially and politically disorganized, as well as a space where
people reproduced poverty, immorality, and marginality. Mobilizing
as a cohesive neighborhood unveiled deep racial, gender, and class tensions. This 1969 journalistic portrayal of Gamboa de Baixo would be
reproduced among various segments of the neighborhood movement:

Dirty and shady men populate the place, a community formed
by thieves, prostitutes, and the feeble-minded. The families
who reside in the streets [near the ocean] complain about the
subworld [near the street]. One of the last victims of the mar-
ginals was attacked in plain daylight. It was an elderly woman,
approximately 70 years old, who was injured by the crook.
Before a man approaches [the neighborhood], the women
seduce him, almost dragging the victims by force to the shacks.
(*A Tarde,* October 4, 1969)

Although leaders promoted a unified political identity within the community, the diversity within Gamboa de Baixo has always been a source
of conflict even before the threat of displacements. Local activists have
had to contend with older residents who have planted roots on the land
and newer residents who have comparatively less history there. The

neighborhood's early affirmation that "we all share the same struggle" was met at times with vehement opposition. For some activists the political goal was to preserve ownership and permanence for those who had traditionally inhabited the land and not for those they perceived as the undeserving poor new settlers who had contributed to the demise of the neighborhood's public image.

Traditionally, being fishermen and fisherwomen has been central to Gamboa de Baixo's identity, of what it means to be a *gamboeiro* or a *gamboeira*. *Gamboa* is an indigenous word with two meanings: "the art of fishing" and "an artificial lake on the coastline or riverbank for collecting fish." When local activists give tours of the neighborhood, they stop at the gamboa located on the oceanfront to explain the indigenous and black history of the land that resounds in the archival documents: "There on the Unhão beach, there was an Indian *gamboa* in the São Simão settlement, the village located in proximity to what is today the Passeio Público" (Carreira 1999). This identification as people of Gamboa is infused with ideas about socioeconomic status and cultural belonging on the coastal land. Throughout the past century approximately three families dominated and controlled the land, and most residents had and continue to have some form of kinship ties that are either biological or material. According to Ana Cristina:

> The truth is that Gamboa de Baixo is practically three families: the Caminha family, the Sapucaia family, and the Bomfim family. Bomfim being the least in number, but the truth is that they are all cousins. If you grab someone right here and go over to the other side of the neighborhood, they're cousins. They might not be close cousins, but they're cousins. I see Gamboa as an occupation, a permitted occupation. Because when they deactivated the fort, the navy gave authorization to a few soldiers to stay here to keep an eye on things. These people started the life in Gamboa, the population. That's why I say "permitted"—they gave them permission to stay. Yes, and they had children, and their children grew up, had children. There are already six or seven generations of the same family in Gamboa. (personal communication, 2002)

FIGURE 8. Ana Cristina da Silva Caminha (top left), Simone Bomfim, and Simone's daughter, Raiane, 2008. Photograph by author.

FIGURE 9. Fishermen prepare their nets in the early morning off the coast of Gamboa de Baixo. In the background a pier for a luxury apartment complex is in the early phase of construction. Photograph by the author, 2003.

Ana Cristina belongs to the Caminha family, one of the largest families in Gamboa (Figure 8). She was born in her mother's home on the beach front near the gamboa. Her relatives have worked as fishermen and fisherwomen and, more recently, as domestic workers, and others work as sailors and divers for local and international industries. Some fishermen fare better in their earnings than those who work outside the community because fish are still a valued commodity. At times throughout the year, however, high tides do not permit fishing, and they are unable to make an adequate living. Even when they face these difficulties, they prefer fishing over other jobs, in which little education and technical skill yield low pay. For local activists, living and fishing on the coast represent key parts of their collective memory, which enhances their self-identification as long-standing black workers (Figures 9 and 10).

With the recent arrival of families who have less affiliation with the fishing profession, Gamboa de Baixo residents have manifested acts of elitism within what they call a traditional community. More specifically, with the influx of laborers from rural parts of Salvador and other neighborhoods over the past few decades, the demographics of the

FIGURE 10. Angela, professional fisherwoman and diver, on a small fishing boat, 2004. Photograph by the author.

Gamboa de Baixo population have changed. A vast majority of these residents are unemployed, meaning that they tend to work in the informal urban economy, where they do not necessarily perform regular services or receive regular wages. One example of this kind of work is the recycling business, in which women like Dona Lenilda and her husband, Gegê, collect plastics, metals, and paper on the streets of Salvador and sell them to recycling manufacturers.

These articulations of class differences are deeply tied to racialized color differences, as well. During the 1980s and the early 1990s, traditional fishing families who lived closer to the oceanfront and traced their direct lineage to indigenous African and European ancestors were in constant conflict with the people who lived in the *malocas,* homes constructed beneath the concrete arches of Contorno Avenue, often shaky wooden shacks. The people living in the malocas, the majority of whom were poor and darker skinned, were considered to be the drug dealers, thieves, and prostitutes who gave Gamboa de Baixo a negative reputation as a criminal and dangerous neighborhood. This view of Gamboa de Baixo exemplifies some of the internal divisions that continue to exist today. For example, some residents avoid walking near the homes located near the central entrance to the neighborhood in order to avoid what they perceive as the dangerous elements who congregate and conduct illegal business. During discussions about the possible expulsion of Gamboa residents, some older residents even suggested that the criminals of the malocas should be the only ones relocated to the distant periphery.

These differences in origins, class, and color have posed serious challenges to community formation in Gamboa de Baixo, and this sense of political unity is essential to the construction and survival of black neighborhoods in the urban center. The newcomers challenge the political strategy of emphasizing generational ties to the land and what it means to be part of the community. Women such as Dona Lenilda and her daughter Lueci were the main proponents of a unified Gamboa de Baixo, leading the neighborhood association in forging a collective political identity and fighting against the removal of all residents despite their origin. Residents who do not belong to the traditional Gamboa de Baixo families have been on the forefront of the community movement, expanding the collective narrative of the neighborhood's history of ownership and belonging to include recent migrants from rural Bahia and other parts of the city (Map 4).

Whether recent migrants to Salvador or descendants of the first inhabitants of the land, they collectively had to grapple with the challenge of only a few residents having legal documentation of land ownership. Claiming native rights to the land in some instances countered

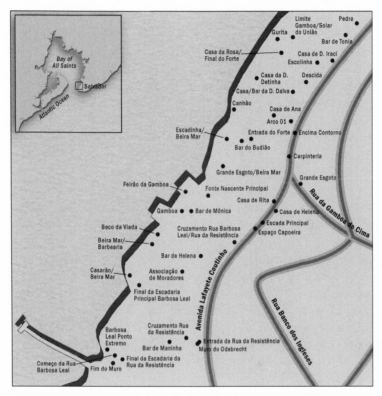

MAP 4. Inside the Gamboa de Baixo neighborhood. Map by Lynn Carlson, Brown University, 2012.

the official discourses that the community was merely an invasion of marginality or an illegal squatter settlement estimated to be less than thirty years old, whereas residents in fact traced their occupancy to slavery times, when blacks lived primarily on undesirable coastal lands. Asserting political power as a cohesive community has meant grappling with the dilemma of mobilizing around an extensive history of residence as a significant part of their cultural difference within the city, as this narrative excludes recent migrants. Ivana, an activist who moved from Rio de Janeiro to Salvador and settled in the neighborhood, suggests melding the interests of newer and older residents:

I do not see Gamboa as an "invasion." . . . There are already six or seven generations of the same family in Gamboa. That is a lot of time to say that it was invaded, that we invaded. Logically, there were other people who came from the outside, but those are few. . . . The great majority have lived here since their grandfathers and grandmothers came here, or their grandparents were born here. . . . That's why when they say it's an invasion, I fight with them. . . . Of course, there weren't this many people here, but it's not an invasion.

Emphasizing their history of settlement on the land, Ivana defends the residents' cultural differences and historical particularities. Her ideas reflect local activists' general sentiment that they represent various families who are historically rooted on the coastal land that they themselves have developed. They have fought to show that Gamboa de Baixo has its own culture that has developed on the coast and in the fort. Also, the neighborhood has grown beyond the original families that have settled there since the colonial period.

Dona Detinha, seventy-eight, recounts that she came to Gamboa at age ten to live with her father, an officer in the Bahian Navy, which gave him a house on the land. She stresses the changes in the community as the population has grown, including the fact that her teenage granddaughters are "so fresh these days," unlike when she was a child. She also wholeheartedly asserts the similarity between Gamboa de Baixo and other poor black neighborhoods in the city of Salvador, saying that blacks formed several other fishing communities like Gamboa de Baixo along the coast of the Bay of All Saints. The most notable difference is the presence of the fort, the area of Gamboa de Baixo in which her family still lives. Though they have had permission to live in the fort area for several decades, her family faces the possibility of removal if the government restores the area, which means that she still has to join forces with residents who have no documentation or little history on the land.

Using history as an interpretive tool of collective defiance, empowerment, and solidarity contests racial hegemony and reinscribes black communities on the coastal lands in the city center. Gamboa de Baixo residents critique dominant notions of the past that exclude them from local and national memories of Salvador. Michel-Rolph Trouillot's recommendation is that oppressed peoples should reject the idea of themselves as "prisoners" of their past and embrace the idea that "history is whatever [they] make it" (1995, xix). By this, Trouillot means that they must rewrite their own histories in order to empower and liberate themselves and their own communities. He writes, "History is the fruit of power, but power itself is never so transparent that its analysis becomes superfluous. The ultimate mark of power may be its invisibility; the ultimate challenge, the exposition of its roots" (xix). As the Gamboa de Baixo activists' dilemma of politicizing history illustrates, "Others' memories must compete with a 'public past' that is itself the result of the ability of a dominant social group to preserve certain recollections [and] *deemphasize* or otherwise *exclude* others" (Hanchard 1994, 151). The power of the historical narrative can be insufficient to overrule contemporary practices of sociospatial discrimination. A radical revision of local and national history needs to be expansive to express a sense of social belonging during urban redevelopment, so that the community movement includes both long-term residents and recent arrivals to the area.

Direct Action and the Gendering of Black Activism

Throughout the past decade, the neighborhood association has been engaged in an ongoing struggle to reverse the exclusionary practices of urban redevelopment practices in Salvador. Gamboa de Baixo activists have recognized that holding on to the historical narrative of being a traditional fishing colony poses political challenges for the women in the movement. As Dona Iraci recalls:

> We used to arrive at the urban development agency, and they would say, "Look here, you have fishermen? Where are they? I only see women. Aren't there any fishermen here?" We were a group of women, only women, that's how it was. They alleged that no one lived here, that only thieves lived here, understand? And we said no, that this was a fishing colony and that only fishermen lived here. . . . You know, it's difficult, isn't it, to say that a woman is a fisherman, too. (personal communication, 2000)

In meetings the lack of male participation and leadership made government officials suspicious of the women's claim that the community was a fishing colony more than a century old. They assumed that only men were fishermen and that a fishing community maintained certain gender norms that would lead to greater male leadership. This gendered perception of political activism was especially significant when they engaged in direct-action protests or confrontational politics with the state.

Late in the afternoon of August 24, 2004, residents of Gamboa de Baixo, armed with whistles, banners, and a megaphone, ambushed the entrance to the state water company, EMBASA (Empresa Baiana de Águas e Saneamento S.A.), in the Federação neighborhood. Dona Maria, a white-haired black woman in her late fifties whom some may consider an unlikely voice of neighborhood activism, led the surprise protest. None of the EMBASA employees, including the security guards, knew about the protest before it happened. No one suspected that the well-dressed group comprising mostly women and children were on their way to a political rally. They stopped at the gates of EMBASA and shouted, "We want water!" Local residents came out of their houses to see what was happening. Thirty-year-old Gamboa de Baixo neighborhood association activist Ana Cristina stepped up to the security guards and demanded to speak immediately with the water company's directors. Gamboa de Baixo residents wanted to discuss the lack of services in their neighborhood. "Water is a human right!" one protester exclaimed. Dona Maria waved her water bill in the faces of the security guards and shouted, "This is absurd! Why am I receiving water bills if there are no pipes installed in my home?" The security guard informed them that the directors were not available. The Gamboa de Baixo activists declared that no one would leave until they met with the directors. They were willing to wait.

The security guards called the administrators, who promptly agreed to meet with the leaders of the Gamboa de Baixo neighborhood association. A few minutes later, one of the directors, a white male in his midthirties, walked toward the crowd blocking the gate. The rally cries became louder: "We want water!" The director asked to speak with the president of the neighborhood association. Securing her baby on her hip, Luciene shouted back at him, "We don't have a president. We only have residents!" She demanded that he address everyone right there in front of the gates. The man turned his back and walked away, claiming that he refused to speak in front of everyone. Back still turned, he shouted, "I can only speak to two people." "But why?" the protesters asked. "There are too many of you, and there is no room inside my office," the man replied, turning to face the Gamboa de Baixo residents. They gave him a brash response: "We are willing to stand. Or we can stand here in front of the gates until tomorrow."

After several minutes of exchanges, the protesters and the director finally agreed to an emergency meeting with ten Gamboa de Baixo residents inside the EMBASA offices. The remaining activists agreed to not block the gates during the meeting, but their verbal exchange with the security guards continued. One woman accused the guards of being *capitães de mato,* a charged racial slur against the lighter-skinned black men. Within the legacy of slavery, the expression translates as "slave catchers" or "bounty men." She criticized them for being on the side of the white "masters" of EMBASA. The security guards were particularly perturbed when another activist, Rita, belted out the provocative lyrics of a hit song by famous Afro-Brazilian singer Elza Soares: "A carne mais barata do mercado é a carne negra" (The cheapest meat on the market is black meat). The crowd joined in. Shortly after, they received a phone call from an activist who was attending the meeting inside, informing them that the negotiations were going well. One important demand had been met: EMBASA directors signed an agreement to reduce water and sewer fees. The meeting attendees later returned to the rally participants in front of the gates and reported that the EMBASA directors had agreed to an emergency visit the following week to the Gamboa de Baixo neighborhood, where they would personally examine the current conditions of the water supply. They also promised to immediately complete the installation of water pipes and sewer systems (Figure 11).

At times Gamboa de Baixo residents found they needed to step up the intensity of their activism to demand social change. One told me, "When we conversed, things were not resolved. They only were resolved when we went crazy."

In the mid-1990s they took a social worker from the urban development company CONDER hostage. A tree fell on a water tank and

FIGURE 11. Ana Cristina and Rita at EMBASA protest, 2004. Photograph by the author.

injured a young girl. Residents had previously demanded that the development company cut down the tree. As Ana Cristina tells the story, "We were so upset that we took a female social worker, a director of the agency, as a hostage. Lueci said that she was going to 'squeeze the blood out of her,' and it was so crazy in the community, everyone mobilized, everyone was so nervous." The activists said that "they weren't going to let go of her as long as the president of CONDER did not arrive—as long as there was not a doctor to attend to the girl." The girl had been waiting in critical condition at the public hospital for more than twelve hours without receiving a doctor's attention and the emergency surgery she needed. "There she was in the hospital, with the bone sticking out, with no attention," says Ana Cristina. "Then, we said that we would only let the director go after she was attended to, when we were certain that the girl was being operated on."

The CONDER workers had gone to Gamboa de Baixo because the community activists had closed down the highway. The activists also surrounded the construction engineer, and "the community was not going to let anyone leave," Ana Cristina continues. All the local newspapers came to cover the "hostage crisis," and the activists realized that only during those moments did development agents take their work seriously. "They only take us seriously when they come to see that we are capable of facing the police, of facing the agency directors, government leaders, of facing the mayor, of cursing out even the governor in the newspaper. That was when they took us seriously," Ana Cristina says.

Protests such as this transform how we conceptualize black mobilization and resistance, particularly our understanding of black antiracism struggles in Brazil. For poor black women in Gamboa de Baixo, getting things done has meant, when necessary, collectively getting in the face of the powerful and demystifying their power and control. This political approach is unlike the culturalist approach that Michael Hanchard argues is the definitive characteristic of black activism (1994, 21, 139), claiming that there are "no Afro-Brazilian versions of boycotting, sit-ins, civil disobedience, and armed struggle" (1994, 139). Gamboa de Baixo protests illustrate that black activists do engage in acts of civil disobedience and violent struggle. During these moments, when even city officials have said that "they didn't think that 'those black women were going to speak'" (Dona Ladi, personal communication, 2000), the black women of Gamboa de Baixo have occupied the streets to speak out against land expulsion and demand better living conditions. Black women's participation in this social movement has become an important assertion of their voices in urban-space discourses that previously silenced them. For these women, contesting racial domination means reclaiming collective power through redefining black womanhood. Reconstructing political identities based on their own understanding of themselves as black is a source of empowerment necessary for political action. As Dona Nice explains:

I thought it was really important to speak about our pride in our skin, in our color, in our race. What I liked was to look a city official in the eye and say, "I am black," with pride. We didn't go to beg them for anything. We wanted our rights. It's important for us to arrive there and say, "I'm black, but I'm black with pride. I'm proud of who I am. I didn't come here to beg from you. I want my rights. The rights are mine." (personal communication, 2000)

To be taken seriously as poor blacks has been an important task for the Gamboa de Baixo community and political organization. Women often explain that their participation in this movement has transformed their previous sense of powerlessness as poor black women within the racist structures of urban governance. As Dona Nice explains, "If they slammed their hands on the table, we slammed loudly, too, looking them in the eye—things I wouldn't have done before but today I do them. . . . I learned that we can't hold our heads down because we're poor, because we're black women" (personal communication, 2000).

Many activists recall when former neighborhood association president Lueci, at eight months pregnant, was forcibly removed from a meeting. Activists immediately got up from the table and fought the security guards.

The Grupo de Mulheres (Women's Group), most active during the late 1990s and early 2000s, was a social movement within the neighborhood association that served as a meeting space for women's physical as well as political empowerment. Their main focus was mobilizing young adult women and teenagers to participate in the community organization and teaching them how to defend themselves and their communities. They organized workshops that included theater, poetry, and arts and crafts, along with other activities that focused on personal development, such as beauty treatments, exercise, family planning, and public speaking. The Women's Group represented a crucial dimension of radical formation in the lives of these women, who spent much time discussing their identities as black women and their social conditions as poor workers who needed to guarantee the survival of their families. They attended women's group activities in other neighborhoods, as well as those organized by black movement organizations such as MNU and UNEGRO.

In a planning meeting, Ritinha brought a book that reflected on the idea of African ancestral knowledge, with a focus on creating models of "new women." Ritinha read and discussed the histories of the Candomblé *orixás* (deities) Oxalá, Nanã, and Ogum. For her these lessons defined how they as black women had been transformed during the process of struggle. Women like Dona Nice opened up about how their experiences as activists had reaffirmed them as black women. They did not always previously have the courage to speak in public, much less invade a public works company. After reading the stories, Ana Cristina says, "I realized that Oxalá tried to create man by himself, but he was unable to. With the help of Nanã, he did it. The movement is like that. When the struggle is individualistic, there are no victories. But when you build with the collective, you have another dynamic." Dona Nice comments, "I don't know if I could have had the same strong will as Ogum, but I have confronted life, looking for faith and getting closer to God. In the association I have come to conquer knowledge. I know things I didn't know before."

During an interview Dona Nice revealed that through the movement she learned the following valuable lesson about Brazilian society: "Half of whites don't like black people. You know this. Racism exists, right? They are really racist, and there I was just accepting it all. I didn't like that. Today, I look at them differently. I say that I love my color. I'm black, and I'm proud of being black."

As shown in the lessons learned by Dona Nice and Ana Cristina, the general sentiment was that the neighborhood movement was a space for openly discussing racism and sexism in Salvador (Perry 2006). For these poor black women, sharing this kind of knowledge offered them the space to reflect on their experiences as workers and activists who generally had government agencies' doors shut in front of them. Their participation in the neighborhood association expanded their knowledge of race relations in Brazil in regard to public policy at the local and national levels. As Ana Cristina states, "The participation and organization of black women in Salvador and in Bahia in struggles against racial discrimination, police violence, and for dignified housing and land rights has been very important for the strengthening of social movements in Brazil. My militancy and that of other black women has revolved around guaranteeing citizenship rights in black communities and valorizing and uplifting the self-esteem of black women in Brazil" (personal communication, 2000).

New Freedom for Women

In 2007 I sat down with Ana Cristina in her living room to talk about how women had influenced the activist movement in Gamboa de Baixo and how their activism had changed them inwardly and in relation to the community. She explained the relationship between black women and the black movement as follows:

> In reality the black movement, some NGOs, and some other groups have contributed a lot, but I think [the base] made things different, which really made the government rethink its interventions. . . . When people begin to organize within the community, they don't know anything. Suddenly, because of the the arbitrary projects of the government, they feel the need to defend themselves, to defend their space. So it was these groups, in an effort to defend themselves, who were able to make changes, who showed that things had to be different. That you can't come to a community ready [to take action]. That projects had to be discussed within, discussed among us—not just with the women but also with the men, and the community as a whole. I think that really, for the most part, the women made a difference: they created change and made the government change the way it works.

I responded, "I think many people in general, at least in the academic world, have not given much value to black women in this sense, by saying, 'These are black women who did this.'" Ana Cristina described the reaction of academics to Gamboa de Baixo:

> The college students who visit the communities to do research for a paper are surprised when they arrive in Gamboa. They're expecting that if a woman is leading the community, she will be of a certain age, never young women, as is our case. They always expect women of forty, you know. They never expect women in their twenties, like we are.

She went on to talk about how women activists were able to change how various groups interacted with the community:

> Not only the government but all these other groups who typically do projects that end up serving the government to make interventions in the community—even they begin to pay more

attention to how the community thinks, what the community wants. So we, as a grassroots movement, the women's movement, really say to them that they have to change how they interact with us, and it really has changed. I can say with complete certainty that it wasn't the black movement that changed this, because the black movement made changes in terms of race and racial identity. But we achieved changes to [public policy]. We are predominantly black communities, all of us here in Salvador, a black majority. We changed this behavior and also changed the interventions.

I asked Ana Cristina if she thought that Gamboa had changed, especially with respect to the freedom that married women began to exercise. She had much to say about the new freedom for women that resulted from their activism:

That has changed a lot! . . . You see, before, women were the most repressed and oppressed. We couldn't do anything. We couldn't talk about anything. . . . The question of women's freedom in Gamboa has changed a lot. People are more at ease, saying what's on their mind. I remember Ivana, for example. Before Ivana started participating in the meetings, going to the street protests, going to a meeting with a bunch of people, more than fifty or seventy people, to speak, to say what she thinks we need to do to defend ourselves—before then, Ivana was always in the house. I never saw her. But today, who is Ivana? She's divorced now. She leaves the house; she gets home in the early morning. Is this what we consider to be freedom? Yes, this is freedom, because before she would never do that. Her husband wouldn't allow it, nor society, nor the community. And it was through this [political] process that Ivana, Rita, I, and Lia learned that we could do anything, that we had the right to certain things. What taught us that? It was the struggle against expulsion from Gamboa. It was the struggle around the racial question, our self-esteem as blacks. It was the struggle around the question of being a woman, of gender—I can do this, I don't have to do that.

Prior to their involvement in political activism, the women of Gamboa de Baixo had little sexual freedom. Ana Cristina described how the movement changed how they conceived of their sexuality and how they came to understand the relationship between sex and their struggle for rights:

And what is gender? For example, the question of sexuality, the discovery of sexuality. Now we have the courage to discuss sex at meetings. Before, we wouldn't talk about it. We didn't have the courage to talk about a lot of things. The neighborhood association and the struggle taught us a lot. It taught us that the struggle for housing is not just about blocking the street and saying that we want houses. It taught us that the struggle for housing is to say that we want houses, we want employment, we want education, we want women's rights. We want to occupy spaces as women, and in order to do this, we have to sit in a circle only as women to discuss our pain. Then we ask, "How is your relationship with your husband? Is it good or bad? If your husband flirts with other women, what does he do when he sees you flirting with another man?" We have to discuss these various kinds of things. We have to talk about the thing that we didn't even know what it was before—sexual pleasure. It was like that for me, for Rita, and for a lot of women in Gamboa, in terms of the freedom that we didn't have. Just the fact that today, any of us can speak with great facility about the question of sex, this shows how much we have liberated ourselves, how the organization of women in Gamboa has given us our right to be free.

Ana Cristina spoke about how this freedom for women also included new financial freedom:

Before, you would come down to Gamboa, you would go into the houses, and normally the men would be working. Most were at sea, of course—Gamboa is a fishing community. Some working on the streets [outside the home], the women working in the home. Today, you might see ten men in the house and women working outside the home. So women learned that one way to ensure their own freedom in relationship to men was financial independence. Because a lot of men did not allow their wives to work; they needed permission. Today, women are freer; they're more beautiful. Women are even more warrior-like, and there are more lesbians.

The new freedom also extended to gays and lesbians in Gamboa de Baixo, according to Ana Cristina:

This freedom has made more women courageous in terms of self-esteem. It was so important in our process, of Gamboa, that women could discover all aspects of themselves. Even the issue of sexual orientation, which we didn't have before: we couldn't say that we did or did not have lesbians, because you didn't see them. It was subtle, hidden, and it made people uncomfortable. They would be afraid. There was a lot of prejudice. Just in the neighborhood association today, I can count three people who the community knows [are gay or lesbian]. But people respect these men and women as community leaders. So you see, this process of organization has made a difference.

Black women grassroots activists expand the definition of the black movement to include the masses who are engaged in direct-action protest. Black communities focus on material issues, such as water, that are not always recognized as racial issues. These communities are the main agents pushing the state toward more-inclusive urban redevelopment policies—policies that have a positive impact on the lives of black people and the places where they create and preserve black culture (Garcia 2006, 2012). This collective sense of preserving community reflects women's ongoing involvement in social groups that they have established with their families and their neighbors in the places where they live. As eighty-nine-year-old resident Nana stated at the peak of the government's threats of expulsion, "From here I only leave for the sky" (Bahia Hoje, August 25, 1995).

Despite disrespectful treatment from city officials and police violence, these women find power in the public assertion of their racial and gender identities. Given black women's position at the absolute bottom of the social strata, their actions during meetings and protests mark the struggle to counter their everyday experiences with racism and sexism in the public sphere. More significant, black women's actions in the face of the government seek to bring attention to the racist core of urban displacement and resistance. Accepting the rapid growth of a large metropolis like Salvador, they adapt to the necessary demographic changes that the neighborhood must experience but fight for neighborhood improvements, such as infrastructure changes. They promote the idea that Gamboa de Baixo is a place where people should want to live, work, and raise their children.

Black women play central roles in forging a sense of community through the social activities they organize and the support networks they create when residents need essential services such as health care or child care. Recognizing the political aspects of maintaining households and communities allows us to understand how these networks reproduce social relations, help to "sustain the social fabric of community" (Feldman, Stall, and Wright 1998, 261), and politicize place-based identities. For many generations women in Gamboa de Baixo have nurtured and provided social services to each other. Like the Women's Association of the 1980s, the neighborhood association and the Women's Group are "intimately connected to ongoing struggles for rights and control over spatial resources to house social-reproduction activities that create and sustain these communities" (261). Neighborhood mobilization forces us to rethink black resistance, as well as reconsider the ways in which blacks offer alternative views on the way Brazilian society operates and should operate. In the following chapter, I explore how fighting police abuse has become an integral part of the neighborhood political project.

4

VIOLENT POLICING AND DISPOSING OF URBAN LANDSCAPES

eu bato contra o muro
duro
esfolo minhas mãos no muro
tento de longe o salto e pulo
dou nas paredes do muro
duro
não desisto de forçá-lo
hei de encontrar um furo
por onde ultrapassá-lo

i beat against the wall
hard
i scrape my hands on the wall
i try to jump over it from far away
i bang against the wall
hard
i don't give up trying to force it
i must find a hole
to get through it

Oliveira Silveira, "o muro" (the wall)

i have been locked by the lawless.
Handcuffed by the haters.
Gagged by the greedy.
And, if I know anything at all,
it's that a wall is just a wall
and nothing more at all.
It can be broken down.

Assata Shakur, excerpt from "Affirmation," 1987

The Wall

"O muro," a 1982 poem by Afro-Brazilian poet-activist Oliveira Silveira, embodies various meanings for the black majority in Brazil, who confront multiple social and economic barriers to their survival and advancement. The term *muro* may allude to the thick glass ceiling in the job market, university entrance exams, police barricades, gated communities, or even the guard with the metal detector at the bank. The wall is a metaphor for understanding the gendered racial and class inequality that governs Brazilian cities—for example, the fact that black women represent the largest segment of unemployed workers (Rezende and Lima 2004; Wilding 2012). Finding a hole in the wall, or even attempting to climb over it, becomes a lifelong struggle for black people and, even more so, for poor black women. Attempting to break down the wall is potentially dangerous and likely to lead to injury or even death.

In Gamboa de Baixo and throughout the city of Salvador, actual concrete walls have come to signify racial boundaries, legitimate and illegitimate ownership, and segregation, and Contorno Avenue is the most important wall structure in the spatial, social, and political formation of the Gamboa de Baixo community. Since the street's construction, walls have evinced exclusion as much as they have suggested inclusion, resulting in the "production of included and excluded bodies" (Razack 2002, 10). Conflicts surrounding the recent construction of O Morada dos Cardeais (The House of the Cardinals), a thirty-seven-story luxury apartment complex, and current challenges to maintaining positive neighborhood relations provide glaring examples of the social, physical, and economic segregation between rich and poor and black and white residential communities in Brazilian cities. A glimpse into the daily lives of Gamboa de Baixo residents illustrates some of the social meanings of walls, specifically as they relate to the unique political dynamics of urban redevelopment in Salvador's city center.

These conflicts must be understood within the context of current urban renewal practices, which many social movement activists argue privilege coastal and vertical construction (high-rises) for white middle- and upper-class Bahians. Although blacks have composed the majority of the coastal population since the slavery period, critics of urban development policies maintain that "the coast will be for those who can afford it" (*A Tarde*, March 15, 2007), meaning those who are rich and white.

Income in Brazil is measured by monthly minimum wage. The current minimum wage is R$678 per month, which is the equivalent of US$317. Sixty-one percent of families in gated communities earn R$12,440 per month (US$6900), or about twenty times the minimum monthly wage. About half of families in poor neighborhoods like Gamboa earn the minimum wage of R$678 per month or less, placing them below the poverty level (*A Tarde,* March 15, 2007). According to Kia Lilly Caldwell, black women, especially those living in the poorest urban neighborhoods, traditionally have been consigned to a "de facto status of non-citizens," occupying not only the spatial margins of cities but also the socioeconomic margins as the poorest of Brazil's poor (2007, 135).

Walls, whether physical or symbolic, push women and blacks to the margins and create disposable subjects. Walls are the first visible sign of the disposal of black coastal neighborhoods during urban redevelopment. As Katherine McKittrick and Clyde Woods state, "Black and poor subjects are disposable precisely because they cannot easily move or escape" (2007, 3). Among Bahia's white elite, urban development also encourages self-segregation behind the physical walls that surround luxury condominiums.

The act of policing is central to constructing, maintaining, and disposing of black marginalized landscapes and the people who occupy them (Fikes 2009). Black feminist theorist Patricia Hill Collins points out that blacks' heightened "visibility can bring increased surveillance" (1998, 51). The increased visibility of Gamboa de Baixo as a target of urban removal and then as a politically organized neighborhood fighting expulsion made it susceptible to increased policing and, as a result, police abuse. Arbitrary police invasions involve illegal searches and seizures, extortion, beatings, and psychological terror (shouting racist, sexist, and homophobic epithets). Pointing firearms directly at residents and randomly shooting at them and into their houses have become routine.

Experiences in Gamboa de Baixo with police violence show that geographic margins should be understood as deeply connected to gendered and racialized socioeconomic status, marginality, and criminalization, echoing Ruth Wilson Gilmore's claim that "a geographical imperative lies at the heart of every struggle for social justice" (2002, 16) and bell hooks's assertion that "this space of radical openness is a margin—a profound edge. Locating oneself there is difficult but necessary. It is not a 'safe' place. One is always at risk. One needs a community of resistance" (1990, 449). Gamboa de Baixo is one such community of resistance, and claiming urban space amid the proliferation of private residential investments and police violence represents a key political focus of black feminist struggles in Brazil. Even as the quality of housing and basic infrastructure has been improving in Gamboa de Baixo since the late 1990s, residents do not have legal rights to the coveted coastal lands. The grassroots struggle for permanence has been forced to grapple with public and private policing that plays a crucial role in whitening coveted urban landscapes such as Gamboa de Baixo.

From the vantage point of black women who live in Gamboa de Baixo and lead the ongoing neighborhood movement against expulsion and for land and housing rights, community relations during urban renewal and land redistribution are more fraught with racial tension and violence than is apparent. O Morada dos Cardeais was built by Odebrecht, a multinational conglomerate that is one of the largest construction, chemical, and oil companies in the world. The construction of the complex threatened not only the neighborhood's permanence but also the livelihoods and individual and collective safety of its residents. Gamboa de Baixo activists consider the complex to be a continuation of recent state-sponsored efforts to revitalize the city center along the Bay of All Saints for tourism and luxury real estate. Such development further creates gendered racial and class hierarchies and heightened security in the region and contributes to the gendered racialization and criminalization of the Gamboa de Baixo neighborhood. The "racial state's aggressively punitive stance" on combating crime in Salvador has meant that the state police apparatus "formalizes inequality" and deepens elitist, racist, and gendered justifications for demolishing this poor neighborhood and relocating its black residents to the outskirts of the city (Gilmore 2002, 21).

The daily acts of police violence stem from the government's view of the entire neighborhood as criminal. Policing black neighborhoods represents not just a politics of containment but also a politics of exclusion tied to urban renewal (Collins 2001; Fikes 2009; Samara 2011; Vargas 2008). Gamboa de Baixo is seen not only as a dangerous part of the city but as simply not belonging in it.

This public view that informs state police actions has shaped how the black women–led Gamboa de Baixo movement couples the gendered and class-based racism embedded in state reurbanization practices with police destruction of black neighborhoods. Private real estate developments with elaborate security mechanisms in the area illuminate the inextricable relationship between the violence of unequal urban development and the violence of policing. Gamboa de Baixo's grassroots struggle to undermine "hegemonic spatial practices" (McKittrick and Woods 2007, 7) of urban land expulsion and segregation reaffirms the need for black women to mobilize around spatial politics as an important strategy to positively transform black neighborhoods.

Fortresses Within: The Politics of Inclusion

Urban theorist Mike Davis describes Los Angeles as a "fortress city" (1992, 225–26). As in Salvador, magnified perceptions of the threat of violence from the so-called criminal underclass (young black men and poor Latino families) dominate the white middle-class imagination. This mobilizes middle-class communities to isolate themselves and build residential fortresses with security systems aimed at keeping out the criminal poor. This fear has less to do with crime rates than with status, for as Davis argues, poor people in cities worry just as much about violent crime as do rich people (224). Furthermore, in cities such as Salvador black women like Simone and Rita in Gamboa de Baixo, the majority of whom head their households and lead social networks in their communities, are the main decision makers about housing design, which increasingly includes physical forms of protection.

As black women in Gamboa de Baixo have fought to stake their claim to the land below Contorno Avenue and around the historic São Paulo Fort, another wall has emerged as a popular feature of neighborhood design. In recent years the number of homes in Gamboa de Baixo that have enclosed their doors, windows, and verandas with burglar bars has increased significantly. This change in the urban landscape has transformed social customs and everyday habits. Traditionally, the narrow streets have always been an extension of residents' homes. Conversations among neighbors take place primarily in doorways and while sitting on front steps or makeshift wooden and concrete benches. The women's association that later became the neighborhood association began with conversations among women on each other's doorsteps, which partly fed male perception of the community organization as something that women do. The burglar bars protecting the houses now limit these kinds of conversations, as well as how freely children are able to play in neighbors' backyards. The bars reduce and control direct access to these spaces, solidifying social divisions between public and private spaces in the neighborhood.

An incident with activist Rita made me understand how fiercely the women of Gamboa de Baixo must protect themselves from predators in their own neighborhood. Rita had installed a steel burglar fence around her veranda (Figure 12). When I would stop in front of her home to speak with her, I found myself talking through the bars of the front gate. One day, as she rushed to open the lock, she saw a young woman she recognized passing by. She grabbed the girl's neck and almost lifted her off her feet. As Rita's sister leaped to separate the two women, Rita said, "Sacizeira!" a term akin to "crackhead." She explained, "She climbed in my back window and stole from me." She said to the girl, "Listen, I'll kill you if you ever come near my house again."

After she let go of the young woman, Rita exclaimed, "Can you believe the nerve of that woman? Do you know how hard I work for someone to just come and climb through my window and rob me?" Rita works as a domestic worker six days a week and is a single parent of two teenage children. "And then just prance by my house as if nothing happened?" Rita shook her head. "Damn, she climbed through the only window without burglar bars."

In decades past, residents of Gamboa de Baixo may have taken their safety for granted in this small community where everyone knew each other, but today, burglar bars protecting entrances, yards, and windows have become a staple security mechanism for homeowners. When they are not available, makeshift security devices like wooden sticks are inserted into windowsills to prevent windows from being opened from the outside. Petty theft, drug trafficking, and intracommunity violence are on the rise, especially violent crimes related to the influx of crack cocaine. "Crack has taken over the city!" residents exclaim. They often remark, "The Gamboa of today is no longer the Gamboa of yesterday," specifically referring to the limitations placed on housing designs and

FIGURE 12. Rita on her veranda in front of the burglar bars, 2008. Photograph by the author.

everyday social habits as a result of the general fear of violence. In the past Rita would not have needed to install grates on her windows, and visitors would have gone directly inside her house to speak with her. The increased violence in these neighborhoods has imprisoned residents, who feel less safe outside the physical confines of their homes. Their fears are real, as demonstrated by the theft at Rita's house. In December 2007 three drug-related murders were reported in Gamboa de Baixo.

A clear relationship exists between increased drug trafficking and use and increased intracommunity violence, a social dynamic that residents have had to deal with on a daily basis. As Rita demonstrated, residents sometimes direct their anger toward the *sacizeiros* who have been coming to the neighborhood in increasing numbers to buy drugs. Rarely do residents use the term *sacizeiro* to describe the upper-class white men and women who come to Gamboa to buy drugs and then quickly take off in their cars and on their motorcycles. As one Gamboa de Baixo resident reports, "I work at a university, and there, a lot of sons and daughters of the rich use drugs. I've never seen the police crack down in upper-class neighborhoods" (*JLC News,* January 6, 2008). The neighborhood's drug addicts, especially those addicted to crack cocaine, tend to be dirty and disheveled young black men and women. They linger in the neighborhood, beg for food, and offer to carry groceries or construction materials in exchange for money. They resell stolen goods that many residents are reluctant to buy because, as a resident says, "when the police invade your house here in Gamboa, they think that if you have nice stuff then it must be stolen." The police commonly ask people for receipts for items found in their homes.

These sacizeiros also are not gamboeiros, a key distinction that residents are quick to make. The day after the first major police raid in January 2008, the city's main newspaper, *A Tarde,* printed a photograph of police hovering over young black boys and girls, supposedly drug dealers, sitting against the wall along Contorno Avenue. When Ana Cristina saw the photograph, she cried, "Look at this! This is ridiculous! *None,* I mean *none,* of these people live in Gamboa." For this activist the front-page story further tarnished her neighborhood's reputation during the arduous political process of trying to secure land rights and permanence (Figure 13).

FIGURE 13. A military police officer jumps the wall of Contorno Avenue to invade the neighborhood. This photograph appears on the cover of the January 4, 2008, edition of *A Tarde.* The caption reads, "Police operation in Gamboa de Baixo, on the Contorno Avenue, to combat drug trafficking. The operation resulted in a minor being shot and 26 suspects being detained." Photograph by Elói Corrêa, courtesy of Agência A Tarde.

Residents are aware of the undermining image of Gamboa de Baixo as an area of poor black drug dealers and users, but they also pay attention to the intracommunity dynamics that produce their fear of violence and the urgent need to construct physical barriers to protect their property. Ana Cristina's best friend, Simone, who recently completed construction on a large two-story house, decided to build three high concrete walls around her property (Figure 14). During a tour of her home while it was under construction, I asked, "Are you building a mansion or a fort?" She replied, "You wait until I put broken glass on top of it. Not even the rats will want to climb over that wall!"

Simone was less worried, however, about the rats than about gunfire, the possibility of theft, and the use of her backyard as an escape route for police fugitives. The need for a physical barrier became even more crucial when, during the January police raid—before she moved in—bullets were fired into the walls of her house. These walls would

FIGURE 14. Simone's multistory house under construction (middle). Ana Cristina resides in the white house two houses to its left, 2008. Photograph by the author.

later become her daughter's playroom, the washroom, and a veranda for sunbathing and parties. She said, "Imagine if the house had been finished and we had been living inside?" For Simone the wall around her home is a matter of life and death for her and her family.

Fear of intracommunity crime and violence, accompanied by the construction of concrete walls and other physical barriers, has become normal and expected in urban communities (Souza 2008). For anthropologist Teresa Caldeira Brazilian cities such as São Paulo have become "cities of walls" where "residents from all social groups argue that they build walls and change their habits to protect themselves from crime" (2000, 297). Security is a basic element of high-rise apartment buildings. Caldeira comments, "Fortified enclaves confer status. The construction of status symbols is a process that elaborates social differences and creates means for the assertion of social distance and inequality" (258). These fortified enclaves exemplify the modern ideal of city living. Davis states, "As a prestige symbol—and sometimes as the decisive borderline between the merely well-off and the 'truly rich'—'security' has less to do with personal safety than with the degree of personal insulation, in residential, work, consumption and travel environments, from 'unsavory' groups and individuals, even crowds in general" (224).

In Gamboa de Baixo burglar bars and walls have become a symbol of both protection and status. Residents' perceptions of neighborhood violence reflect repeated statements by Simone, Rita, and Ana Cristina that they would much rather live in Gamboa and that what happens here is nowhere near as bad as what happens in some other neighborhoods in the city. The Gamboa of today may not be the Gamboa of yesterday, but the neighborhood continues to be a desirable place to live, perceived by its residents as better than most neighborhoods throughout Salvador. It is not uncommon to hear these sentiments among activists and residents, which is the primary reason that the grassroots movement against land expulsion has been so strong. Residents make statements like, "I don't see myself living anywhere else," and, "From here, I leave dead." As one woman recounts, "How many times have I even heard police officers going down the hill talking among themselves, saying, 'It's way too beautiful here'?"

Comparative neighborhood surveys on violent crime in Salvador would probably undermine depictions of the neighborhood as a labyrinth of drugs, violent crime, and prostitution. Three violent deaths in Gamboa de Baixo during December 2007, however, challenged political efforts to undo the public image of the neighborhood as a place of terror where the police battle the criminalized poor (see Davis 1992, 224). For some local residents the walls and gates protect them from both internal and external terror, specifically from the police, whom many residents believe contribute to the everyday increase in crime and a generalized culture of fear (Souza 2008; Vargas 2006).

Urban theorists have given little attention to precisely how poor people perceive fear and the fortresses and other mechanisms of security they construct around themselves. Even with limited means, residents of neighborhoods such as Gamboa de Baixo see walls and gates as necessary housing-design features. Thus, fortresses are not limited to the rich. This scholarly tendency to focus on upper-class communities takes us back to the common assertion among Gamboa de Baixo residents that rarely are rich people in Salvador criminalized, but also to Mike Davis's argument that certain security technologies are available only to the rich. Poor people depend on the security provided by the police, but as I show in further descriptions of police operations in Gamboa de Baixo, neighborhood residents believe that the state contributes more to the destruction of their neighborhood than to its betterment during the ongoing public battle for urban land rights. In cities like Salvador, "'Security' becomes a positional good defined by income access to private 'protective services' and membership in some hardened residential enclave" (Davis 1992, 224).

The walls and burglar bars of Gamboa de Baixo illustrate the fear that poor black people experience, but they also show that residents refuse to allow their fear to make them accede to what development agents have argued is the inevitable removal of residents from that area of the city. They build the security mechanisms necessary to remain on the urban land to which they claim rights. In other words, they build walls and gates as a way of containing themselves safely within their homes. A key dimension of the political struggle, this represents a practice of self-inclusion on the coastal lands rather than exclusion from it.

High-Rise Power, Low-Rise Defiance

On February 28, 2008, a disastrous flood damaged the home of neighborhood activist Adriano, one of two men active in the association at the time. Ana Cristina was stuck in traffic on the waterlogged streets of Salvador, standing on a hot, crowded bus of panicked passengers. She did not reach Gamboa de Baixo until two o'clock in the morning, and as soon as she arrived, wet and exhausted, she was called to the eastern side of her neighborhood, which shared a wall with the O Morada dos Cardeais residential community. A landslide from the hillside of the luxury apartment complex had torn down a portion of the wall that separated the two communities. As a young woman heard the wall collapsing onto her house, she leaped on top of her children to protect them. While her children escaped uninjured, she was hospitalized with head injuries.

Gamboa de Baixo activists contacted representatives of Odebrecht, the company that built the high-rises, and Odebrecht immediately agreed to take responsibility for the cleanup and reconstruction. This dialogue was the result of years of struggle and Gamboa de Baixo's demands for respect as neighbors who had lived on the land for many years before the apartment complex was built. Since construction of the apartment community began, local residents have insisted that attention be paid to the environmental safety of the landscape. These sorts of disasters are not natural but rather, as some residents have always expressed, the consequences of environmental shifts due to mass construction on the coastal lands. In this instance the wall between Gamboa de Baixo and O Morada dos Cardeais failed both communities. Odebrecht's willingness to promptly rebuild the house and the wall speaks volumes about the wall's origin in wealthy residents' need for spatial segregation and the construction company's financial resources to enforce such segregation (Figure 15).

Walls in Gamboa de Baixo generally have been perceived as necessary forms of protection, but residents have asserted that the wall that separates them from O Morada dos Cardeais was constructed to contain as well as exclude Gamboa residents. The wall demarcates the space and the place of Gamboa de Baixo residents; they have no rights to the land beyond the wall. The self-containment of O Morada dos Cardeais residents operates differently from the self-containment that Gamboa de Baixo residents practice. The self-containment of Gamboa de Baixo residents is more about belonging, rather than exclusion; they are creating security mechanisms to guarantee their safe permanence in the area.

A low wall built by the Archdiocese of Bahia, the previous landowners, existed on the eastern perimeter of Gamboa de Baixo before Odebrecht bought the property. Odebrecht extended the height and width of the wall, however, before the construction of O Morada dos Cardeais began in 2003. The wall was immediately met with suspicion on the part of Gamboa de Baixo residents, who lost significant access to space in their backyards and to open views of the bushy hillside. The previous wall did not extend all the way to the oceanfront, whereas the new wall made access to the shore and the land in front of their homes extremely difficult. Residents were no longer able to grow vegetables and fruits there, and one Gamboa home was demolished during construction.

FIGURE 15. A concrete wall separates Gamboa de Baixo and O Morada dos Cardeais. Photograph by Ana Cristina da Silva Caminha, 2011.

The extension of the wall was just the beginning of numerous problems that surfaced as a result of Odebrecht's acquisition of the coastal land for the luxury apartment community. The name of the community refers to the mansion on Contorno Avenue that had housed some of Brazil's most important cardinals for almost a century. Gamboa de

Baixo activists negotiated with the Catholic Church for several years to take ownership of the part of the land that was in their community. Instead, the church sold the former cardinals' house and the land to Odebrecht, including an area where Gamboa residents continued to live. This transaction occurred without the knowledge of the community, exemplifying years of strained relationships between the community and the Archdiocese of Salvador.

Community activists were particularly disappointed because they believed that the transfer of land rights from the church would have further legitimated their rights to permanence in the area and would have strengthened their movement against the state government's land-expulsion plans. As the lawyer for Odebrecht confirmed during meetings with Gamboa de Baixo activists, "Priests certainly don't sell anything for cheap," which supported the activists' claims that the land sale to the corporation was primarily for capitalist gain, contradicting claims by the church that it sought to defend the interests of marginalized groups in Brazil. In fact, the Catholic Church in Bahia and throughout the country has always struggled to come to terms with its history of land usurpation from indigenous and black peoples but has been unable to make proper reparations for these past actions, even when communities like Gamboa de Baixo have presented their cases for land ownership. As a result the Gamboa de Baixo neighborhood association has redirected its efforts toward negotiating the return of community land from Odebrecht. The corporation has never publicly suggested that they plan to displace the local population, but representatives have admitted that as a result of the political organization of the neighborhood, they had to change some of their original construction plans, which included the destruction of more than the two Gamboa residences for which owners were compensated. The relationship between the neighbors who share Contorno Avenue, the beach, and the waters of the Bay of All Saints remains tenuous.

Ana Cristina, critical of the church's historical land usurpation, affirms that with the construction of the new wall, Odebrecht physically reinforced what already existed symbolically. Though the previous wall hardly posed a barrier to residents and the cardinals had no security mechanisms, the previous wall also served as a marker of spatial and social separation between the elite house of white cardinals and the poor black fishing community. Another resident activist explains the inconveniences of the wall as follows:

> The archbishop's wall was low, which made it difficult for rats to get into our homes. Now rats climb up to the roof. And you never know what they're going to throw down on us from up there. One day they threw a rock from a building on the other side of the street. It hit the middle of my house. If someone had been passing by, the person could have been injured. (*A Tarde,* August 4, 2004)

The new wall is much different in size than the previous wall, which was barely noticeable and hardly posed a physical barrier to residents who planted and cultivated the land on the other side. Nor did the wall pose any sanitation danger, such as rodent invasions. As Ana Cristina suggests, however, a wall is a wall is a wall—to borrow Angela Gilliam's statement that a "slave is a slave is a slave" (1992), meaning that oppression by any other name is still oppression. Regardless of its size, the previous wall served as a marker of spatial and social separation. Now, it is a constant reminder that even though residents previously freely moved about the land—as had their ancestors well before the cardinals settled there—without land titles, it is no longer their land.

Coastal Luxury and Spatial Entitlement

In the luxury apartment residences of O Morada dos Cardeais reside some of Bahia's and Brazil's wealthiest citizens. The most famous resident lives in the multimillion-dollar penthouse, *axé* singer Ivete Sangalo. Gamboa de Baixo residents like to jest that they are "Ivete's neighbors," which should give status to their neighborhood. They constantly report Ivete sightings, but they admit that it is probably unlikely that Ivete boasts of Gamboa de Baixo as an ideal neighbor. The gated luxury apartment communities overlooking the Bay of All Saints are some of the most desirable forms of housing for Salvador's elite, including famous artists and executives from development agencies such as Odebrecht. Historically, the Vitória neighborhood has had some of the largest and fanciest closed condominiums for upper-class

Bahian and foreign residents, most of whom are white. The majority of blacks who transit these spaces tend to be housekeepers, drivers, landscapers, and security guards.

Several cable cars have been constructed to transport the residents from these buildings down the hillside to the docks, where they access their boats, swim, or spend leisure time. There are already twelve cable cars along the coastline of the Vitória neighborhood, and these apartment buildings are extending their piers farther and farther into the ocean. In 2003 several condominiums signed an agreement with the Ministério Público to protect the natural environment of the coastline by limiting the number of cable cars they build and to replant trees and other vegetation to recover the traditional landscape destroyed during the cars' construction. Odebrecht's use of the land to build a cable car and a pier for O Morada dos Cardeais suffered severe public scrutiny before the construction was completed, but the company did not eliminate its plans to develop the coastline for leisure activities such as boating. In fact, the developed coastline remains a key aspect of the luxury lifestyle that the complex offers. The modern pier rises and lowers into the water depending on tide levels, helping boaters to board their yachts. This elite group of residents can afford not only to live in the apartments but to purchase the goods necessary to take full advantage of amenities like a modern pier. The complex is located near two well-established yacht clubs. Gamboa de Baixo continues to be one of a few poor fishing communities in the city center remaining on the coast, all of which are engaged in fierce battles with the state and private enterprises such as the yacht club for land rights.

Before the building was completed, in 2004 neighborhood activists secretly obtained copies of the property's marketing information that Odebrecht distributed to potential wealthy buyers. The pictures are seductive, and the layouts of the different apartment models are spectacular. Gamboa activists jokingly suggested that the family that Odebrecht displaced should have requested an apartment instead of accepting payment. Odebrecht does not mention Gamboa de Baixo anywhere in the booklet, which includes a detailed history of the church's historical affiliation with the land. In fact, in an enlarged photograph of the building that covers four pages in the booklet, Odebrecht has deleted some of the area where Gamboa lies and replaced most of the neighborhood with an image of a lush green landscape that includes houses from the Solar do Unhão neighborhood and the São Paulo da Gamboa Fort.

These false representations resemble the tactics that Bahian development agencies have used to demonstrate that the revitalization of Gamboa de Baixo has been successful. Gamboa de Baixo is visibly absent from the revitalized landscape in state urban development brochures, or photographs of the Solar do Unhão neighborhood are shown to represent Gamboa de Baixo. Odebrecht's brochure includes an image of the modern cable car that links the apartment building to the pier on the beach in front of land where actual Gamboa de Baixo residences are located. (The photograph was taken from the ocean, looking onto the landscape, and was altered to replace the Gamboa de Baixo neighborhood with trees.) A purposeful and clever marketing strategy, as black movement activist and resident of Gamboa de Baixo Leo notes, "the building's blueprint showed all this to be full of trees. When the buyer comes to live here they will see that it is not so green" (*A Tarde*, August 8, 2004). The marketing materials represent a state-supported ideal for the land, a place for the white elite to live and play without black and poor neighbors, reflecting broader urban development efforts to cleanse the area of its marginal population.

Along with the presentation of the beauty of the clean, lush coastal landscape without the presence of the Gamboa neighborhood, Odebrecht provides the following description of the buyer's future neighbors:

> It is on this stage that the curtains open to the Morada dos Cardeais. In the neighborhood are the Museum of Modern Art (MAM), Solar do Unhão, the imperial Vitória, monasteries, and century-old churches, with modern replicas such as the Castro Alves Theater and the Bahia Yacht Club. All of these represent the most traditional area of the city. (Odebrecht 2004)

The description fails to mention the century-old fishing community of Gamboa de Baixo, which is located closer to the complex than the selected historical and modern sites.

In this most public sense, Odebrecht refused to acknowledge that the more than 250 families in Gamboa de Baixo were as significant a part of the natural landscape as the fort, the museum, and the wealthy

Vitória neighborhood. This is the kind of public erasure that poor black communities experience in Salvador. Black people and the spaces they inhabit are written out of popular discourses on Bahian history, as well as out of the local geographic history of Salvador's urban center. These communities are simultaneously visible and invisible. They are visible enough to pose a threat to elite housing developments but invisible to urban developers such as Odebrecht, who have private and state support for ignoring them.

The marketing brochure continues, "Bahia, sanctuary of art and beauty. Fertile land, open sea toward an enterprise that seals a venture with tradition, quality, and sophistication. A landmark in the life of those who are sure to live in grand style." Bahian cardinal Dom Geraldo Majella Agnelo contributes the following to the brochure, "May the Beloved Senhor do Bonfim, Our Savior and Lord of Peace, bless and protect the future residents of the bold undertaking of Odebrecht." In addition to blessings from the cardinal, residents of O Morada dos Cardeais received the protection of sophisticated security apparatuses installed on the property, a necessary aspect of their luxurious lifestyle. During construction armed security guards worked twenty-four hours a day to prevent trespassing and theft of construction materials. Gamboa de Baixo residents believed that the security was meant for them, part of the constant depiction of their neighborhood as poor and criminal.

Activist Leo states that he anticipated that residents of Gamboa de Baixo were going to pay the price for Odebrecht's plans to privatize access to the coastline by extending its pier far out into the ocean. This was not just a security concern, as local residents had already criticized the Bahia Marina Yacht Club for destroying the bay's ecosystem when they built their pier in the mid-1990s. One contentious issue was the yacht club's construction of a stone breakwater that changed the ocean's natural currents and negatively affected fishing activities along the coastline. More significant, the club's security guards often prevented fishermen from fishing from the breakwater, a previously unregulated area. Gamboa de Baixo residents who scuba dive or snorkel in the waters around the Vitória neighborhood are often harassed by security guards. In some instances boaters have ignored buoys that divers use to indicate their presence and have endangered their lives by recklessly speeding over them. Some apartment residences use buoys in the water to demarcate their territories. Though Gamboa de Baixo residents primarily use the waters for fishing, some security guards discourage any type of physical contact with the piers—an extension of the luxury apartment communities that require protection. As Angela, a professional diver and an activist in the neighborhood and the fishing associations, says, "They think we're pirates, that we'll jump out of the water to rob them, and then row our boats back home." Her accounts of violent encounters between these security guards and Gamboa de Baixo fishermen and fisherwomen further express the ridiculous nature of these assumptions about the residents' criminality. As Leo's previous statement reveals, this price is one that Gamboa de Baixo residents are paying for the increased privatization of public lands and beaches along the coast of Salvador, to which the white elite feels entitled. These sentiments are widespread enough for luxury condominiums to invest significant amounts of money into security mechanisms that illegally keep Gamboa de Baixo residents out of public waters.

For Gamboa de Baixo activists engaged in a decade of struggle against forced removal and for land rights and participatory urbanization, the construction of Morada dos Cardeais meant heightened fear of displacement. "Gamboa de Baixo is on a tightrope," Ritinha affirmed in a meeting with Odebrecht representatives. Another resident added,

> We have to be alert. Alert to everything, because . . . they [the state] have the revitalization of the commercial district; they have the revitalization of the historic center. Gamboa is in a dangerous zone. And just because it's Odebrecht doesn't mean we are not going to think about these things. . . . We know what the history of residential removal has been in the violent form that we have had to deal with it. (*A Tarde,* August 8, 2004)

The Gamboa de Baixo community is effectively under siege from all sides, as Ritinha emphasized in a later evaluation meeting with neighborhood activists. Both state and private urban developers envision a lush green landscape below Contorno Avenue, the restoration of a fort accessible from the Bay of All Saints, and the consumption of coastal luxury.

The Spectacle of State Violence

Concrete walls (and not black people) have now become part of the ideal natural coastal landscape. Safe spaces created by walls are a way of life for residents of these types of luxury apartment communities. The Salvador elite's preoccupation with security in this region of the city is the direct result of public stigma attached to Gamboa de Baixo and poor black neighborhoods in general as being violent. Other neighbors, such as residents of the upper-class condominiums of Gamboa de Cima and Banco dos Ingleses, have contributed to this criminalization of the neighborhood. A Gamboa de Baixo resident told the story of an older white woman, whom I will call Dona Vera, who lives in Gamboa de Cima. After Vera's apartment was robbed, she immediately approached a member of the neighborhood association to ask if she knew who might have committed the crime. This Gamboa de Baixo resident was clearly upset and explained that whenever any crime happened in the homes above Contorno Avenue, it was immediately assumed that Gamboa de Baixo residents were responsible.

The media also contributes to this negative representation of the neighborhood when they report crimes committed along Contorno Avenue. If a crime occurs in Gamboa de Cima, they report that it happened in Gamboa de Baixo. If a crime happens a mile down the road, they report that it took place in Gamboa and that Gamboa residents committed it. For example, a murdered man was found a quarter mile up the road from Gamboa de Baixo in 2004, but the newspaper reported that he was a victim of criminal activities in the neighborhood. The man was not a resident of Gamboa de Baixo, and his death was not related to anyone in the neighborhood. As one resident claims, "A man dies in Campo Grande, what does that have to do with Gamboa? We have to pay the price for crime in the city." As a newspaper reporter affirms, "All black people continue being perceived as potential bandits or drug dealers without justification or explanation" (*A Tarde,* June 9, 2008). In June 2012 tourists were robbed and assaulted on their yacht in the middle of the bay, and the military police relentlessly invaded the community for two weeks, claiming that they were certain to find their culprits in Gamboa de Baixo.

Gamboa de Baixo residents believe that the construction of Ode-brecht's wall and the installation of security demonstrate public acceptance of these disparaging ideas about their community. As some residents have stated, part of the ongoing political struggle is to prove that they are people, too, and that people in Gamboa de Baixo work and raise healthy families in an environment they have enjoyed for generations. As another resident states, "Everyone has to live her life. If they are rich boys and just defend their rights and want everything to themselves, that's not going to work. They have to think about others too" (*A Tarde,* August 8, 2004). This statement affirms that Gamboa residents do not plan to leave the land and that the neighbors of O Morada dos Cardeais have to share the land, the beach, and the waters of the Bay of All Saints.

Residents of both O Morada dos Cardeais and Gamboa de Baixo are forced to grapple with almost daily state policing and a normalized lack of privacy. But the two communities experience policing quite differently: in O Morada dos Cardeais the wall and the private police work to protect the residents, whereas in Gamboa de Baixo neither the walls nor the gates can protect them from the violence of the state police. Police violence has become a spectacle for residents of O Morada dos Cardeais, who look down from their thirty-seven stories onto the Gamboa de Baixo residents who are living the violence. Thus, the wall alone does not account for the spatial difference between the communities; the actual height of the building becomes an inherent geographic difference in how the two communities view each other. In everyday life, especially during moments when ordinary policing in Gamboa de Baixo becomes an extraordinary event, O Morada dos Cardeais residents have a unique and safe perspective from above. Gamboa de Baixo residents never have access, however, to the everyday lives of those who live above them in the high-rise apartments or the spatial privilege of safety and privacy. They cannot climb over the wall, whether real or imagined.

This spatial difference in protection became very evident in Gamboa de Baixo during the last violent police raid of 2007, in December, and the first raid of 2008, in January. Police operations in Salvador's poor black communities increase during the summer, particularly in preparation for the city's carnival festivities. Known as Operação Pente

Fino (Operation Fine-Tooth Comb), police comb these neighbor-hoods for criminals whom they perceive as a possible threat to tourists. The two raids were not the first times I witnessed the everyday violent use of police force in Gamboa de Baixo, but they were extraordinary moments. Residents commented that some of the police technologies used were new to them. For example, a couple of days after Christmas, they witnessed the unprecedented use of helicopters flying low over the bushes and trees of the Odebrecht land on the perimeter of Gamboa de Baixo. The police rappelled out of the helicopters onto the beach, which some residents described as "a scene out of a war zone." The military police used new techniques to invade the community and fight their war against perceived *marginais*. At the beginning of January 2008, residents learned that the December operation was only one battle in this longer war.

Witnesses to the January 2008 war on Gamboa de Baixo realized that police actions had a direct impact on O Morada dos Cardeais residents, who primarily participated as spectators. The violent and noisy police invasion disrupted their daily activities, leading the curious among them to watch the scene from their balconies. Their vantage point differed from that of Gamboa de Baixo residents, who were witnesses rather than spectators—an important distinction that makes explicit their full engagement with the violence as observers from within their community. They were unable to observe from outside the community, out of harm's way.

The January 2008 War

The following personal account of the police war on Gamboa de Baixo brings home the terror that residents go through in this community.

It was a beautiful morning. The sun was hot, the sky clear, and the ocean bright blue. Children were home on summer vacation, and small doorway shops had already opened. Life in Gamboa de Baixo was already in full swing. Simone, who was a domestic worker in the Vitória neighborhood, had taken the day off work to wait for the delivery of sand and gravel for her construction project. As usual, around nine thirty in the morning she stopped at Ana Cristina's house before walking to Contorno Avenue to meet the truck and help some local men (and some *sacizeiros*) bag building materials and carry them to her "fortress" under construction. I opened Ana's gate and let her in. Her seven-year-old daughter followed. As Simone stood in the middle of Ana Cristina's small living room, its single window open to the ocean, the gate and the door open, we heard a noise like firecrackers: BAP BAP BAP.

We heard men's voices yelling words that were unintelligible from where we were, but it sounded like they were close to the house. Simone's husband, Zequinha, pushed the door closed while Ana grabbed the little girl, who had already begun to scream, and ran into the kitchen.

We heard quickly running footsteps pass the house, followed by what we now know was automatic-weapon fire.

I fled to the bathroom and knelt in the shower. Ana Cristina and the little girl were in the stairwell behind the rear wall of the house. Simone stood against the kitchen wall, next to the refrigerator.

"It sounds like bandidos," Ana Cristina said. I was sure the memory of the three December murders was flashing through all of our minds.

"I don't know if they're bandidos or the police," Simone said.

"Stay on the ground!" we heard the police command on the street above Ana Cristina's house. The phone rang. Nicelia, Ana Cristina's sister, was calling from the other side of Gamboa. She could see several dozen Companhia de Operações Especiais (COE; a SWAT-like special military police unit) officers on Contorno Avenue dressed in black, some with black bags over their head. A full assault on the community had begun. "Stay inside," Nicelia ordered. "They're firing automatic guns from Contorno Avenue down on the houses." She warned us not to go upstairs. Almost all of the homes in Gamboa de Baixo had ceramic tile roofs, which did not protect the residents from police bullets.

As the firing continued, Simone ran to close the front window.

"Quick, Simone!" I yelled from the bathroom.

"Stay on the floor!" Ana Cristina shouted back at me. "Get behind that wall, Simone!"

The guns fired again and again. I could not stop shaking. The little girl grabbed on to Ana Cristina for dear life. The phone rang; Nicelia, again. The police had invaded the eastern side of Gamboa de Baixo. Parents scooped their children out of the water. Divers and fishermen rushed back to shore. Some were being ordered by policemen to get out of the water. Residents of O Morada dos Cardeais who were on the pier ran into the boathouse while those inside their apartments watched the war from their balconies. The balconies in Gamboa de Cima and Banco dos Ingleses were also crowded with spectators.

Volleys of automatic-weapon fire were followed by silence.

I moved from the shower over to the toilet seat, where I sat and put my hand on my jaw, my sign since I was a child that I was deeply worried.

"Coitada de Keisha-Khan!" (Poor Keisha-Khan), Ana Cristina sighed.

"Coitados de nós" (Poor us), I retorted, my voice and body shaking.

The phone rang again. Rita was calling from her job as a domestic worker and wanted to know what was going on. Her daughter had called her, screaming into the phone that she was scared that the police were going to break down the gate and enter their house. Rita lived close to Contorno Avenue near the entrance where the police had come in, and her daughter could hear that they were invading houses, most of which were occupied.

The gunfire stopped, and we cautiously moved into the living room, staying clear of the wooden door. I knelt under the window to peek through the wooden planks.

"Don't open the door, please," I pleaded. Ana opened it anyway. The police had descended to the beach front.

"Why are they in my mother's alley?" Ana Cristina asked nervously.

"Don't even think about going down there!" I responded.

She called Crispina, her other sister, on the phone. Crispina reported that a young man who had been shot had run into the alley. The police were looking for him, but no one knew where he was. Crispina was locked inside and knew nothing.

"Call me if you know anything," Ana Cristina ended the call.

Someone called for Simone and Zequinha from outside. The police had apprehended their construction workers, who did not have their identification cards on them. Simone ran down to her house to get their wallets to show the police and to vouch for them as workers. When she returned, she reported that the entire Contorno Avenue perimeter, including all three entrances to Gamboa de Baixo and the neighboring Solar do Unhão, had been blocked by police cars and wagons.

"There are a lot of police of all kinds, but I saw mostly COE," she said. She also saw several officers with black cloth bags over their heads.

I peeked out the window again. Several fully armed COE officers walked by the house with a young man in their grip. They were armed with weapons that could cut open all kinds of locks and gates and break down any door. They were equipped to fight a war, an urban war.

Bits and pieces of information reached us about the gravity of the situation. Bullets had penetrated Dona Vilma's roof. She later told newspaper reporters, "The police arrived here firing gunshots. I had to hide underneath the bed." Her dog hid with her. Camilo, a former activist with the neighborhood association, also recounted that the "police came already firing" directly from Contorno Avenue down onto the houses in Gamboa de Baixo. Bullets came through his roof and lodged in his bathroom sink. The police fired shots into the walls of Simone's house, almost hitting the construction workers. They invaded the bar owned by Ana and her sister, demanding to search for drug dealers on the second floor. They had a list, and they asked for everyone's documents. They also had detailed aerial photos of the neighborhood.

"Did you let them in?" Ana Cristina asked.

"What was I supposed to do?" Nicelia responded. "I'm not a criminal. I don't have anything to hide." She could not challenge men and women armed with machine guns who had openly threatened to kill anyone who made a sound. Hours later, she was still visibly shaken.

One woman reported that an armed officer with his face covered said to his partners as he walked past her house, "This is a good place to live. I used to live here and I loved it."

Speculations about the entire operation dominated conversations in the neighborhood for days afterward. Most agreed that it was the most violent police operation that residents had ever witnessed. The neighborhood, they said, had been terrorized. Almost none had ever seen the COE team, known for high-risk operations, in action in their neighborhood; that kind of police action was what happened in violent neighborhoods, like those in Rio de Janeiro.

"It was like a movie, but real, you know," one man said.

I recalled attending a screening of the movie *Cidade de Deus* (*City of God*) with Ana Cristina when the film was first released in 2002. The film depicts the war between drug traffickers and military police officers in a Rio de Janeiro neighborhood and is often described as containing barbaric, unnecessary violence. As we left the theater, Ana Cristina said, "I don't identify with this kind of movie. At least Gamboa and Salvador haven't gotten that bad." But in fact what we experienced on that day in January 2008 was frighteningly similar to scenes in the film.

Police actions like the January 2008 operation have made some in Gamboa de Baixo identify with another recent popular Brazilian film, *Tropa de Elite* (*Elite Squad*; 2007), now one of the most-watched films in Brazilian history. Most Gamboa de Baixo residents have bought or rented the movie. The film portrays the personal and professional experiences of two members of Brazil's most elite police squad in Rio de Janeiro, focusing on their violent encounters in the shantytowns. Prior to the police operations in January, Gamboa de Baixo's experience with this "elite squad" had been limited to the movie screen. After the raid some tried to lighten the seriousness of the COE operations by joking that *Tropa de Elite* was filmed in Gamboa.

The details of *City of God* and *Elite Squad* are important insofar as they illustrate the importance of vantage point—black people's spatial perspective on living in urban communities and understanding their social conditions and how the white elite sees and interprets the everyday policing of neighborhoods like Gamboa de Baixo. From one perspective the neighborhood and its people are undeserving of such inhumane, violent treatment; the entire neighborhood was being criminalized and destroyed. From another perspective the police carry out the much-needed job of cleansing the area of criminals as part of the process of improving the social landscape. As many residents have affirmed, they feel increasingly displaced from the land and waters of the bay by the white elite. They believe that the increased policing of their neighborhood is directly related to residential shifts in the coastal landscape. The public police serve to protect not Gamboa de Baixo residents but the elite who live around them. The situation in Salvador resembles how Brazilian anthropologist Teresa Caldeira describes poor urban residents in São Paulo:

Rich people are perceived as being outside the law and society; their social position assures that they will not be punished.

Perception of this additional inequality, which perverts clas-
sifications and social contracts, is at the center of the total
pessimism many residents of São Paulo feel about creating a
more just society in Brazil. Since it is difficult to impose order
through existing institutions, which are unable to control evil
and therefore unable to build a better society, people feel that
they are constantly exposed to the natural forces of evil and to
the abuse of those who place themselves outside of the law. To
protect themselves, they have to rely on their own means of
isolation, control, separation, and distancing. In order to feel
safe, that is, they have to build walls. (2000, 101)

The Struggle for Space

The spatial difference in protection that exists between luxury apartment communities and poor black neighborhoods is evident in the
relationship between Gamboa de Baixo and O Morada dos Cardeais.
The extraordinary moments in urban policing I describe are part of the
everyday experience of residents of Gamboa de Baixo. Local residents
have witnessed violent police invasions and many have come face to
face with elite COE teams equipped with firearms and machinery that
residents imagine are used to demolish, eliminate, and kill. In this
type of urban war, the police shoot first and ask questions later while
O Morada dos Cardeais residents watch the war from the safe confines
of their balconies.

Black Brazilian sociologist and feminist militant of the black movement Vilma Reis wrote a few days after the January 2008 operation
in Gamboa de Baixo, "In Salvador, second-largest black city on the
planet, where to be black is still synonymous with dangerous, undesirable, out of place, and fundamentally *descartável* [disposable],"
violence against poor black people has become routine and, for some,
an expected element of urban governance (Reis 2008b; see also Cardoso 2004; Flauzina 2008). Black neighborhoods like Gamboa de
Baixo are portrayed as morally, socially, politically, and spatially out of
control. Many residents feel they are being unfairly criminalized—they
often state, "Não sou marginal" (I'm not a criminal). Contrary to public perceptions that the police are cleansing the area of criminals as a

necessary part of the process to socially improve the urban landscape, local residents understand that they do not deserve such inhumane, violent treatment. The entire neighborhood is being marginalized, criminalized, and destroyed simultaneously.

This perspective bridges the theoretical gap between analyses of the violence of unequal urban development and the violence of urban policing. The overlap between the two processes shows the emergent need for black social movements in Brazil and elsewhere to combat the image of collective pathology while struggling to gain access to vital urban resources such as housing, land, and basic sanitation. For black communities urban renewal campaigns can be radically exclusionary and dangerously violent. The black women–led struggle for citizenship constitutes an urgent demand for racial inclusion in development discourses and practices and a call to take urban grassroots antiracism strategies, such as fighting police abuse, seriously.

5

"PICKING UP THE PIECES"
Everyday Violence and Community

In socially excluded communities women live out their lives
against the backdrop of constant criminal and police violence.
The impact of this violence on their lives is complex and profound, yet their stories are rarely heard. In a debate that has
traditionally centered on gun violence, the focus has invari-
ably been on young men—the overwhelming majority of those
involved in gun crime, both as perpetrators and victims. This
report focuses on the largely untold stories of women struggling to live their lives, to bring up their children and to fight for
justice amid police and criminal violence.

Amnesty International, *Picking Up the Pieces:*
Women's Experience of Urban Violence

Dona Iraci: Die While Fighting

Six years before the January 2008 police operation, on Saturday, September 21, 2002, at about midday, residents of the Gamboa de Baixo
neighborhood were terrorized by yet another extraordinary police invasion that has marked the Gamboa de Baixo community as well as
political history. Caravans of fully armed military and civil police descended on the community searching for drug dealers, beating everyone in their path. Women abandoned their wash pans and rushed with
their children into their homes, and young men with identity cards
in hand were violently pushed against the wall and searched. The police pressed guns close to young black men sweating from fright. Rita
closed her steel gate and sat on the floor in her living room. She was
too frightened to move and feared that any movement or sounds might
stir reaction from the raging policemen already breaking down her
neighbors' doors. Unlike what the population above Contorno Avenue
imagines and the media portrays, police invasions in Gamboa de Baixo

are never expected, nor are they perceived as normal policing. They are considered arbitrary and random acts of violence that can have deadly consequences. On that Saturday, while children were playing, women were washing clothes, and men were cleaning their boats, the whole community stopped. Most residents stayed inside their homes or stood on their doorsteps paralyzed while they watched the police take over.

Iraci Isabel da Silva (called Dona Iraci) ran out of her house, located near one of the entrances to Contorno Avenue, and saw a policeman beating her ten-year-old grandson, who was playing in front of her door (Figure 16). She confronted the policeman and told him to let go of her grandson. The policeman screamed at her, and when she screamed back, he threatened to beat her, too. The violent confrontation went on for several minutes, until she finally suffered a heart attack. Dona Iraci died that Sunday morning at the age of forty-five, and as is customary in Bahia, she was immediately buried on Monday. She was the treasurer and founding member of the neighborhood association, the mother of six adult children whom she had moved as small children from the interior of Bahia to Gamboa de Baixo, and the wife of her childhood sweetheart.

The violent loss of community leader Dona Iraci is representative of police violence in Gamboa de Baixo and throughout Salvador's black communities. Dona Iraci's individual act of courage in her last fight against police terror mobilized local residents in the wake of her death. The neighborhood association founded the Council for the Defense of Gamboa de Baixo with the participation of activists from other neighborhoods, human rights groups, black movement organizations, and scholar-activists. Inspired by the antiviolence politics of the former U.S.-based Black Panther Party for Self-Defense, the organization linked their struggle to other black neighborhoods in Salvador, as well as to the global black struggle against police abuse. In meetings they began to document personal stories of police abuse, and they wrote letters to public officials demanding radical changes in police tactics. One of the first documents they produced was an open letter to the Brazilian public that was published in the local newspaper and in an online Afro-Brazilian national magazine. The letter begins by describing the violent death of Dona Iraci and continues by linking police

FIGURE 16. Dona Iraci sits near the window at a neighborhood association board meeting in the community school building. Leo and Lueci sit to her right, circa 1995. Courtesy of Gamboa de Baixo neighborhood association archives.

violence to a long history of socioeconomic and spatial marginalization and violence in Gamboa de Baixo:

> This history of aggression dates back to 1960, when Contorno Avenue was constructed, segregating the community of Gamboa in relationship to the rest of the city, which perpetuated the violence of "amnesia" by state agencies—such as the Secretary of Health, when there was a cholera outbreak in 1992 that victimized Senhor Geraldo Ferreira de França, community leader known as Gegê, after whom the neighborhood association was later named. Then in 1995, the people of Gamboa de Baixo faced more violence when the state government initiated the Revitalization of Contorno Avenue Project, which envisioned the expulsion of families from the community where they live and where their ancestors lived in a fishing community proven to be centuries old.

With a long struggle in search of citizenship, we, the people of Gamboa de Baixo, have fought against these acts of violence and many other acts of social and racial discrimination. We are black men and women who have had our history denied, we comprise the masses of unemployed workers, and even worse, we are the preferred targets of institutionalized violence, in order words, of the police. Our community lives terrorized, without security, with no one to turn to in order to guarantee our rights. As if that were not enough, many of us have been victimized by the continued violence of the absence of public services, the abuses, physical and psychological torture, that are happening with greater frequency in our community.

Dona Iraci's resistance and death and the subsequent antiviolence mobilization illustrates the broader preoccupation of the community with antiblack racial violence, which includes exclusionary acts of urban redevelopment, as well as state abandonment and poverty. After Dona Iraci's death, one Gamboa resident said to a newspaper reporter, "We're treated as if we were a den of thieves, when in reality, we are a community of citizens who demand respect and know our rights" (*A Tarde,* September 29, 2002). In memory of Dona Iraci, the neighborhood association created a landscaped square on Contorno Avenue at the main entrance to Gamboa de Baixo's and named it Iraci Isabel da Silva Square.

Although 97 percent of the documented cases of residents being killed by police involve black men, as Rita states, "Women are beaten [by the police], too," both physically and psychologically (Alves and Evanson 2011; Amnesty International 2005, 2008; Athayde and Bill 2007; Rocha 2012; Wilding 2012). As Dona Iraci's case shows, women and children in Gamboa de Baixo are not exempt from police violence. Activists in the neighborhood deliberately argue against those who would label Dona Iraci's death an unfortunate case of poor health and minimize the intentional trauma inflicted on her black body when she questioned the routine police violence in her neighborhood. The police's capacity to dehumanize Dona Iraci and the black residents of Gamboa de Baixo stems from established understandings of these residents as gendered and racialized others undeserving of respect, dignity, and the benefits of full citizenship in Brazil. Amnesty International reports that "the reality for women in Brazil's slums is catastrophic. They are the hidden victims of the criminal and police violence that has engulfed their communities for decades." The report also states that "women who fight for justice on behalf of their sons or husbands end up on the front line, facing further threats and harassment from the police" (Amnesty International 2008).

Os Homens (The Men)

Two years before her death, Dona Iraci described an example of police action during a Gamboa de Baixo protest on Contorno Avenue at the beginning of the neighborhood struggles, when women activists blocked the street with their bodies and debris:

> We didn't let them pacify us. Only women were there at the time. The men all ran. Only the women stayed that day. That made us stand out, because there are times when we women have more courage, more strength than the men. They ran for real. Only women stayed. We resisted there. We didn't run. We went to fight the police with punches and kicks, all of us at once. . . . When they tried to arrest the woman, we surrounded the car and we all screamed, "Let her go, let her go." . . . When the police said, "We're going to shoot," we said, "Go ahead, you can kill us, but we're not leaving her, no. We're staying right here." We kept saying, "Let her go," but they didn't let her go. They said, "She's going to jail because she disobeyed," and we said, "No way. You disobeyed us, too." We had our truth to say to them. Isn't that right? And it went on and on. When they saw that we weren't going to give in, they let her go. They took her out [of the police car] and returned her to us. The struggle went on, and other people came to support us. (personal communication, 2000)

Dona Iraci's final confrontation with the police was not her first. Fighting the police had always been a part of protests that involved direct action like disrupting traffic or standing in front of the water company, as described in chapter 3. The police play the state's key role in criminalizing and subsequently destroying the community as part of its urbanization plans. Aggressive policing in the neighborhood accompanies bellicose actions against activists engaged in preserving the community. Contrary to what Dona Iraci's actions suggest, however, most people in Gamboa de Baixo are too afraid to confront the police. Police resistance normally occurs within the context of street protests, where there may be participants from nongovernmental organizations and human rights groups, who offer a measure of protection to protestors. During the many police invasions when there are no witnesses to the violence, most residents are rendered passive and silent out of fear.

Gamboa de Baiso refer to the police as *os homens* (the men). They report to each other that "os homens" are coming or that "os homens" were here and took someone away or beat up someone. They often report that the police steal money or goods from their persons or from their homes. At the end of the year, just before Christmas and New Year's, police activities in Gamboa de Baixo increase significantly. They arrive with their machine guns and pistols drawn and ready to fire. "They come shooting," as the residents say. They harass those in their path and are notorious for kicking small children or shoving old women out of their way. No one is exempt from their wrath, and as one woman affirms, "They have no respect for anyone, not men, not women, not children, not even old people" (personal communication, 2003). Some feel the police are doing their jobs, whereas others see their actions as proof of overt abuses of power. But it is clear that the police violate the people more than they protect them.

There is no police station in the neighborhood, but the military and the civil police forces invade the community several times a week, sometimes every day. Several carloads may appear at once, but single police officers also go into the community. They almost always claim to be looking for drug dealers, but they also appear in response to specific incidents such as robberies that occur on Contorno Avenue or violent crimes reported in the community. Many residents express the belief that Gamboa de Baixo is a training ground for new recruits in the civil and military police because it is a "controllable space." It is a small neighborhood with only three entrances by land. At times, hundreds of fully armed police officers occupy all areas of the community for several hours, testing new tactics and technologies, like helicopter rappelling. They have entered Gamboa de Baixo by sea with new speedboats. Residents have observed that during mass police raids, like the ones described in this and the previous chapter, many of the officers are inexperienced and have little knowledge of the area. They do not know how to identify who is and who is not a criminal. They tend to be more frightened and often react impulsively and indiscriminately, such as by firing into spaces where there are innocent bystanders.

At one of their weekly board meetings, the neighborhood association's secretary, Maria José, stated that the police had shot at her house while they were chasing some alleged drug dealers. While she and her family slept, bullets hit the wall a few inches from her window and beside her daughter's bunk bed. Adriano states that the police threatened him as he sat on his windowsill. On one occasion, as the police frantically ran by his house with their guns drawn, he nervously tapped his feet against the wall. They shouted homophobic epithets at him and demanded that he stop shaking, even though their actions terrified him and other onlookers.

The police extort all kinds of goods from Gamboa de Baixo residents. It is not unusual to see them take money out of men's wallets during pat downs. In Gamboa de Baixo, throughout the day fishermen take their catches to the fisheries to sell. After stopping them and accusing them of being drug dealers, the police often take either the fish or the money earned from their sale. Children tell stories of going to the store to buy bread and coffee for supper only to be robbed and harassed by officers on the way. Other residents say they have lost electronics such as televisions and video players to the police, who accuse them of stealing the items. "How can I show a receipt so long after I bought them?" one woman asked after she was required to show proof of purchase for appliances in her home. The police who invade Gamboa de Baixo are infamous for extorting money, as much as several hundred or several thousand reais, from drug dealers in exchange for their freedom. Drug dealers negotiate with the police before they are even arrested.

Quantifying the people injured or murdered during police actions is difficult because the police have invented many ways to disguise statistics—statistics often provided by the same people responsible for the crimes. Human rights organization Comissão Teotônio Vilela prepared a report claiming that between 2000 and 2001 the number of police victims grew from 1,479 to 3,017. These numbers compare with those under seventeen years of Chile's military regime, during which approximately 3,197 people were assassinated (Kalili 2003, 20). The following is an excerpt from the U.S. Bureau of Democracy, Human Rights, and Labor's 2004 country report on human rights practices in Brazil:

> State police forces [both civil and military] committed many extrajudicial killings, tortured and beat suspects under interrogation, and arbitrarily arrested and detained persons. Police also were implicated in a variety of criminal activities, including killings for hire, death squad executions, extortion, kidnappings for ransom, and narcotics trafficking. Despite new powers to intervene in certain types of human rights cases in 2001, the federal police failed to act in the numerous human rights violations by state authorities.
>
> The U.N. Special Rapporteur on Torture noted that the majority of the victims of torture were of Afro-Brazilian descent (see Section 1.c.). Research by the Institute of Applied Economic Research (IPEA) noted a disproportionately high rate of police killings of Afro-Brazilians. Persons of color were five times more likely to be shot or killed in the course of a law enforcement action than were persons perceived to be white. During the year, the São Paulo police ombudsman repeated his 2002 claim that the majority of victims of police killings were young black men from impoverished areas on the periphery of major cities. (U.S. Bureau of Democracy, Human Rights, and Labor 2005)

In Bahia, reports on human rights abuses committed by the military and the civil police emphasize that these abuses provide state support for the "extermination" of the black population. More than 70 percent (approximately one thousand) of all homicides—primarily by firearms—from 1996 to 1999 involved the participation of at least one policeman (Machado and Noronha 2002; Oliveira, Ribeiro, and Zanetti 2000). In the first six months of 2011, 77 homicides had been committed by the police. Between 2007 and 2010, there were 74, 148,

245, and 136, respectively, all justified by the police as being the result of "acts of resistance" (*Correio,* July 14, 2011).

Ivan Brandão of the Secretary of Justice of Bahia adds, however, "This is not exclusively Bahian, this is the general portrait of violence in the country" (Oliveira, Ribeiro, and Zanetti 2000). The aforementioned statistics from various reports on human rights show that police violence, in its various forms, is a national trend. Between 1980 and 2010, Brazil had approximately 1.1 million homicides, averaging 36,000 per year. This compares with the combined numbers for the Israel/Palestine conflict (125,000 over fifty-three years), the Guatemalan Civil War (400,000 over twenty-four years), and the Angolan Civil War (550,000 over twenty-seven years) (Waiselfisz 2010).

In the 2003 Gamboa de Baixo community census, the neighborhood association interviewed representatives from approximately 250 families. Though they mentioned other forms of violence, such as domestic violence, child abuse, and fights among residents, all identified police abuse as the number-one form of violence in the neighborhood. These men and women whispered to local activists when they spoke about the police, but they also cited graphic examples of the terror they dealt with every day. They implored the neighborhood association to address the problem with the government. Although no official documentation of the number of cases of police abuse exists, like Dona Iraci almost everyone has a story to tell.

When asked, "Have you ever experienced any form of violence?" Camilo, a thirty-five-year-old father of two, a former activist in the neighborhood association, and a husband to current activist Lu, was eager to discuss his first violent confrontation with the police. Like many black men, he had experienced police abuse throughout his youth and adulthood, and he reassured the census taker that "no one forgets that first time." He was fifteen years old, and the incident occurred on his mother's birthday. It was raining hard when he went to his sister's house on the opposite side of Gamboa. The military police were in the neighborhood investigating a robbery that they believed had happened on Contorno Avenue. As he was walking, they grabbed him and put him in the back of their car. Camilo's mother heard that her son was being held and went to the police to ask them to let him go. She explained to them that he "had nothing to do with anything and that he was not a vagabond." They refused to let him go, and additional police arrived on the scene to provide backup. The police threatened Camilo, "Hey, big black man, I'm going to get you. I'm going to paint your hair blond and call you Blond Devil." Camilo sat in the police car for almost an hour as his mother and other relatives protested. He was finally let go, but today, as an adult, he is still approached by the police and asked to identify himself. He shows his worker's card as well as his national ID. When asked whether this had to do with being black or with living in Gamboa de Baixo, he replied:

> It has to do with the fact that I am black, that I live in a neighborhood like this one that has its highs and lows, negatives and positives. This place has a good side and a bad side. . . . The negative side is the drugs. They think that everyone who lives here has some involvement with drugs, which isn't true. Because there are many family men, hard-working people here. [There are drug dealers] like everywhere else, even in the big mansions of rich neighborhoods. (personal communication, 2003)

All residents of Gamboa de Baixo have had negative encounters with the police at some point, if not on several occasions throughout their lifetimes. As Camilo's statement illustrates, the police's criminalization of Gamboa de Baixo connects with their racialization of its inhabitants.

Os Meninos (The Boys)

In general residents express that they are more afraid of the police than they are of *os meninos* (the boys), the neighborhood drug dealers. The daily struggle to prove that Gamboa de Baixo is not a crime-ridden community is stymied by random acts of violence by the drug dealers. In their political aims, the neighborhood association faces the challenge of deconstructing the community's identity as a drug-trafficking zone. Though the majority of Gamboa de Baixo residents are not involved in the drug trade, the association has to admit that drug sales occur in the neighborhood day and night. Men and women from the upper- and middle-class apartment buildings above Contorno Avenue walk down to Gamboa to purchase drugs. Others park their motorcycles and cars and hurriedly descend under the street to purchase their goods and drive off. These transactions are so quick that an uninformed observer would not recognize them as drug sales. It is a known fact that drugs exist in the neighborhood, but only the sellers are policed and receive punishment for their involvement.

Crime in Gamboa de Baixo stems directly from socioeconomic conditions imposed on the neighborhood. Young black men enticed by the drug trade have little access to paid work in the city, leaving them with few resources to take care of themselves and their families. One of the very few options open to them is fishing. Local activists have encouraged young men in the community to learn commercial fishing and diving, with the support of the Fishermen and Fisherwomen's Association. A few young boys have abandoned the drug trade to work as fishermen and divers, usually after a violent encounter with the police. One boy, speaking about his transformation, says that although the money is significantly less, he feels a lot safer on the ocean and knows his money is clean. He says that fishing affords him more freedom than did his previous life of constant fear and running from the police. More important, he had felt trapped in the neighborhood and rarely felt comfortable going to the shopping mall, the movies, or other neighborhoods. Providing alternatives to young men in Gamboa de Baixo who want to escape selling drugs is difficult, especially given the government's lack of support for subsistence and small commercial fishing, in contrast with widespread economic support for large-scale commercial fishing.

Drug dealers who falsely claim to be fishermen make it difficult for the neighborhood movement to preserve the integrity of Gamboa de Baixo as a centuries-old fishing colony. The police are suspicious of residents' claims that they are fishermen and fisherwomen. They frequently question the validity of this identity, even when it is obvious that residents are engaged in fishing activities or are known fishermen and fisherwomen in the city.

Many residents believe that they are more likely to die as a result of violent crime involving the police than from conflicts among drug dealers. Few overt tensions exist between the general population and the drug dealers, because many have strong family ties to the neighborhood. They grew up in the neighborhood and tend to maintain certain traditions, such as respect for and loyalty toward family members, no matter how distant the link. Some residents refuse to describe in detail their feelings about the drug dealers but mention that their presence causes problems with the police that will not disappear until residents collectively deal with the issue of drug trafficking in the community. They feel constrained and trapped by the generalized criminalization of the neighborhood and by their political impotence. They respond to activists' attempts to engage them in antipolice actions by asking, "How are we supposed to fight the *homens* when we also have to fight the *meninos* and vice versa?" Resolving these issues intricately tied to social abandonment and economic marginalization is not an easy task, and it cannot be completed overnight. In the meantime local activists demand that the state reexamines how it treats the vast majority of the Gamboa de Baixo population, who are not involved in any form of criminal activity.

"Now Gamboa Is Going to Become Hell"

The daily struggle to prove that Gamboa de Baixo is not a crime-ridden community is stymied by random acts of violence among the drug dealers. When one act of violence occurs in the community, the repercussions are immediately felt by all residents because of family ties and the violent police response.

On September 14, 2003, one year after the death of Dona Iraci, a gun battle involving drug dealers removed any remaining trace of the tranquility and security that might have traditionally been associated with a small fishing community. The exact cause of the violent confrontation is unknown, but it began with a fight in a bar between the owners of the establishment and the drug dealers. Shots were fired, and the drug dealers ran home to retrieve their weapons. The combatants fired more than fifty shots at each other, including from Contorno Avenue down into Gamboa de Baixo. Residents frantically ran for their lives as volley after volley was fired. Several young men involved in the battle were wounded. A man who had nothing to do with the fight but was nonetheless a friend of some of the drug dealers was killed. He begged for his life as a gun was pointed at him, crying, "Don't kill me! I'm a father with children!" He was shot in the head at point-blank range. The next day, the funeral for the deceased man was tense. Fear overshadowed the sadness of losing a brother, father, and boyfriend because some of the drug dealers had promised retaliation for the injuries inflicted and the death of their friend.

The incident caused tremendous anxiety in Gamboa de Baixo. Residents had come to tolerate the presence of the drug dealers to a certain extent, and no one expected this kind of violence from them. Suddenly, they realized that the drug dealers and the owners of the bar had a full arsenal of assault weapons in their houses.

Prior to September 14, 2003, many local residents would not have described Gamboa de Baixo as a violent place to live, even with the drug traffickers, and most today would agree that it is still safer than most other neighborhoods in Salvador. People said, "In Gamboa, there's no violence. Other neighborhoods are violent, but not here. You might have some petty drug dealers, but that's nothing—it's safe here."

The gun battle threw the neighborhood into a state of fear. This kind of barbarity among residents was previously unheard of. They said that in all their years of living in Gamboa, they had never seen anything like it. "It was really cruel," one said. "Now Gamboa is going to become hell," another said.

Residents were left with many unanswered questions. How many weapons were in Gamboa de Baixo? How were the drug dealers planning to use them? What had caused the gun war? What would come next?

The generalized feeling of fear in Gamboa de Baixo dramatically increased after the battle between the drug dealers. People now feared their neighbors and for the police's response. The day after the battle, the streets were silent and empty. Everyone had taken refuge in their homes.

Intracommunity violence is pervasive, which requires critical political intervention by community leaders, who try to encourage peaceful living through the social and political activities they organize. But intracommunity violence is only one part of the problem that Gamboa de Baixo faces: innocent citizens are also subjected to police abuse in response to local crime. Human rights violations at the hands of the police occur more often than does drug trafficking–related violence. Admitting to some of the complexities of neighborhood violence, Camilo points out that most residents are not opposed to the police fighting crime or doing their jobs, "as long as they carry out their jobs properly" (personal communication, 2003). As the 2003 document "Letter from the Black Youth of Salvador"—to which youth from Gamboa de Baixo contributed—affirms:

> The situation of black youth in the job market is extremely fragile. We don't have the right to a life without racial and sexual violence. In sum, we don't have the right to exercise our citizenship. For us, this citizenship means the right to frequent public spaces, like shopping malls, buses, parks, etc., without the imposition of police beatings. We do not accept the destruction of our image as a community. We, black youth, want the right to meet in public spaces without being apprehended by the police.

Citizens' right to exist without fear of racial or sexual violence is tied to their right to a dignified image of the communities in which they live. They hope for this aspect of full citizenship in a city that demonizes poor black communities. The struggle against police abuse and intracommunity violence is a long and arduous one that involves a radical transformation of the police's treatment of these urban spaces, as well as increased access to resources that prevent black youth from engaging in criminal activities in the first place. Grassroots activists in these communities continue to demand widespread social, economic, and political inclusion of poor black people.

The Funeral Rite (Right)

In death, as in life, poor black people throughout the African diaspora struggle to maintain some basic forms of dignity. Burial practices for the residents of Gamboa de Baixo illustrate what Nancy Scheper-Hughes calls "death without weeping" (1992), which is the presence of human suffering as a routine part of daily life while trying to provide respectful burials for the dead. After the death of Dona Iraci, the entire community was overcome with sadness, and everyone wept. Many had known her as a strong black woman who was always full of energy, a feisty, stout woman with a high-pitched voice and an unforgettable smile and laugh. After almost two decades of organizing with her as neighbors, they were attending her funeral. She lay in a small, plain wooden coffin. Flowers were spread all over her body and around her round, glowing, dark-brown face. They had sprayed lavender perfume on her. She was resting. A busload of family members had traveled overnight from the interior of Bahia to attend the funeral, even though some had wanted her to be buried on family land there. Her children cried uncontrollably, and her husband wept into a gray handkerchief. They were devastated. Dona Iraci's daughter sat feebly leaning on a female relative, eyes swollen, and every now and then she blurted out an emotional "My mother!" and "Why?" Dona Iraci's young grandchildren grabbed onto the legs of their sobbing parents.

Almost all of Gamboa de Baixo's residents crowded into the viewing area of the Campo Santo cemetery, located about two miles from the neighborhood. Some had taken the bus, but most had walked there. Strangers, curious about the large numbers of people, asked about the person who had died, and some remarked that she must have been someone important. Ana Cristina purchased a large wreath outside the cemetery but declined to write a farewell message to place on the wreath, instead finding someone with better penmanship.

After the blessings from the priest, Ana Cristina spoke about how Dona Iraci had died fighting for dignity and human rights in her community. Before they closed the casket, everyone cried and sang the community hymn out loud: "I will not leave here. / No one will take me away from here. / Does the Lord have the patience to wait?" The large crowd walked Dona Iraci's body to her final resting place. They placed her coffin inside a concrete drawer and sang a few hymns as the gravediggers sealed it with cement. In Salvador the buried are usually exhumed after two or three years, and their bones are cremated. A year later, Dona Iraci's children removed her bones and buried her in Jacobina, the town of her birth.

After Dona Iraci's funeral, the Gamboa de Baixo neighborhood was a quiet place for several days. No one played music of any kind, which was unusual in a noisy neighborhood. Residents blamed her death on the violent actions of the police, and they were revolted. They did not close down Contorno Avenue that Monday morning, because her family did not want to protest on the day of the funeral.

At the weekly neighborhood board meeting, Maria José said that she woke up late one night to find herself embodying the spirit of Dona Iraci, speaking just like her, with the same expressions and gestures. Such experiences after funerals used to be commonplace, but today, this kind of reaction is not commonly reported in Gamboa. As Ana Cristina recounts, in the past, after returning from funerals, everyone used to jump into the ocean fully clothed. After a family member died, many women used to cut their long hair.

Dona Iraci's funeral was not a typical funeral for Gamboa de Baixo, nor was it characteristic of funerals for most poor black people in Salvador. In 2003 the funeral for Dona Jacira, Rita's former mother-in-law, showed how poverty shapes the funeral process. After years of alcohol abuse, she suffered from liver failure and passed away in Rita's home. With her son dead, brutally murdered the year before, and without any other family to support her, she had been living with Rita. When she died, Rita called on Ana Cristina, who sought government assistance for indigents (the term the government uses for impoverished people—in this case, people who die and do not have money for a proper burial) to attain a free casket and a plot in which to bury her. Only a few people, about fifteen women and Adriano, a leader in the neighborhood association, attended this funeral in the Quinta dos Lázaros cemetery. The neighborhood association gave money to a few people who could not afford the bus fare to travel the forty-five minutes from Gamboa de Baixo.

In the cemetery they also went to view the body of a one-year-old girl who was about to be buried. The family of the little girl was mourning her death but also arguing about who was responsible for it. The child's father lashed out at the grieving mother, accusing her of not properly feeding the child and not taking her illness seriously. The parents were arguing with the funeral home director for providing a casket that was too small. The baby's head could not fit inside the casket properly, and when it was time to close it, they had to turn her head to the side. It was a depressing scene, and Gamboa de Baixo onlookers consoled the grieving family members, people they did not know.

When Dona Jacira's body arrived, Rita and the cemetery directors discussed the high cost of having the priest pray over her body before it was buried. She reluctantly paid for the priest, and they placed a few flowers on the body. When the priest arrived, he began a loud and dramatic eulogy, and the mourners grumbled when he mispronounced Dona Jacira's name, correcting him in unison. They appeared eager for him to finish. The women carried the casket to the shallow grave at the far end of the cemetery. The smell of death was overwhelming, and they covered their mouths to protect themselves from the flies that swarmed around them. Observing the women struggling to carry the heavy coffin, Adriano blurted out, "Where are the men of Gamboa?" Rita's daughter cried on her mother's shoulder when they placed the coffin into the shallow grave. After the gravediggers covered it, Rita stuck a numbered white cross into the dirt mound as a grave marker. Around them were several fresh mounds of earth with similar crosses. They walked past the other graves and descended single file through the neighborhood below the cemetery. As soon as they reached the main street, a city bus arrived and took them back to Gamboa de Baixo.

Gamboa de Baixo residents tend to be buried in the cemeteries in Campo Santo and Baixa das Quintas. Whereas Dona Jacira's burial had few attendees, Gamboa de Baixo came out in droves for the funeral of former fisherman Raphael. A man in his early forties, Raphael had apparently abandoned professional fishing to work as a runner for the local drug kingpin, whom I refer to as Ferrão. Because Ferrão no longer lived in Gamboa de Baixo, he sent his runners to collect and distribute drugs to local dealers. One afternoon in late August 2004, witnesses claimed that Raphael had come to Gamboa to collect money from some of the dealers when a car stopped him on Contorno Avenue. He apparently got in the car, and that was the last time he was seen alive. He disappeared for several days, which led to a frenzy of rumors and speculations about what had happened to him. Finally, his body was found partially burned on the side of the road on the outskirts of Salvador, with one bullet in the head and three more in other parts of his body. The entire community was devastated because he had lived in Gamboa de Baixo all of his life. Since he had only recently become a runner, his role in drug trafficking was not considered to be very important. He had been a member of the Gamboa community since his birth, and everyone knew him very well. He was a single parent of two children who had lost their mother a few years before to illness.

Raphael's funeral demonstrates some key aspects of the way the community is organized. During the early morning of the funeral, women in his family walked through the entire Gamboa de Baixo neighborhood, knocking on doors to write down the names of those who were attending the funeral. Around ten o'clock in the morning, everyone met under a tree on Contorno Avenue. The family then distributed money to everyone on the list. Ferrão had apparently sent money to pay for the bus fares. Most affirmed that they had no money, and they filled an entire city bus in Campo Grande and rode to Baixa das Quintas.

When they arrived at the stop near the cemetery, they got off the bus and made the long walk of about two kilometers down the main road and up the long, steep hill. Before they reached the top of the hill, they bought flowers to put on Raphael's grave. When they arrived, his body was already on display, which immediately led to a debate about whether his face was also burned. Some refused to enter the viewing room, unsure of whether to look at him. One woman reported that the body in the coffin was in a black plastic bag, with the exception of the head.

A short time later, the family informed everyone that the grave had not yet been paid for and that no money had been sent to contract a priest. They waited for another hour while they resolved the paperwork and payment for the burial. The drug dealers from the neighborhood were noticeably absent from the funeral, which many criticized, considering that their actions had led to Raphael's death. The family sat together on a tree stump, and they covered their faces with tissues to protect themselves from the flies.

Finally, without the blessing of a priest, the men in attendance, mostly fishermen, carried the coffin to a drawer in one of the interior lanes of the cemetery. The smell was overbearing, and the flies threatened to enter ears, mouths, and noses. As they sang hymns at Raphael's gravesite, attendees were busier fanning away the flies than they were worried about singing the right words. They could not concentrate on anything but the flies and the stench.

Discussions about Raphael's death continued on the bus ride from the cemetery, particularly whether he was partially or fully burned. "What difference does it make?" one woman asked. She stressed that it was a terrible way for any person to die. There was much speculation about which one of the drug dealers would be tortured and murdered next. Questions about who was responsible, whether they were drug dealers themselves or hired hit men, or if they were part of an organized death squad all remained unanswered. They talked about the intense police presence in Gamboa de Baixo that would be inevitable in the coming days.

Dying in poverty stinks, literally and figuratively. Burials for Gamboa de Baixo residents exemplify how poor blacks struggle even to bury their dead. Friends and families come together during these moments and gather the resources necessary to cover basic funeral expenses. In the case of Dona Iraci, the mass attendance at her funeral illustrates how significant she was to her family and neighbors. The community politicized her death and subsequently mobilized against police abuse in the neighborhood. In death Dona Iraci reminds us of poor black women's fight for the right to live in peace and in communities without violence. The burial of Dona Jacira was an example of a community's attempt to lay her to rest in dignity. The death of Raphael was a critique of the senseless violence in their neighborhood, as well as the importance given to a former fisherman whom people had known for decades. He was remembered less for his participation in the drug trade and more for his years of hard work and care for his family. This is not the relationship that the community has with all of the drug dealers. In fact, Raphael was not considered to be one of them. They saw him as a casualty of others' misdeeds. He meant a great deal to the people of Gamboa de Baixo, unifying a community to think critically about the future generation of black males who may have abandoned fishing as a viable option for work.

Picking Up the Pieces

Ana Cristina studied at night at a university almost an hour by bus from Gamboa de Baixo. It was the only schedule available for the courses she needed to graduate. In January 2008 when she registered for her last year of courses, she was the only member of her community to be enrolled in college and one of the few to have pursued education beyond high school. As I watched her sister Nicelia meticulously comb her hair for a night out with her boyfriend, she said, "I hope that Ana is able to change her schedule this year. I don't understand why they can't offer courses during the day." She abruptly stopped combing her hair and dialed Ana Cristina's cell phone. "Were you able to change your course schedule?" she shouted into the phone. From Nicelia's facial expression, I imagined that Ana responded that she hadn't been able to. "Damn, I'm tired of this. She needs to quit this university. She's always coming home at midnight. Another year that no one will be able to sleep until she gets home."

I tried to stress that university was important, that it was her sister's last year, and that she would be okay, but I agreed with her that it was a dangerous sacrifice for her sister to make. Nicelia dropped her head, looked at me, put down her comb again, and with tears welling up in her eyes, told me, "I don't want to go out anymore. I'm going to call him and tell him I don't want to go out. I'm tired. I can't take this anymore." She reached for the phone. I told her, "If she wants to take the risk, then let her live her life. She'll be okay. Don't stop living your life because of Ana. Go take advantage of *your* life!" She shrugged her shoulders and continued to comb her hair. "Thank God he's already told me that he's not even thinking of living in Gamboa."

Being black, female, and a resident of a poor neighborhood in Salvador's city center is stressful. According to Amnesty International, "Many of the residents who spoke to Amnesty International in May 2007 were suffering from extreme psychological problems caused by stress" (2008). Their lives have been disrupted. The life experiences of black women activists—whose experiences of violence I aim to contextualize as interconnected processes of state dominance—teach us that violence internalized in black communities cannot be understood as separate from the violence of class-based spatialized racism such as the construction of walls around luxury apartment communities (Caldeira 2000; Flauzina 2008; Smith 2009; Vargas and Alves 2009; Wilding 2012). Unless one is aware of the context of Nicelia's emotional reaction against her sister's decision to continue her studies amid public threats of physical violence and even death, as well as an ongoing struggle against neighborhood cleansing, it may be easy to depict her emotions as individual trauma rather than the collective experience of the women of her neighborhood, of black communities throughout Salvador.

As Bruce B. Lawrence and Aisha Karim write in the introduction to *On Violence*:

> There has never been a period or a group or a place free from violence, whether defined as a product or a process, as internal or external to individuals and their worldview or experience, but the range of data can be and should be focused on specific questions, local projects, and collective strategies that neither ignore violence nor surrender to its inevitability. (2007, 10)

In the city of Salvador, the local newspaper *A Tarde* reported on February 25, 2008, that "murder has become routine in various neighborhoods of Salvador." On that day ten people were killed during a period of eight hours—all in black neighborhoods. Though the majority of the victims of violence are young, black, and male, we cannot ignore the impact that urban violence has on black women.

The violence of displacement through private and state-sponsored urban development is inextricable from the private and public security mechanisms that police employ in neighboring communities of the elite. The space of the neighborhood itself and the Bahian police's treatment of it are crucial aspects of ongoing state efforts to expel Gamboa de Baixo residents from the coastal lands during the gentrification of the city center of Salvador. Thus, intracommunity violence equally affects neighborhood stability and black women's personal and political lives. The examples in this chapter illustrate how the police routinely commit violent acts against poor blacks and that black urban communities led by black women simultaneously internalize and contest that violence. Police terrorism in poor black urban neighborhoods is both routine and extraordinary, employing the most sophisticated techniques of urban warfare. Because of these daily barriers, black women neither wholly accept nor are able to wholly contest the violence they experience. Amnesty International reports that "poor communities remained trapped between the criminal gangs which dominated the areas in which they lived and the violent and discriminatory methods used by the police" (2008), which reflects the general frustration experienced by black communities throughout Brazil (Flauzina 2008; Perlman 2010; Reis 2005). Yet everyday and structural forms of violence shape their political consciousness, their gender and racial sensibilities, and their actual ability to organize their community and resist that violence. In essence, while they have to confront the violence within their community and from the state, they see fighting violence as a key aspect of preserving their right to occupy the urban landscape. This detailed description of intraviolence also illustrates a general feeling of a lack of protection within their community and from the state. Sherene Razack argues in her analysis of the death of an aboriginal woman in Canada that racist and sexist ideologies are accompanied by spatial practices such as violent land expulsions and the containment of black and poor peoples in marginalized areas of the city (2002). In Gamboa de Baixo local activists organize against land evictions and for land rights within this context of everyday violence.

That black women experience police violence in ways that lead to trauma and death and how they respond to that violence challenge how we think about the gendered nature of police repression. Intracommunity dynamics shape their activism as they are forced to simultaneously grapple with the reality of fighting both the *homens* and the *meninos*. In addition to real fear, violence on the part of residents tarnishes the positive image of Gamboa de Baixo that activists have worked hard to construct for the public above Contorno Avenue. Yet local residents express that as they fear the police more than they fear drug traffickers in their communities, they see both forms of violence as an interconnected state-supported process. This violence is detrimental to the overall struggle for black permanence on coastal lands and in the city center.

6

POLITICS IS A WOMEN'S THING

Política é coisa pra macho
ouvi isso a vida inteira

Politics is a man's game
I heard that all my life

Benedita da Silva, in *Benedita da Silva:*
An Afro-Brazilian Woman's Story of Politics and Love

Vamos pra Reunião!

"Vamos pra reunião!" (Let's go to the meeting!), Ana Cristina shouts.
She clutches her purple notebook as she passes Rita's house on her
way to the weekly Tuesday night board meeting of the neighborhood
association.

Rita opens her front door and responds, "In a little while. I'm washing clothes."

Ana Cristina presses her to hurry; they have important business to
discuss and it's essential that the meeting start on time.

It is 2004 and the citywide network of neighborhood activists has
become influential. The Odebrecht building is under way, and the
Gamboa de Baixo association has initiated negotiations with them to
compensate residents for lost houses and land. These meetings have
come to be known as what women do in the neighborhood.

Ana Cristina walks up the steps next to Rita's house and notices
that to her left the staircase that leads to Contorno Avenue is dark.
LIMPURB, the government agency responsible for collecting trash as
well as replacing the hard-to-reach lightbulbs, has been promising for
months to complete this service but has not followed through. When she
reaches the street above, she pauses to look into one of the street's arches
where the local capoeira team practices. It is hot inside the concrete
arch, and the young capoeiristas sweat profusely while they perform

their complex martial arts moves. A little boy who can't be more than five years old impresses her as he cartwheels across the slippery floor.

Ana Cristina continues down another staircase that leads to the beachfront on the side of the neighborhood referred to as Gamboa. Residents have named the other side, where Rita and Ana Cristina live, the Fortress, referring to the São Paulo da Gamboa Fort. Ana Cristina comments on the excessive amounts of garbage in her path and on the overgrown embankment. "It's absurd!" she exclaims, expressing her disgust with both the government's neglect and the residents' lack of care for their environment. She thinks about proposing an immediate mass cleanup because they cannot wait until LIMPURB begins trash collection and sweeping in the neighborhood. Two-thirds of the way down the hill, she reaches the one-story neighborhood association building where the meeting is to be held. The windows are closed, and the lights are off. "Where is everybody?" Ana Cristina grumbles under her breath as she opens the door. The building consists of one main room and a small office/library furnished with donated furniture, a kitchen, and a tiny bathroom. There is a pink plastic coffee thermos on the side table in the main room, and glass cups have been rinsed and placed on a tray beside it. Two large plastic bowls of popcorn covered with paper napkins have been neatly placed next to the thermos. The prepared coffee and the tidiness of the room let us know that Adriano has already arrived but is probably waiting in his home a few steps down the hill.

Ritinha arrives a few minutes later. Ana Cristina steps out onto the balcony and shouts for Maria José, who lives in a house facing the building. No one answers. She asks a small child lingering on the building's front steps to call Adriano. A short time later, Adriano comes up the hill and immediately states that if the meeting is not going to start on time, he can continue watching his favorite soap opera. He comes up the steps and enters the main room, saying that the building was dirty when he arrived earlier and that all the brooms were either broken or missing. He also points out that some of the glass cups have disappeared. Ritinha looks at him guiltily and promises to return his silver serving tray, which she borrowed a while back for a party. Adriano sits down across from Ana Cristina at the long black table and looks directly at her when he suggests that the association directors convene a meeting with all of the groups who use the space on a regular basis, including the local dance and capoeira groups, as well as a church organization.

Lula, the only other man who actively participates in the association, arrives with several receipts in hand. He stops in front of the door to finish his cigarette. Dona Marinalva, a petite elderly woman, comes in and sits in a chair with her back to the window. Her small black purse hangs across her body, as usual.

Shortly after, Rita loudly announces her arrival: "I'm here! What is there to eat? I didn't eat lunch, and I had to leave my dinner at home."

Adriano chastises her as she walks over to the food table, "Is food the only thing you think about?"

"Yes," she doesn't hesitate to respond, pouting and jutting her hips out to exaggerate the size of her round belly. Everyone laughs.

Lu arrives with her baby girl in her arms and her toddler son trailing behind. Maria José follows behind them with her baby son latched onto her breast. With the exception of Dona Nice and Joelma, who are both working late, all of the directors of the neighborhood association are in attendance.

It's already half past eight, and a frustrated Ana Cristina asks, "What's the agenda for tonight's meeting?" She reads from her notebook some of the issues she thought should be on the agenda: (1) the organization of a general assembly; (2) payment to Lula for the construction materials he purchased and for his labor when he repaired the neighborhood association building; (3) the two upcoming Iemanjá celebrations; and (4) the scheduled meetings with Odebrecht, EMBASA, and CONDER. Before they discuss the issues on the agenda, Adriano begins with the announcements. He says that the day before, he attended the weekly meeting with Voices for Communities Fighting for Housing Rights. During that meeting the group agreed to organize a political formation workshop to include the participation of Gamboa de Baixo residents. They should continue to be active in the citywide network of neighborhood activists, and "not just the leadership" will participate. Other community members will benefit from this workshop.

Second, Adriano says that there is a neighborhood association meeting with Odebrecht the following morning. Only board members and the families negotiating with the company will attend. The payment amounts for the banana trees that two residents have cultivated on the property have basically been agreed upon. Adriano reports, however, that the family who owns the house that partially sits on "so-called Ode-brecht's land" has agreed to remove their home and has raised the asking price from its original R$25,000 (about US$12,000) to R$50,000 (about US$24,000). Adriano says that this was a small defeat for the neighborhood association because they had fought with Odebrecht for the permanence of this home and those of all other residents who occupy the land the company claims to own.

In a clear sign of discomfort, Rita and Ana Cristina shift around in their seats, and a few of the other women grumble under their breath. A brief discussion ensues about the role of the neighborhood association in these kinds of negotiations, as well as the future of financial incentives for land seizure and expulsion.

"What will happen if more families feel that they can sell their homes for high prices?" Dona Marinalva asks. In a near whisper, she recounts that she has overheard conversations among her neighbors that they want to sell their houses, too.

"And who is going to buy their tiny little houses?" Rita rebukes, explaining that Odebrecht is interested in one particular house because it needs that small piece of land for the boathouse.

Everyone agrees that the vast majority of residents are unwilling to sell their homes and relocate elsewhere and that it is likely that the displaced family will rebuild on land within the neighborhood. Adriano intervenes in the heated discussion with another announcement of a meeting with the secretary of urban habitation that has been scheduled later in the month. He says it is essential that the majority of the board members attend.

It's almost a quarter past nine when the board shifts its focus to the organization of the general assembly. Ana Cristina expresses a need to return to the bimonthly general assemblies, a political event that promotes debates and discussions on the current happenings of the community and the neighborhood association. Ritinha suggests that at least one of the general assemblies each month be local, taking place in different areas of the neighborhood. Everyone nods in agreement, and Rita suggests that the first assembly be held in the community school and center, located underneath Contorno Avenue on the Fortaleza side of the neighborhood. Meeting in that building, Rita says, would reclaim the political use of the community center. Before the construction of the neighborhood association building, the community school was the main space used for meetings. Rita adds that with the recent reorganization of the community school by a few "greedy" residents claiming to be its new directors, the space has been represented as a separate neighborhood association.

Rita explains, "It seems like it's an association with a president and vice president and not just a school."

Ana Cristina replies, "But our association is the only legally recognized representative entity of the neighborhood chosen by the people."

Ritinha clarifies that even though Gamboa residents agree that the neighborhood association is the democratically elected body chosen to represent the interests of the community, the school's directors indeed misrepresent themselves as leaders of the neighborhood. The misuse of the titles "president" and "vice president" by nonelected individuals when they negotiate with the state for benefits for the community school suggests that they are representatives of the entire neighborhood, as well. This action, Ritinha warns, threatens to delegitimize the neighborhood association's activities, especially if residents receive material incentives such as food baskets, construction materials, or salaried jobs.

As a solution it is suggested that a general assembly in the school would increase the participation of the residents in that area, while also reclaiming the space as a community space operating in conjunction with ongoing activities of the neighborhood association. Lu and Maria also suggest that future meetings take place in the São Paulo da Gamboa Fort, thereby encouraging the participation of the residents who live there. Also, a meeting on the shorefront and another on Rua da Resistência (Resistance Street, named by the founding members of the neighborhood association), where Gegê lived, might quell residents' complaints that they are often unaware of the happenings in the rest of the neighborhood.

Everyone agrees with Rita when she challenges, "Let's see if they attend a meeting in front of their homes."

"Let's see," they all concur.

The board schedules the next general assembly for two Saturdays from tonight's meeting. Ana Cristina suggests that the agenda include an open discussion about ongoing negotiations with Odebrecht, the incomplete construction of sewers by EMBASA and Bahia Azul, CONDER's responsibility for repairing poorly constructed homes, community participation in the political formation workshop, the restoration and future use of the *casarão* (historic mansion), and celebrations for Iemanjá, the Candomblé goddess of the waters. Ritinha offers to prepare and copy flyers to distribute a few days before the general assembly. Adriano agrees to pick up the flyers from Ritinha and pass them out on the Gamboa side. Lu promises to pass out flyers on the Fortaleza side. Rita offers to publicize the meeting in front of her house with a bullhorn and flyers, while Ana Cristina proposes to reinforce the announcements by making personal door-to-door stops on the day of the meeting.

Around a quarter past ten, Dona Nice arrives at the meeting from work. "It must be really late!" Adriano exclaims. Ana Cristina says that Ritinha has to catch her bus home. The discussion of Lula's receipts and payment will have to wait until the next meeting, but they still need to iron out the details of the two Iemanjá celebrations. One of the celebrations follows the tradition of the citywide commemoration of the Yoruba goddess associated with the sea. This year it needs planning because the fisherman who normally organizes the baskets of flowers and gifts to be taken out to sea has been hospitalized. The neighborhood association will take the lead by purchasing the basket during the week and then collecting gifts from the residents on the day of the celebration. A discussion begins about the difference between the two celebrations. The fishermen's celebration, Ana Cristina highlights, tends to be a simple celebration in which most of the local fishermen and residents participate. They also take the longer boat ride down the coastline to participate in the massive celebrations in the Rio Vermelho neighborhood. During this discussion, Maria José, who organizes a *presente de Iemanjá* (offering to Iemanjá) a week after the citywide event as a part of her own religious obligations, suggests that the group wait until the following week to talk about the details of her preparations. Practitioners and nonpractitioners of Candomblé tend to participate in both events, but some residents make a clear distinction between the secular fishermen's celebration and Maria José's sacred presente de Iemanjá, which involves Candomblé rituals.

Independent of what people choose to believe, Ritinha chimes in, "Iemanjá é de Candomblé." They agree with Ritinha that Iemanjá is from Candomblé.

Before the meeting ends, Ana Cristina writes down the names of neighborhood-association directors who will attend the next day's meeting at Odebrecht: herself, Adriano, Dona Marinalva, and Ritinha. A brief debate ensues about their role in that meeting, with Ana Cristina emphasizing that they will not sign any document that states they agree with the company's construction project. In previous meetings Odebrecht representatives had suggested that they sign such a document, but Ana Cristina underlines that they have no comprehensive knowledge of the project or the company's future intentions for the community. She also notes that agreeing with the company might compromise their political image within the neighborhood and that they could be accused of being on the side of *os barões* (rich boys), a potentially dangerous image that might feed into current opinions that the neighborhood association is being bought off by Odebrecht. The only document they will sign, she vehemently adds, will be the future agreement to transfer collective land ownership to the community.

On that final note, they begin to lock the windows, and Rita washes the glasses and bowls in the kitchen. They pick up the bits of popcorn and throw them in the outside trash bin. Maria José, Dona Marinalva, and Dona Nice head down the hill toward their homes. The others slowly walk up the hill, including Adriano, who complains that he is late to visit a "friend," who his smirk suggests is more than a friend. They stop in front of a local bar that is blasting reggae music while a few regulars play pool and drink. They dance to the infectious music while they continue to climb the hill. "Que bom" (How great), Ana Cristina sighs in relief when she sees Ritinha's husband waiting in his car on the other side of Contorno Avenue.

As this description suggests, organizing and completing a weekly board meeting represents no easy task for community leaders in the Gamboa de Baixo neighborhood association. Most Tuesday evenings, the board meeting conflicts with personal and professional responsibilities of working women like Rita, who works as a domestic worker from sunrise to sunset and takes care of her own household duties at night. Her dedication to the neighborhood association meeting illustrates her willingness to take on the triple duties of worker, mother, and activist. Dona Nice and Joelma both work until late at night and usually arrive after the meeting ends. Ana Cristina often misses meetings because she attends college at night, while Maria José sometimes sells *acarajé,* a fried bean pie that originated in Candomblé religious practices, in front of a local bar. Simultaneously managing both the domestic and the political spheres poses a tremendous challenge for this group of women activists.

For similar reasons small children are almost always present at meetings and other political activities. Many are breast-feeding, and in most cases these mothers have no one to leave their children with, nor would they want to if they did. The work of the neighborhood association is not always divided equally. For example, Ana Cristina, when she is unemployed, handles most of the daily happenings of the neighborhood, such as the visit of state technicians. Adriano has a more flexible work schedule as a tutor for local schoolchildren and can often reschedule or cancel classes on short notice. How these courageous women (and a few good men) lead this community organization amid these challenges dismantles the myth that the lack of male leadership in the neighborhood is the result of men's work outside the home and that the predominance of female leadership results from women's work at home. Though some of these women are unemployed outside their homes, many work and still actively engage in community politics, and building community is intimately tied to political struggle.

Domestic Work, Insider Knowledge, and Grassroots Politics

In a class system that relegates black women to the bottom of the socioeconomic hierarchy, domestic workers give special insights into how gendered racism operates in Brazil and the challenges in resisting that racism. More than 80 percent of working adult and adolescent females in the Gamboa de Baixo neighborhood are domestic workers. Despite carrying out one of Brazil's least valued and most dehumanizing forms of work, many of these women carve out political space from their everyday lives in order to organize a resistance movement and, in doing so, act as the predominant leaders of Gamboa de Baixo's community politics.

At a board meeting of the Gamboa de Baixo neighborhood association in 2003, Rita recounted the story of her work conditions in the home of a wealthy Bahian musician who lived in the elite Rio Vermelho coastal neighborhood. The meeting took place a few days before Christmas, and Rita sadly remarked that her employer said he would not pay her the state-mandated thirteenth-month year-end salary bonus. She had been fully expecting the money, and she asked the other neighborhood association board members what her legal rights were as a domestic worker and whether this category of worker traditionally received the bonus. Her boss had already refused to sign her worker's card, which documented her work history and salary, leaving her without any legal recourse, and he was paying her below the legal minimum wage. She earned R$200 per month, whereas the national minimum salary was R$240 (about US$70). Rita explained that three generations lived in her employer's household and, therefore, the work was hard. She hand-washed clothes for five adults and two children. Like most domestic workers, she complained that she suffered acute back pain from the cleaning and ironing and that her hands were raw from all of the washing. "They can afford to buy a washing machine," Rita affirmed, but like most Bahians, they preferred to have their clothes washed by hand. Black women provide an available and cheap labor alternative to the expensive technologies that make domestic work easier.

Being cheated out of a fair salary was a usual complaint of domestic workers in Bahia. It led to the political organization of the Sindicato dos Trabalhadores Domésticos da Bahia (Domestic Workers' Union of Bahia, or Sindoméstico) and the Sindicato das Lavadeiras (Washerwomen's Union) during recent decades. A more common complaint of domestic workers is employers' refusal to pay the necessary social security taxes, obstructing workers' ability to receive retirement benefits after many years of work. After hearing Rita's story, Ana Cristina told of her own mother's enduring struggle to retire even though her hands were severely damaged from many years of hand washing. Ana Cristina also admitted that for several years as an adolescent and young adult, she worked as a domestic worker in her light-skinned sister's house in Gamboa de Baixo without receiving a salary. The job provided her with shelter and food, as well as the freedom to move about her neighborhood and to participate in community politics. Ana Cristina perceived her unpaid labor, however, as a form of racial exploitation common to other black domestic workers in Gamboa de Baixo and throughout Salvador.

A discussion about what Rita should do about her exploitative working conditions erupted during the meeting. Ritinha suggested that they contact a lawyer, and Rita said that she was already planning not to return to her job after the holidays. The women of the Gamboa de Baixo neighborhood association regularly confront the police and shout at state officials during meetings and group demonstrations, but they individually struggle to overcome the oppressive conditions they face in other aspects of their lives. As Ana Cristina reminded Rita during the meeting, the Gamboa de Baixo struggle is not just about the empowerment and improvement of the neighborhood but also about reinventing themselves as black women and realizing their own *projetos de vida,* their own "personal life projects," a term they repeated regularly in Women's Group meetings. The incident with Rita raises the question of how and why black women have been able to mobilize on a collective basis in their communities around issues of housing and land rights but have not been able to resist on an individual level at the workplace or even at home. In addition to tales of everyday struggles for fair salaries, accounts of employers who try to sexually exploit young Gamboa girls are commonplace.

Domestic work continues to be one visible reminder of Brazil's neoslavery attitudes and practices toward black women's work. The following excerpt from the Declaration of Black Brazilian Women's Organizations explains this relationship between domestic work and black women's servitude:

> Domestic work still is, since enslavement in Brazil, the place that the racist society has destined to be the primary function of black women. In this domain, there are relatively few gains to be made in the work force and the relationships are charac-terized by servility. In many places, forms of recruitment are predominantly neoslavery. These women play an essential role

in the development of sustainable production and in the consumption of goods and provision for services for their family and community.

As this declaration affirms, this form of enslavement maintains similar racial, gender, and class hierarchies as were prevalent during slavery times. At the same time, black women use this form of work to sustain their families and communities, often because it's the only option open to them.

Similarly, Carolina Maria de Jesus presents in her childhood memoir *Bitita's Diary: The Childhood Memoirs of Carolina Maria de Jesus* (1997), a personal testament of black women's struggle against poverty and racial oppression. De Jesus locates her experiences within the broader community when she writes of the everyday challenges black women face as domestic workers in the homes of white families, as well as the difficulty of raising their own children. She writes, "Poor women didn't have any free time to care for their homes. At six in the morning, they had to be in their mistresses' houses to light the fire and prepare the morning meal. What a horrible thing! Those who had mothers, left their children and their homes with them" (22).

Although women express the various ways that they try to resist these kinds of exploitation, the vast majority continue to work under difficult circumstances, do not participate in unions, and are not registered with the Brazilian government as formal workers. They are often unaware that unions exist or that there are certain rights guaranteed to workers in their profession, even when working without legal documentation. To my knowledge, no woman in the Gamboa de Baixo neighborhood is affiliated with a domestic workers' union or a union that addresses their needs. These black women workers in Bahian society are viewed as disposable, rendered invisible, and undervalued as real workers. In 2012, as the federal government augmented the rights of domestic workers to equal those of other workers in areas such as maternity leave and retirement contributions, many still worked informally and outside contractual agreements (Carneiro 1995; Figueiredo 2011; Silva and Lima 1992). Even with these recent advancements, many poor women throughout the country are usually afraid to resist because domestic work is the only kind of job they can find (Mori et al. 2011).

Regarding the struggle against the oppressive conditions of domestic work, social movement theorists encourage rethinking those conceptualizations of black women's resistance that privilege mainstream politics (Davies 2008; Kelley 1993; McDuffie 2011). Daily acts of resistance and survival, such as quitting unexpectedly or working slowly, have a "cumulative effect on power relations" (Kelley 1993, 78). Black women lead grassroots organizations in the battle against exclusionary urban policies and state aggression in various ways, including direct action protests and meetings. From this perspective black women's political consciousness in neighborhood movements stems from the very strategies, actions, and experiences that drive Ana Cristina to work in exchange for food and shelter and Rita to abruptly leave her job. Some women who work in the high-rise buildings that overlook Gamboa de Baixo explain that working in close proximity to their homes allows them to stay abreast of their neighborhood's everyday happenings and attend to emergencies in their homes and community.

This approach to politics refocuses discussion on why (rather than how) people participate in social movements. According to Patricia Hill Collins, "U.S. Black women's critical social theory lay in the common experiences they gained from their jobs" (1990, 10). In forging strong "familial" ties with their white employers, black women construct "insider relationships" (10). These women witness and understand racism firsthand, however, and know that although they are navigating the intimate terrains of white people's lives, they "could never belong to the white 'families'" (11). In fact, domestic workers remain what Collins calls "outsiders-within," socially and economically marginalized from white society. Black women who work as domestics not only maintain relationships within their all-black communities but also develop complex relationships within the homes where they work. Navigating the homes of white families on a daily basis, they belong as workers, but they are permanent economic and social outsiders-within.

In another essay Collins emphasizes that black women are never "like one of the family," which reflects how racial and gender power operates within the private realm of domestic work (2001). This form of social organization also illustrates the "politics of containment," which for black women "marked with the status of subordinated work-

ers" means that they are "tolerated as long as they remain in their pro-
scribed places" (5). At the same time, domestic workers gain access to
the particularities of racial ideologies and practices, which they take
back to their home spaces and share with each other, thereby developing a collective social critique of gendered, class-based racism. For
example, in Gamboa de Baixo mainly domestic workers argued that if
local residents accepted being removed from the coastal lands to the
distant outskirts of the city, they would lose access to the sea as an
important resource. "Which wealthy white condominium will allow
us to leave our boats here and walk through daily to go fishing?" they
asked. Black women domestic workers consistently expressed that
they observed firsthand the intricacies of how the white elite thought
and acted. They experienced the very strict hierarchies of race, gender, and class every day as they walked through neighborhoods such
as Vitória and entered their employers' homes through kitchen doors
and service elevators.

As blacks, women, mothers, and workers, these workers constitute the *superexploited,* producing a kind of political militancy necessary to lead social movements (Davies 2008; Jones 1974; Kelley 2002;
McDuffie 2011). Drawing upon the ideas of radical leftist thinker and
activist Claudia Jones, Carole Boyce Davies explains that the issues of
material neglect affecting black women make them "both pivotal and
vulnerable to struggles" (2008, 38). This positions black women, "the
most exploited and oppressed," at the vanguard of black struggles (40).
In Brazil, as throughout the African diaspora, "since black women are
often heads of households, entire black communities will remain in
poverty if the black women stay underpaid and superexploited" (41).

This understanding of black women's standpoint constructed from
their experiences on the margins of the political economy elucidates
the collective action of black women in Brazilian urban communities.
In Gamboa de Baixo the knowledge black women gain as domestic
workers is a source of political empowerment and organizing creativ-
ity. Women like Rita might not overtly resist their employers' actions,
but they share their critiques with their neighbors in spaces like association meetings. Understanding that colonialism and racism are
the root causes of their exploitation, these black women contemplate

collective ways to overcome that exploitation and transform society. Still, Collins's black women's standpoint theory does not explain the relative lack of political action in the workplace.

One explanation may be that in cities like Salvador labor organizations rarely concern themselves with racial justice and housing rights. This absence of a class consciousness that includes the racialized poor discourages black communities from organizing around a shared class position. From this perspective black women in Gamboa de Baixo prefer to mobilize as *moradores* (residents of a neighborhood) and not as *trabalhadores* (workers). In their neighborhood organizations black women link their class positions as poor workers to their racial and gender conditions in a structurally unequal city. They understand that they are poor because they are black women, an understanding gained through their heightened racial and gender sensibilities at work and at home. They self-identify as residents of an urban neighborhood under siege by the police, development agencies, and private companies because Gamboa de Baixo is black and poor. The neighborhood, unlike the workplace, is an important site of political autonomy and liberation for poor black women in Salvador's communities (Perry 2008).

"If We Didn't Have Water": Spirituality, Land, and Environmental Justice

Although most domestic workers are black women who are underpaid and continue to live in poverty, they make up the majority of the participants and the leadership of terreiros. In addition to the knowledge black women gain as domestic workers, what drives the Gamboa de Baixo struggle for land rights during recent threats of mass eviction and forced displacement, or what neighborhood activists have termed the "wave of black clearance," is, in part, their love for and spiritual connection to the sea that is the backyard of their urban neighborhood. It is important to recognize that the sea and African religious traditions shape black women's everyday culture and environmental politics in Gamboa de Baixo and in black neighborhoods throughout Salvador. This privileging of the spiritual in understanding the intricate relationship between black diaspora culture and grassroots politics represents a key aspect of the broader issues with which I grapple in my interdisciplinary research on black women as cultural producers and political agents in Brazil. Black women workers in urban neighborhoods in Salvador carve out geographic, social, and political spaces for themselves while expanding notions of cultural belonging and citizenship at the levels of the city, the nation, and the diaspora (Butler 1998; Harding 2003). Black women's central role in urban social movements must be seen as a part of a larger diaspora pattern of black women's oppositional politics vested in property rights for both cultural and material gain.

To begin to comprehend this inseparable connection between black women's religious culture and politics, the words of the late Brazilian literary scholar of Bahian culture Jorge Amado, in his novel *Sea of Death* (1984), come to mind: "The ocean is large, the sea is a road without end, waters make up more than half the world, they are three-quarters of it, and all that belongs to Iemanjá." In the African diasporic religion of Candomblé, practiced by the vast majority of Bahians, Iemanjá is the highly revered goddess of the sea, commonly known as A Mãe das Águas (The Mother of the Waters). Each year in Salvador, February 2 marks one of the most important days of celebration in Candomblé, the Festa de Iemanjá, which takes place in the Rio Vermelho coastal neighborhood. With more resources today, particularly government sponsorship, the festival has been transformed from a community practice into a massive cultural project of interest for both locals and national and international tourists. The dominant ceremonial presence of black fishermen and Candomblé religious leaders (most of whom are women) reminds us, however, that although Rio Vermelho is now a predominantly white, elite neighborhood, black fishing colonies have historically occupied the coastal lands of Salvador and have carried out these traditions since the slavery period (Figure 17). Gamboa de Baixo is now one of the few black urban fishing colonies that exist on the Bahian coast, and two Iemanjá festivals still occur simultaneously, a large one in Rio Vermelho and a smaller one in Gamboa de Baixo. Like in most fishing communities, local residents pay homage to the goddess of the sea for protecting the fishermen and fisherwomen while they work and for supplying the sea with sufficient fish, an important natural resource that sustains the local economy and African-inspired culinary traditions. More important, Gamboa de Baixo residents express their gratitude to Iemanjá for protecting their children while they play on the neighborhood's beaches.

FIGURE 17. Festa de Iemanjá in Rio Vermelho neighborhood. Photograph by Javier Escudero.

Approximately one week after the February 2 festivals, another Iemanjá festival is carried out in Gamboa de Baixo. Maria José organizes an offering of gifts to Iemanjá, a personalized celebration that has become a neighborhood custom. She receives relatives and friends from all over the city and state, as well as her Candomblé family from Itaparica Island, located in the bay and visible from Gamboa de Baixo. The neighborhood association has been active in preparing her offering each year, from raising funds to creating traditional gifts, many of which became biodegradable after much discussion within the organization about the harmful environmental effects of plastic presents such as dolls and perfumes. When asked why she joined the community struggle, Maria José explained that living close to the resources of the city center, such as schools and hospitals, was very important. Then, she added that there were few places in the city where she could have access to her own beach to carry out her yearly religious obligations to Iemanjá and celebrate with her neighbors, many of whom were her family members. She would continue to fight for this right to own and live on these coveted coastal lands (Figure 18).

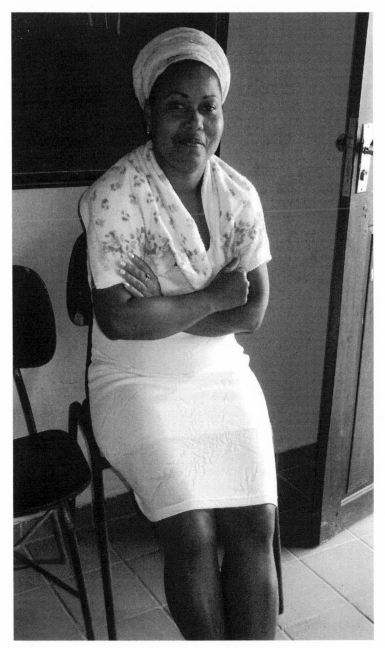

FIGURE 18. Maria José (nicknamed "Preta") inside the neighborhood association building, 2004. Photograph by the author.

In Candomblé female deities such as Iemanjá have long been considered a source of black women's political power, which is evident in present-day grassroots movements (Carneiro and Cury 2008; Garcia 2006; Hautzinger 2007; Aryá 2009; Santos 1995; Sterling 2010; Werneck 2007). From within African religious communities comes a collective imagining of Africa "that is as real as it is translated through the patterns of organization and political organization" in which women's leadership is recognized as crucial for spiritual and material transformation (Werneck 2007, 203). Rachel Harding has similarly argued that Candomblé has served as "a collectivizing force through which subjugated peoples"—and I would emphasize black women—"organized an alternative meaning of their lives and identities that countered the disaggregation and the imposed subalterity to which they were subjected by the dominant social structure" (2003, 1).

From this perspective local activists assert that the Iemanjá festivals in Gamboa de Baixo should be understood not only within the context of African religious traditions and their reverence for the sea but also as an aspect of black women's deliberate actions of staking claims to urban land on the Bahian coast. In terreiros throughout the city, black women have inherited not only African religious practices but also the rights to the land on which they practice these traditions. Historically, to speak of these terreiros has meant to speak of black women's land. Thus, black women have been uniquely positioned in these communities as having both collective memory and legal documentation of ancestral lands. This memory extends beyond the Bay of All Saints to the practice of women as landowners in Africa, where they served as the primary mediators of family relations within their communities, influencing the distribution of important resources such as land. Signifying more than just the physical space where families live, work, and forge political networks, urban land in contemporary Brazil represents the ability of black women to pass spiritual and material resources from one generation to the next. Land has become one of the greatest social and cultural assets for black people, particularly for women, who are the most economically marginalized. In essence the neighborhood fight for land rights has integrated their political demands to legalize collective property rights with demands to preserve the material and cultural resources the sea provides.

I am deliberate about not detailing Candomblé practices or its specific African-derived cosmologies and mythologies. Rather, the ethnographic examples of the Iemanjá festivals are intended to bring attention to the political formation of a black urban neighborhood located on the geographic and socioeconomic margins of a Brazilian city. The terreiros as sociopolitical spaces are understudied, but the political actions of black women in grassroots struggles bridge the relationship between black struggles for self-definition and the freedom of African cultural expression and social movements that make territorial claims to urban space. The case of Gamboa de Baixo supports my theoretical claim that African religious traditions are indissociable from black women's political actions in the local, national, and global black struggle for material resources such as land, employment, and education. As black Canadian feminist M. Jacqui Alexander asserts, "Ultimately, excising the spiritual from the political builds the ground at the intersection of two kinds of alienation: the one an alienation from the self; the other, which is inevitable, alienation from each other" (2005, 326). In other words, black women's religious matters are political matters, and black women's collective resistance against the violence of land evictions and displacement is deeply connected to what womanist theologian Dianne M. Stewart terms "the liberation motif" of African-centered traditions in black diasporic communities (2005). This emphasis shows that black women in Brazil and throughout the black diaspora are cultural producers as well as political agents in their own right, with their own African-inspired sensibilities of gendered racial liberation and social transformation in Brazilian cities. Spirituality, I reaffirm, must acquire a privileged space in the broader understanding of how black women have responded to the barbarous reality of class-based and gendered racism in Brazil and throughout the black diaspora.

Scholars of black social movements have emphasized the importance of culture in antiracism and anticolonialism politics. Similar to the aforementioned ideas by Werneck and Harding, Kim Butler argues that adaptations of Candomblé have been "rooted in the conscious choice of Afro-Brazilians to use African culture as a mode of support and survival in modern Brazilian society" (1998, 195). The ethnographic focus on the political mobilization of black urban communities contextualizes black cultural practices within the ongoing processes of gendered racial and economic oppression that mark the black Brazilian experience. The black majority in Bahia and the predominance of African religious traditions do not obscure the lack of gendered racial inequality. In many respects the black population, particularly black women, carries the burden of centuries of enslavement and social marginalization. The terreiros have been spiritual spaces of racial and gender solidarity where black women maintain cultural identity and community in the city of Salvador.

From this perspective we cannot ignore that, historically, the main protagonists, such as Makota Valdina Pinto in Salvador, in antiracist environmental justice movements in Brazilian cities have primarily been black women leaders of Candomblé communities (Nascimento 2008; Perry 2006, 2009). Makato Valdina has been, since her youth, a neighborhood activist and one of the city's most outspoken voices against environmental racism, linking the increased lack of public access to unpolluted lands and natural water sources to the widespread neglect of black urban communities. Makato Valdina's actions echo Jomo Kenyatta and other diaspora scholar activists who argue that water and land are two of the greatest natural resources for black people socially, economically, and spiritually. In Afro-Brazilian communities, gaining access to these resources or protecting them from privatization and destruction has been an ongoing focus of community-based activism. Black women environmentalists in Salvador have also focused heavily on the urgent need for environmental reform while fighting to eradicate the violent religious intolerance many Afro-Brazilian religious communities suffer. Violence against these communities has targeted the built environments of the terreiros, such as the frequent defacement of the metal gates of the historic Casa Branca terreiro located in Ogunjá and the ongoing encroachment on the lands of the Terreiro do Cobre in Federação. The state demolition of the terreiro Oyá Onipó Neto in February 2008 further illustrates the gendered implications of these violent attacks on black women's lands, and their organic leadership in combating such violence locally (Figure 19).

The leadership of black women in environmental justice movements should also be understood within the larger context of emerging neighborhood movements. Black urban spaces are racialized,

FIGURE 19. The terreiro Oyá Onipó Neto, located in the Imbuí neighborhood, was demolished by the municipal government. The terreiro's priestess, Mãe Rosa, sits beside one of her spiritual daughters crying. Protests afterward would lead to it being rebuilt. Photograph by Fernando Vivas. Courtesy of Agência A Tarde.

gendered "terrains of domination" in which black women's politics are deeply connected to resistance against "geographic domination" as practiced in environmental neglect, land evictions, and displacement in Brazilian cities (McKittrick 2006). In addition to making demands to the state for clean water and basic sanitation, Gamboa de Baixo activists have adopted good environmental practices, such as scuba diving to remove garbage from the ocean and using biodegradable materials in Candomblé ceremonies. Environmental reform and the building of sanitized spaces matter to poor people as much as they matter to the state to create clean modern cities, but black neighborhoods desire clean urban spaces that include black people rather than exclude them. Thus, environmental reform should be viewed as intertwined with the struggle for the legalization of black urban lands, recognizing that property rights continue to be a crucial aspect of black claims to Brazilian citizenship. Furthermore, black women's political leadership in issues of land and sanitation in Salvador's *bairros populares* is important for understanding everyday grassroots actions of the black movement.

The sea, specifically its relationship to African cosmologies, yields an indispensable source of spiritual, material, and political nourishment in the lives of black women in Bahia. It is not by accident that clean water continues to be a key political demand for neighborhood activists and that black women lead this fight. Land rights must be considered within the broader quest for water and an overall healthy, clean urban environment. Politicizing the need for water, as illustrated by the previously described cholera and EMBASA protests, has been integral to Gamboa de Baixo's ongoing fight for urban land rights and neighborhood improvement amid state threats of land expulsion. Water, specifically the waters of the Bay of All Saints, has been a spiritual source of black women's political empowerment in Gamboa. Water has been at the center of Gamboa de Baixo's political organizing around issues of land and housing reform since its inception, and poor black women have been key to those discussions.

Black Women's Leadership as a Challenge to Hegemony

The intricate relationship among racial, gender, and class structuring as well as spiritual forces sheds some light on black women's ethics in urban social movements and shows a crucial reason why neighborhood associations are female led and why they have been relatively successful in preserving collective community interests such as land and improved social conditions. In diasporic religious traditions, black women also learn and practice a feminist ethics that encourages a focus on the collective rather than on the individual. Patricia Hill Collins argues that these kinds of moral and ethical principles stem from women's experiences in religious institutions and underline their ideological position in black political struggles. She writes that this follows the black feminist tradition in community activism:

> This moral, ethical tradition, especially as expressed within
> black Christian churches, encouraged black women to
> relinquish their special interests as women for the greater
> good of the overarching community. Rejecting individualist

strategies that they perceived as selfish, black women came
to couch their issues as black women within the egalitarian,
collectivist ideological framework of black women's community work, an approach that works well within womanist
approaches to black women's politics . . . . Within this inter-
pretative framework, fighting for freedom and social justice
for the entire black community was, in effect, fighting for one's
own personal freedom. The two could not be easily separated.
(1998, 27)

Similarly, in Brazil black women's morality—informed by Christian-
ity and, more important, by Afro-Brazilian religious traditions, also
heavily female dominated—encourages them to abandon their special
interests and fight on behalf of the entire community. Activists in Gamboa de Baixo see the collective community interests as coinciding with
their own individual needs as poor black women—thus, women have
had sustained leadership over time and the neighborhood movement
has not been co-opted or dismantled by politicians.

Former Gamboa de Baixo activist Camilo, Lu's husband, explained
to me why he thought the neighborhood and its movement had gained
the reputation of being "of women." He began by clarifying that Gamboa de Baixo is "of men," too, but it was different from other neighborhoods in the city:

Gamboa has been an example for many communities, and we
have heard people making it a point to state that the majority of
leaders in Gamboa are women. That isn't what made me stop
participating in the struggle. For me it's a great honor to know
that our neighborhood is seen as an example. For me it's positive because any struggle expects most participants to be male.
So if the majority here are women, it's because we are different.

Men are present, though, during key moments, such as street protests.
Women take greater risks, however, because of how the society and
policing operates. For example, black men are more likely to get arrested, and in a fishing community women are more educated and
prepared to engage in negotiations with the state over policy issues.

Another key distinction between men and women is that men sell out a lot faster to the politicians and development agents, to the detriment of the entire community. When politicians approach neighborhood groups to garner votes, they almost always approach male residents, some of whom have bargained with the state for personal gain, such as political appointments. Camilo supports this idea by describing the neighborhood activists in Solar do Unhão, located adjacent to Gamboa de Baixo and also threatened by land expulsion:

> Here, on this side in Solar do Unhão, the people didn't know anything. When we started, they didn't know anything, but thank God, we found advisers who wanted to help us, and the knowledge that we got, we passed on to them. Afterward, they aligned themselves with politicians on the right. After we found out, they distanced themselves from us. I believe that yes, they sold out.

The majority of the leadership in Solar do Unhão was men who were willing to negotiate with politicians. Some would later be hired to work for the government in exchange for accepting development plans that included partial eviction. Today, Solar do Unhão is oftentimes upheld as a model revitalized neighborhood. These kinds of political relationships show that male leaders are more willing to take advantage of their male privilege and any accompanying benefits when dealing with the state. In turn, they forego group advancement and consent to racial, gender, and class domination for individual interests such as jobs.

Like in the case of Gamboa de Baixo, the government has similar plans to evict the residents of Solar do Unhão, who also consider themselves to be a traditional centuries-old fishing colony. In fact, the geographical configurations of urbanization plans considered both neighborhoods to be one, and residents say that only in recent decades have they claimed separated identities. Family ties between the neighborhoods are historical; since the construction of Contorno Avenue and the increased settlement by immigrants from rural regions of Bahia and other neighborhoods, however, Gamboa de Baixo has been relatively poorer. Whereas Gamboa de Baixo residents have tended to embrace newcomers, who oftentimes build improvised housing out of wood, Solar do Unhão residents have resisted this settlement and protested the construction of such poor structures. In general the income levels and the quality of housing have been better in Solar do Unhão, but they have shared the struggle against the threat of expulsion and displacement to the distant urban periphery and also for basic sanitation and other resources.

At the onset of the movement in the mid-1990s, the major difference between the political organizations of the two neighborhoods was that a majority poor black women's leadership emerged in Gamboa de Baixo while men, some of whom worked as civil servants and were formally educated, assumed leadership in Solar do Unhão. As some of the Gamboa de Baixo activists boldly recall, the sexist leadership of men in Solar do Unhão undermined the possibility of joining collective forces as two black communities facing similar actions by the state. They assert that the survival of both communities is the direct result of women activists' determination to protect the collective interests of both communities that extend geographically as well as across familial lines. They also remember that the male activists were unwilling to take seriously and engage with the women of Gamboa de Baixo in political strategizing. To further compound the problems, state officials offered benefits such as government posts to individual male leaders, which led some to abandon the movement or act in ways that were detrimental to the overall political project of both communities.

As the movement in Gamboa de Baixo strengthened, the movement in Solar do Unhão steadily declined, culminating in the false representation of incomplete urbanization projects in the area as a success. Gamboa de Baixo activists refused to participate in any government-sponsored celebrations. Also, Solar do Unhão has suffered from land speculation with the increase in the numbers of outsiders, primarily foreigners, who have come to settle on the Bahian coast.

Gamboa de Baixo activists have refused to align themselves with state officials and have worked to prevent the demolition of their neighborhood. This underlines the specific challenges black women grassroots leaders face that are different from those of their male counterparts. An important part of this challenge is how political co-optation is used as a way of undermining that leadership and dismissing the diverse dimensions of black women's knowledge. Black women experience co-optation differently, usually in the form of sexual seduction, resting on the belief that all black women, especially poor ones, are sexually available and are willing to sell their bodies in exchange for money, goods, and jobs. There were many occasions of improper touching, passing of telephone numbers on slips of paper, and offers of car rides home. Another aspect of this attempt to weaken black women's leadership was the constant referring to activists as "girls," even in the case of elderly women, and not respecting or accepting their political participation in Bahian society outside expected service and sexual roles. In this instance, women simply became "their little friends," who were being put in their place as "poor promiscuous black women" (Ana Cristina, personal communication, 2007). This sexualized treatment came not just from the state representatives but also from both white and black male activists in leftist and black movement organizations that interacted with local activists. Ana Cristina recounts that ultimately these were attempts to create intimate relationships with individual women with the aim of destroying the collective movement and weakening the struggle for land rights. This form of co-optation has not been successful, however, and when compared with male-led organizations, black women activists' unwillingness to either sell their bodies or negotiate on an individual basis has proved to be beneficial to the overall community struggle for material resources (Perry and Caminha 2008, 140).

Gamboa de Baixo pushed forward with its collective claims for further improving local social conditions and for the regularization of land rights, which has benefited Solar do Unhão residents, as well. Today, a new group of male leaders has emerged in Solar do Unhão who are trying to take advantage of the political gains made by neighboring women activists and attempting to open dialogues with these women, who now have more than a decade of political experience and knowledge, as well as respect from state officials. As Gamboa de Baixo activists affirm, these leaders have much to learn about how the government operates and how it has changed since initial conflicts around land expulsion arose. The challenge for these male activists is how to revert previous co-optation practices in ways that allow them to dialogue with the state for collective rights, similar to what Gamboa de Baixo activists have been able to achieve as a result of years of hard work.

They have been able to resist attempts at co-optation in ways that positively benefit themselves as a community (Perry and Caminha 2008). Black women in Gamboa de Baixo's grassroots political movement identify the contributions of women such as Ritinha as being among the primary reasons why they have not been so easily co-opted and that they have been able to focus on collective social change that benefits entire black communities. As David Covin writes in his description of the black movement, "In the political world, local, state, and national, those who decided the fates of these black people were white. One feature of a racialized society was that this white monopoly of political power was seen as perfectly normal" (2006, 40). Most discussions led by black movement activists in the neighborhood highlight the systemic nature of Brazilian racism and emphasize where blacks and black women are socially and economically located in Bahian and Brazilian society. For example, as in the rest of society, black women have the least formal education, which means that ultimately what they have to gain in better housing and land rights outweighs what little resources they may gain individually in jobs or other goods in exchange for abandoning the struggle against the state. This knowledge fuels black women's political interest in claiming rights that transform their social conditions and form a new, equal society. As Sueli Carneiro writes, "Black women's struggle is for a multiracial and multicultural society, where difference is experienced not as inferiority but as equality" (1999, 228).

Furthermore, political work around black identity and Afro-Brazilian culture has been fundamental to how black women understand their political potential amid widespread racism, sexism, classism, and homophobia. The black movement plays a crucial role in what local activists identify as rescuing key aspects of their identities as black women—specifically, empowering them to feel capable of waging struggle against the state. Some say that they have learned to not depend on white nor male leadership, which means they do not need to give in to the co-optation attempts by male politicians and other government agents.

Hence, the gendered differences in grassroots organizing affect the outcome of negotiations with the state. As seen in the experiences of female Gamboa de Baixo activists, their relative success is the result of the women's reluctance to deal with the state individually and their preference for collective social transformation. Furthermore, black women leaders of the Gamboa de Baixo neighborhood association have been unwilling to negotiate on an individual basis because they see their community's collective interests as congruent with their own. This represents a crucial reason that female-led organizations tend to be relatively successful in preserving collective community rights, such as access to land and improved social conditions for the entire community. The challenge remains, however, to negotiate between personal and communal transformation as part of their overall political projects. This challenge reflects a complex relationship to the gender and racial oppression that black women experience as invisible workers, while underlining their vision for liberation from this form of enslavement.

Defying Expectations

In 2004 a group of mostly male Swiss graduate students visited Gamboa de Baixo to learn about grassroots organizing in Salvador and throughout Brazil. After traveling to other parts of Brazil, including the Amazonian region, they were greeted by a group of female community leaders in Gamboa de Baixo. I served as the interpreter for the Swiss group. Many of the students asked questions about the age and the gender of the local activists. In large part the activists comprised young women like Lu, a woman in her early twenties, and Ana Cristina, then thirty years old. Shocked, to say the least, the students commented that they had expected older men to be at the forefront of the movement. In fact, they had brought with them a men's Swiss watch for the neighborhood association's president, whom they had expected to be male.

When presenting the gift, they apologized for their assumptions and said that the female leadership and participation challenged their own internalized social prescriptions of women's political agency. Furthermore, they stated that to see black women in these positions of leadership signified a brave defiance of the overt racism they were surprised to have witnessed during their trip to Brazil. With knowledge of social movements in indigenous and black communities, their previous conceptions of Brazil's racial democracy had been shattered.

Moreover, as one man expressed emotionally, having been previously bombarded by negative, oversexualized representations of black women as prostitutes, female-led political mobilization in Brazil made him face his own racism and sexism. This interchange exemplifies the global perception of black women and the lack of knowledge of black women's politics throughout the African diaspora. Though I find it difficult to believe that these men's experiences during one day in Gamboa de Baixo completely changed their views of black women, my understanding of this global invisibility of black women was heightened. Although black women have always been key figures in black liberation struggles worldwide, the likes of Fannie Lou Hamer, Luiza Mahim, Lélia González, and Amy Jacques Garvey have been ignored. Thus, sexist and racist notions of black women's inability to produce political knowledge and lead political organizations are reproduced.

Defying expectations of their roles as workers, mothers, fisherwomen, and activists, poor black women in Gamboa de Baixo, with their unique political assertion, have disrupted the usual social and political order in Salvador. Black women, who represent the largest numbers in domestic work, are viewed on a daily basis as subservient, submissive, and obedient. In fact, the only black women with whom most of the city's elite whites interact, often throughout their lifetimes, are the housekeepers and babysitters who work in their homes. For black women to occupy a dominant political space in meetings and protests as leaders of their communities challenges prevalent disparaging stereotypes of poor black women and forces their consideration as important agents of social change.

The experiences in Gamboa de Baixo show that the neighborhood association represents an important political space for black women to assert their local power and leadership. Women's everyday interactions, such as removing their neighbors' clothes from the line when it starts to rain or discussing land disputes on each other's doorsteps, provide a visible example of just how much the personal and the political mingle at the community level. Organizing in the neighborhood enacts radical social change from the homes where black people live, work, and play. Furthermore, as leaders of these kinds of organizations, black women bring to the forefront their unique ideas and methods of social protest, which expands our knowledge of racial and gender consciousness at all levels of society. Gamboa de Baixo activists organize as blacks, women, and poor people, leading to more expansive definitions of black womanhood and social movements on a global scale.

Moreover, the Gamboa de Baixo neighborhood association shows that black women's political actions constitute a continuation of their everyday acts of community building. The participation of black women in grassroots organizations is not an anomaly, but visible female leadership continues to be sparse in most neighborhood associations. Domestic workers are key to the development of female leadership as a result of their knowledge gained as "outsiders-within." These women have common interests as workers; their work experience affects the maintenance of their home spaces. More important, poor black women choose to organize as residents of their neighborhoods rather than as workers because they understand that the dominance of domestic work, oppressive at its core, should not be preserved. In their social movement to improve their neighborhood, they demand improvements in their social conditions, primarily for access to education that will prepare them for other areas of employment.

The political actions described throughout this book are courageous, but they are hardly what is expected of women who primarily work as housekeepers and nannies. Defying expectations, they are invisible in domestic work but visible in neighborhood associations. Thus, domestic work provides the knowledge and wisdom necessary to understand systemic gendered antiblack racism, as well as to organize against land expulsion. The neighborhood, not the workplace, offers liberatory possibilities. Related to this is the centrality of Candomblé as a social and political force in black communities, particularly the spiritual importance placed on the built environment.

Conclusion

ABOVE THE ASPHALT
From the Margins to the Center of Black Diaspora Politics

> Is it possible that one day my children and the children of my
> children will lie down on the old walls and rocks of Gamboa
> de Baixo, to fish and admire the moon, as I have done in the
> past? Or will they be dead? Yes, dead! Or perhaps, who knows,
> expelled from their community, like what happened to the
> population of the Pelourinho, Água Suja, and Ogunjá and so
> many other poor black communities in Salvador.
>
> Ana Cristina, lecture at Brown University, 2011

A Luta Continua

On August 4, 2007, at an official ceremony in the open space of the
historic São Paulo Fort in Gamboa de Baixo, community leaders celebrated what they thought was the landmark agreement that would
eventually lead to the possession of land for local families. The agreement was between the state navy and the mayor's office to transfer the
land to the city government. This political act was the result of decades
of struggle over land tenure that promised to benefit residents who had
been living on and using the land since the colonial period. The mu-
nicipality would then have the power to transfer collective land titles to
the Gamboa de Baixo community neighborhood association. Collective rather than individual land titles would make both mass removal
and real estate speculation difficult.

The legal possibility of land tenure sparked much discussion among
the Gamboa de Baixo residents in attendance. They questioned the
meaning of the city government signing a contract "allowing the use of
naval land." Dona Vilma, having lived in the neighborhood for over fifty
years, asked government representatives present at the ceremony, "Is
my house considered to be on naval land? Will I be able to receive my
title?" Dona Vilma's question reflected the concerns of other residents

who were distressed for the same reason. They began asking a series of other questions, like, "What exactly are the boundaries of this naval land?" They inquired about the possibility that the land agreement was partial—in essence, authorizing use but not ownership—and that some parts of the neighborhood would be kept out of the agreement. The agreement regularized only land owned by the state for local use and control, leaving out significant portions of land belonging to other legal entities, such as the Catholic Church (and now the Odebrecht construction firm). In addition to the navy, several competing owners of the land were missing from this legal agreement. Doubts about the meaning of the collective right to land in the city of Salvador have caused many residents to view the tenure and titling process with suspicion and call into question the viability of partial land ownership of some areas of Gamboa de Baixo.

Black women neighborhood association leaders in Gamboa de Baixo are at the forefront of these debates on land rights, and this official document was not the one for which they had waited so long. Though signing the agreement inside the fort was important symbolically, what they really wanted was, however, a document that made it legal for all local residents to stay in their homes permanently and that acknowledged collective ownership. How would the city government pass on ownership to the neighborhood if the neighborhood only had the right to use the land?

Several of the activists present pointed out this inconsistency and began to shout about the underlying racial injustice at the heart of the issue. Ritinha led chants of the names of black national heroes: "Zumbi, Dandara, and Luiza Mahim!" and, "Long live the black people!" She wanted to remind residents of blacks' and black women's tradition of resistance when fighting for the right to live with dignity and material resources such as land. Dona Lenilda began, in typical style, to sing the Gamboa de Baixo political anthem and was promptly joined by the other residents: "From here, I will not leave. No one can take me away."

The neighborhood anthem expressed the resident's determination that the many-decades-long struggle of those with no rights of citizenship for land in downtown Salvador could not end with a partial government contract. The black women–led struggle for land rights in Gamboa de Baixo brings up the following question that has troubled popular movements in predominantly black communities in Salvador: How do you claim rights in a context where government actions generally ignore gendered racism as a structural element of social inequalities and disregard the participation of this segment in the articulation and implementation of public policy? This question reflects how the representatives of government have contributed to stereotypical views of urban black communities, generally, and black women, specifically, who are seen as unable to negotiate their own demands.

Six years later, without collective land titles Gamboa de Baixo continues to face the possibility of spatial displacement even with recent state investment in their everyday living conditions, such as the construction of hundreds of new homes. Activists continue to participate in solidarity with other communities around issues of urbanization and land rights. Everyday struggles revolve around efforts to maintain and increase improved conditions in the community. The future development of Salvador's urban waterfront is still probable, and urban renewal for tourism continues to pose a threat of expulsion for Gamboa de Baixo residents. Their exclusion will again produce fear and stir powerful sentiments of mass mobilization in defense of their territorial rights.

The black struggle for collective permanence and land rights is ongoing. The 2009 displacement of Vila Brandão, a coastal black community among the upper-class neighborhoods of Barra, Graça, and Vitória, continues to galvanize the women activists of Gamboa de Baixo, and the struggle is even more urgent since the August 2010 government demolition and cleanup of traditional beach cabanas (Figure 20). Many Gamboa de Baixo residents say it is only a matter of time before the bulldozers come to clear their coastal lands, as well.

Why Focus on Housing and Land as Human Rights Issues?

The inequalities within Bahia's urban redevelopment practices make apparent the need for globally disseminating knowledge about these practices, as well as their colonial roots. Mass displacement in the name of revitalization threatens Salvadoran neighborhoods such as Marechal Rondon, Alto de Ondina, and Gamboa de Baixo and, on a smaller scale, resembles practices faced by millions in China, Jamaica,

FIGURE 20. Demolition of beach cabanas in Salvador, 2010. Photograph by Fernando Vivas. Courtesy of Agência A Tarde.

Zimbabwe, Colombia, and many other countries (Angel-Ajani 2004; Khagram 2004; Koonings and Kruijt 1988; Ng'weno 2007; Patillo 2007; Vine 2009). In the United States the removal of poor people and people of color for gentrification and the construction of highways and airports has become so commonplace that little public outrage exists. Afro-Brazilian geographer Milton Santos (1987b, 1996), who carefully studied Harlem's gentrification of the 1980s and 1990s, predicted the destruction of Salvador's Pelourinho and the relocation of its residents. The restructuring of cities has come with a monumental price for poor blacks, as it exacerbates existing problems of violence, poverty, and social abandonment. The struggle against this global problem must be intensified.

In response to these violent acts of urban displacement, the black struggle for the human right to housing has increased. Demolition and land expulsion are among the most important human rights issues facing blacks today. Amid rapid growth and increased rural–urban migration, global cities must grapple with the basic right to decent and dignified housing, as codified in Article 25 of the Universal Declaration of Human Rights:

> Everyone has the right to a standard of living adequate for the health and well-being of himself and of her family, including food, clothing, housing and medical care and necessary social services, and the right to security in the event of unemployment, sickness, disability, widowhood, old age or other lack of livelihood in circumstances beyond her control.

The United Nations' consistent reiteration of its commitment to urban populations' right to adequate housing illustrates this point. At the opening of the 2012 World Urban Forum in Naples, Italy, UN secretary-general Ban Ki-moon stated:

> We can usher in the future we want by heeding the Rio+20 call for an integrated approach to sustainable cities that better supports local authorities and involves the public, especially the poor, in decision-making.
>
> As experts, you are well-versed in responding to the problems facing cities and optimizing their potential opportunities. Your work has even more impact as you focus not only on systems but people—the children who travel to school, the elderly who navigate various challenges, the mothers and fathers struggling against poverty and others who make up the fabric of daily life. They need affordable and sustainable transport and energy. They need safe and green urban spaces. They deserve decent shelter, drinking water and sanitation. When you work for healthy air quality, job creation, improved urban planning and better waste management, you are working for better living conditions for millions of people.

More than a decade ago, housing movement activists in Salvador demanded these mechanisms for their direct involvement in urban planning:

(a) Discussions with the community, by way of their representative organizations, in order to avoid distortions about the origin, nature, and range of the initiatives that will be adopted;

(b) Meetings with the residents on each street, with the presence of technicians, about the specific requirements of each public works project;

(c) Prior planning including clarification of phases and timelines for the beginning and the conclusion of public works projects. (Articulação de Comunidades em Luta Por Moradia 2003)

This method for community participation during urbanization processes speaks to the limitations of democracy in Brazilian cities. Contrary to international recommendations, developers create housing schemes for displaced people on the outskirts of major cities like Rio de Janeiro and Salvador. Instead of improving living conditions for communities like Salvador's quilombo Rio dos Macacos in the spaces they have traditionally occupied, displacement and relocation become the means to distance them from prosperous city centers. As Rio de Janeiro prepares for the 2016 Olympic Games, residents in the poorest neighborhoods have already been organizing against threats of mass removal, as well as increased militarization and violence. The demolition and removal of residents from Duke Street in Kingston, Jamaica, was overshadowed by national celebrations of the country's fiftieth anniversary of independence and unprecedented success at the London games (*Gleaner,* August 21, 2012).

A global response to this common practice was most visible in Zimbabwe in 2005, during events that received international media attention and resulted in numerous meetings on the violent implications of urban renewal. President Robert Mugabe authorized a massive reurbanization plan, called Operation Murambatsvina (Drive Out Rubbish), that demolished the homes of more than 700,000 poor blacks in the city of Mutare in that year alone. This unjustified eviction and displacement has affected millions more, as people were displaced in other cities and sent to areas that were unprepared to house them. In a 2005 statement on Zimbabwe, UN secretary-general Kofi Annan called this "slum blitz" the most "catastrophic injustice" ever committed against the poorest people—specifically, women and children—in Zimbabwe. A young woman who was evicted from her home in early June 2005 stated, "I gave birth yesterday. We have been sleeping in the open for three weeks." She also claimed, "For now, I am sleeping with the newborn in this shack while my husband and two other children sleep outside. We don't know what to do" (*BBC News Online,* July 22, 2005). Some of the residents in targeted urban enclaves were injured or killed when they did not vacate their burning or bulldozed homes in time. When called on to put a stop to the destruction, a prominent African leader was quoted as stating that "Africa has bigger problems than that." In fact, many African leaders are cited as viewing this mass expulsion as a cleansing and a solution to the problems of growing urban populations. Similarly, the removal of homes and market stalls has been linked to "fighting crime" and creating new "hygienic" spaces in these cities (*BBC News Online,* July 22, 2005). These reports exemplify that the widespread international practice of cleansing the poor from prominent urban centers is seen as an acceptable form of urban renewal and development. The need for international solidarity among grassroots movements is urgent. Examining the black diaspora locally and comparatively is a crucial aspect of waging this struggle, particularly in contributing to the production of knowledge on urbanization policies in Brazil and elsewhere.

Maintaining the delicate balance between developing modern spaces and implementing new technologies, on the one hand, and not destroying existing homes and local cultures, on the other, remains a challenge for modern engineers and architects. Gamboa de Baixo's political work illustrates that community participation must be a component of urban renewal projects. Local governments often fail to consider and incorporate the specific needs of poor black people. Gamboa de Baixo activists show that they experience the cities in which they live in vastly different ways from other segments of society. In this instance, their location on coastal lands in the city center affects their access to material resources such as fishing, hospitals, and schools. Though they lack financial resources, they have the resilience learned from ancestral knowledge as African-descendant peoples to give them the courage to continue fighting for those resources.

The right to one's own backyard is the right to practice cultural traditions, as well as the freedom to walk out one's door or swim in the ocean without the threat of displacement or police or drug violence. Amid those threats, local activists demonstrate that it is possible to construct, as the national government advertises, "um Brasil para todos" (a Brazil for everyone). Today, when the Odebrecht mansion and the Bahia Marina Yacht Club are viewed from a local fishing boat, the permanence of Gamboa de Baixo seems quite a significant political achievement in the struggle over coveted coastal land and urban space. The local residents are small fish in a large pond filled with sharks, as Dona Telma said while defending her home against a bulldozer.

Diasporic Futures

While I was completing research for this manuscript, I invited interviewees to ask me questions. They almost always asked why I decided to focus on land rights and black women's political activism. In addition to discussing my ongoing activist work with homeless women, I would lightly retort that all Jamaicans living abroad are deeply involved in some land dispute or another. Over the past two decades, my grandmother endured a fierce legal battle against land eviction in rural Jamaica that strained family relationships, as well as revising Jamaican land laws. Her victory in securing her childhood home was the direct result of the transnational efforts of my aunts, who mobilized Jamaican political support, and my mother's key role as an attorney on the legal team. My identification with land struggles came from personal experience, and my intellectual focus on these issues was an attempt to deepen these connections politically.

Localized community struggles for housing, land, and clean water take place against the backdrop of blacks' historical struggles for emancipation and the global black struggle against enslavement and the multitudinous symptoms of colonialism and racial domination evident in modern-day society. In other words, this book has been as much about the political organization of black women in Salvador and Brazil as about black women's search for freedom in diaspora communities worldwide. My understanding of Brazil has been informed by a global perspective on urban policies and urban social movements around land and housing. It would have been equally valid to study slash-and-burn approaches to revitalizing modern cities in the country of my birth, Jamaica, or in Providence, Rhode Island, the city where I currently reside. As Miessha Thomas, Jerry Pennick, and Heather Gray of the U.S. Federation of Southern Cooperatives of Land Assistance Fund write, "From the senseless murders of African-American landowners, to the public sale of family land, African-American land ownership has rapidly declined in the 20th century, and continues to steadily decline in the 21st century" (2004). Black land loss in the United States has been systemic but not isolated from the rest of the black diaspora.

In April 2011 when Ana Cristina gave her lecture at Brown University alongside Libia Grueso, a longtime Afro-Colombian activist, many students and faculty were surprised to learn about mass land eviction in Latin America. Audience members asked, Why is there no global outrage about the more than three million Afro-Colombians who have been violently displaced from the country's Pacific coast? Should we be concerned about the millions of poor blacks who occupy Rio de Janeiro's urban neighborhoods during efforts to "cleanse" and "beautify" the city for an international audience in the upcoming Olympics? Others cautioned that these diasporic processes should not be geographically distanced from U.S. cities like Providence and Los Angeles, especially where homeless people, corporations, and even universities have been engaged in strenuous conflicts and political struggles over claims to space (Boyd 2008; Soja 2010; Williams 2005). In the anthropological tradition, this ethnographic exploration of Brazil facilitates a deeper look into the spaces we occupy in the United States and what those racialized, gendered, and class processes can teach us about our own conditions as blacks globally. How we transform our social conditions will depend on this diasporic view. *A luta continua*, and the struggle will undoubtedly continue with black women's participation and leadership as they fight against injustice and for the right to live with dignity and freedom.

REFERENCES

Agier, Michel. 2000. "Um debate sobre o carnaval do Ilê Aiyê." *Afro-Ásia,* no. 24, 367–78.

Alexander, M. Jacqui. 2005. *Pedagogies of Crossing: Meditations on Feminism, Sexual Politics, Memory, and the Sacred.* Durham, N.C.: Duke University Press.

Alves, Maria Helena Moreira, and Philip Evanson. 2011. *Living in the Crossfire: Favela Residents, Drug Dealers and Police Violence.* Philadelphia: Temple University Press.

Amado, Jorge. 1984. *Sea of Death.* Translated by Gregory Rebassa. New York: Avon.

Amnesty International. 2005. "Brazil: 'They Come in Shooting': Policing Socially Excluded Communities," http://www.amnesty.org/en/library/info /AMR19/025/2005.

———. 2008. *Brazil: Picking Up the Pieces: Women's Experiences of Urban Violence in Brazil.* London: Amnesty International.

Andrews, George Reid. 1991. *Blacks and Whites in São Paulo, Brazil, 1888–1988.* Madison: University of Wisconsin Press.

Angel-Ajani, Asale. 2004. "Out of Chaos: Afro-Colombian Communities and the Realities of War." *Souls* 2, no. 6, 10–18.

Articulação de Comunidades em Luta Por Moradia. 2003. *Como Salvador se faz: Dossiê das lutas das comunidades populares de Salvador—BA pelo direito á moradia.* Salvador: Articulação de Comunidades em Luta Por Moradia.

Asher, Kiran. 2009. *Black and Green: Afro-Colombians, Development, and Nature in the Pacific Lowlands.* Durham, N.C.: Duke University Press.

Assies, Willem. 1994. "Urban Social Movements in Brazil: A Debate and Its Dynamics." *Latin American Perspectives* 2, no. 21, 81–105.

Associação Amigos de Gegê dos Moradores da Gamboa de Baixo, Associação dos Moradores do Nordeste de Amaralina, Conselho de Moradores do Bairro da Paz, and Grupo de Mulheres do Alto das Pombas. 2001. "Carta aberta dos(as) moradores(as) das comunidades populares de Salvador." *Cadernos do CEAS,* no. 194 (July–August): 91–94.

Athayde, Celso, and M. V. Bill. 2007. *Falcão: Mulheres e o tráfico.* Rio de Janeiro: Editora Objetiva.

Avé-Lallemant, Robert. 1961. *Viagem pelo norte do Brasil no ano de 1859.* Translated by Eduardo de Lima Castro. Rio de Janeiro: Institute Nacional do Livro.

Azeredo, Sandra. 1994. "Teorizando sobre gênero e relações raciais." *Estudos Feministas,* February, 203–16.

Ayrá, Valnizia de. 2009. *Resistência e fé: Fragmentos da vida da Valnizia de Ayrá.* São Paulo: All Print Editora.

Bacelar, Jeferson A. 1982. *A família da prostituta.* Salvador: Fundação Cultural do Estado da Bahia.

Bailey, Stanley. 2009. *Legacies of Race: Identities, Attitudes, and Politics in Brazil.* Palo Alto, Calif.: Stanford University Press.

Baiocchi, Gianpaolo. 2005. *Militants and Citizens: The Politics of Participatory Democracy in Porto Alegre.* Palo Alto, Calif.: Stanford University Press.

Bairros, Luiza. 1991. "Mulher negra: O reforço da subordinação." In *Desigualdade racial no Brasil contemporâneo,* edited by Peggy Lovell. Belo Horizonte, Brazil: MGSP Editores.

———. 1995. "Lembrando Lélia Gonzalez." In *O livro da saúde das mulheres negras: Nossos passos vêm de longe,* edited by Jurema Werneck, Maisa Mendonça, and Evelyn White, 42–61. Rio de Janeiro: Pallas/Criola.

———. 1996. "Orfeu e poder: Uma perspectiva afro-americana sobre a política racial no Brasil." *Estudos Afro-Asiáticos,* no. 17, 173–86.

———. 2002. "III conferência mundial contra o racismo." *Revista Estudos Feministas* 10, no. 1, 169–70.

Beato, Lucila Bandeira. 2004. "Inequality and Human Rights of African Descendants in Brazil." *Journal of Black Studies* 6, no. 34, 766–86.

Bourdieu, Pierre, and Loïc Wacquant. 1999. "On the Cunning of Imperialist Reason." *Theory, Culture, and Society,* no. 16, 41–58.

Boyd, Michelle R. 2008. *Jim Crow Nostalgia: Reconstructing Race in Bronzeville.* Minneapolis: University of Minnesota Press.

Brandão, Maria de Azevedo. 2002. "Salvador: Da transformação do centro à elaboração de periferias diferenciadas." In *Quem faz Salvador?,* edited by Ana Maria de Carvalho Luz, 151–65. Salvador: EDUFBA.

Butler, Kim D. 1998. *Freedoms Given, Freedoms Won: Afro-Brazilians in Post-abolition São Paulo and Salvador.* New Brunswick, N.J.: Rutgers University Press.

———. 2011. "A nova negritude no Brasil: Movimentos pós-abolição no contexto da diáspora africana." In *Experiências da emancipação: Biografias, instituições e movimentos sociais no pós-abolição,* edited by Flávio Gomes and Petrônio Domingues, 137–56. São Paulo: Selo Negro.

Caldeira, Teresa P. R. 2000. *City of Walls: Crime, Segregation, and Citizenship in São Paulo*. Berkeley: University of California Press.

Caldwell, Kia Lilly. 2007. *Negras in Brazil: Re-envisioning Black Women, Citizenship, and the Politics of Identity*. New Brunswick, N.J.: Rutgers University Press.

Camara, Evandro. 1998. "*Racism in a Racial Democracy: The Maintenance of White Supremacy in Brazil* by France Winddance Twine." *American Journal of Sociology* 3, no. 104, 911–13.

Capone, Stephania. 2010. *Searching for Africa in Brazil: Power and Tradition in Candomblé*. Durham, N.C.: Duke University Press.

Cardoso, Edson Lopes. 2004. "Pesquisas, extermínio e omissões." *Ìrohìn*, no. 8 (December/January): 2.

Cardoso, Ruth Corrêa Leite. 1992. "Popular Movements in the Context of the Consolidation of Democracy in Brazil." In *The Making of Social Movements in Latin America: Identity, Strategy, and Democracy*, edited by Arturo Escobar and Sonia A. Alvarez, 291–302. Boulder, Colo.: Westview Press.

Carneiro, Sueli. 1995. "Gênero, raça e ascensão social." *Estudos Feministas* 3, no. 2, 544–52.

———. 1999. "Black Women's Identity in Brazil." In *Race in Contemporary Brazil: From Indifference to Inequality*, edited by Rebecca Reichmann, 217–28. University Park: Penn State University Press.

Carneiro, Sueli, and Cristiane Cury. 2008. "O poder feminino no culto aos orixás." In *Guerreiras de natureza: Mulher negra, religiosidade e ambiente*, edited by Elisa Larkin Nascimento, 117–43. São Paulo: Selo Negro.

Carreira, Mauro. 1999. *Bahia de todos os nomes*. Salvador: Grupo de Apoio à Criança com Câncer–Bahia.

Castillo, Lisa Earl. 2011. "O terreiro do Alaketu e seus fundadores: História e genealogia familiar, 1807–1867." *Afro-Ásia*, no. 43, 213–59.

Castro, Mary Garcia. 1996. "Family, Gender, and Work: The Case of Female Heads of Households in Brazil (States of São Paulo and Bahia), 1950–1980." PhD diss. University of Florida–Gainesville.

Collins, John. 2008. "'But What If I Should Need to Defecate in Your Neighborhood, Madame?': Empire, Redemption, and the 'Tradition of Oppression' in a Brazilian World Heritage Site." *Cultural Anthropology* 23, no. 2, 279–328.

Collins, Patricia Hill. 1990. *Black Feminist Thought: Knowledge, Consciousness, and the Politics of Empowerment*. New York: Routledge.

———. 1998. *Fighting Words: Black Women and the Search for Justice*. Contradictions of Modernity 7. Minneapolis: University of Minnesota Press.

———. 2001. "Like One of the Family: Race, Ethnicity, and the Paradox of U.S. National Identity." *Ethnic and Racial Studies* 24, no. 1, 3–28.

Cordiviola, Chango. 2002. "Quem faz Salvador uma cidade invisível." In *Quem faz Salvador?*, edited by Ana Maria de Carvalho Luz, 35–40. Salvador: EDUFBA.

Corrêa, Mariza. 2008. Review of *Negras in Brazil: Re-envisioning Black Women, Citizenship, and the Politics of Identity*, by Kia Lilly Caldwell. *Signs* 34, no. 1, 200–203.

Cortés, Jose Miguel G. 2008. *Políticas do espaço: Arquitetura, gênero e controle social.* São Paulo: SENAC.

Covin, David. 2006. *The Unified Black Movement of Brazil: 1978–2002.* Jefferson, N.C.: McFarland.

Crenshaw, Kimberlé Williams. 1991. "Mapping the Margins: Intersectionality, Identity Politics, and Violence against Women of Color." *Stanford Law Review* 43, no. 6, 1241–99.

———. 2002. "Documento para o encontro de especialistas em aspectos da discriminação racial relativos ao gênero." *Estudos Feministas* 10, no. 1, 171–88.

Davies, Carole Boyce. 1994. *Black Women, Writing, and Identity: Migrations of the Subject.* New York: Routledge.

———. 2006. "'Con-di-fi-cation': Transnationalism, Diaspora and the Limits of Domestic Racial or Feminist Discourse." *JENdA: A Journal of Culture and African Women Studies*, no. 9, http://www.africaknowledgeproject.org/index.php/jenda/issue/view/13.

———. 2008. *Left of Karl Marx: The Political Life of Black Communist Claudia Jones.* Durham, N.C.: Duke University Press.

Dávila, Arlene. 2004. *Barrio Dreams: Puerto Ricans, Latinos, and the Neoliberal City.* Berkeley: University of California Press.

Dávila, Jerry. 2003. *Diploma of Whiteness: Race and Social Policy in Brazil, 1917–1945.* Durham, N.C.: Duke University Press.

Davis, Angela Y. 1981. *Women, Race, and Class.* New York: Random House.

Davis, Helen. 2004. *Understanding Stuart Hall.* Thousand Oaks, Calif.: SAGE.

Davis, Mike. 1992. *City of Quartz: Excavating the Future in Los Angeles.* New York: Vintage.

———. 1998. *Ecology of Fear: Los Angeles and the Imagination of Disaster.* New York: Vintage.

———. 2007. *Planet of Slums.* New York City: Verso.

Dunn, Christopher. 1994. "A Fresh Breeze Blows in Bahia." *Américas* 46, no. 3, 28.

Dzidzienyo, Anani. 1979. *The Position of Blacks in Brazilian and Cuban Society*. London: Minority Rights Group.

Espinheira, Gey. 1989. "Pelourinho: A hora e a vez do centro histórico." *Cadernos do CEAS*, no. 119, 35–45.

———. 2008. *Sociedade do medo: Teoria e método da analise sociológica em bairros populares de Salvador: Juventude, pobreza e violência*. Salvador: EDUFBA.

Fagence, Michael. 1995. "City Waterfront Development for Leisure, Recreation, and Tourism: Some Common Themes." In *Recreation and Tourism as a Catalyst for Urban Redevelopment: An International Survey*, edited by Stephen J. Craig-Smith and Michael Fagence. Westport, Conn.: Praeger.

Farias, Juliana Barreto, Giovana Xavier, and Flávio Gomes. 2012. *Mulheres negras no Brasil escravocrata e pós-emancipação*. São Paulo: Selo Negro.

Feldman, Roberta M., Susan Stall, and Patricia A. Wright. 1998. "'The Community Needs to Be Built By Us': Women Organizing in Chicago Public Housing." In *Community Activism and Feminist Politics: Organizing across Race, Class, and Gender*, edited by Nancy A. Naples. New York: Routledge.

Fernandes, Sujatha. 2007. "Barrio Women and Popular Politics in Chavez's Venezuela." *Latin American Politics and Society* 49, no. 3, 97–127.

Ferreira Filho, Alberto Heráclito. 1999. "Desafricanizar as ruas: Elites letradas, mulheres pobres e cultura popular em Salvador (1890–1937)." *Afro-Ásia*, nos. 21–22, 239–56.

Figueiredo, Angela. 2011. "Condições e contradições do trabalho doméstico em Salvador." In *Tensões e experiências: Um retrato das trabalhadoras domésticas de Brasília e Salvador*, edited by Natalia Mori, Soraya Fleischer, Angela Figueiredo, Joaze Bernardino-Costa, and Tânia Cruz, 89–131. Brasília: Centro Feminista de Estudos e Assessoria.

Fikes, Kesha. 2009. *Managing African Portugal*. Durham, N.C.: Duke University Press.

Flauzina, Ana Luiza Pinheiro. 2008. *Corpo negro caído no chão: O sistema penal e o projeto genocida do estado brasileiro*. Rio de Janeiro: Contraponto Editora.

French, Jan Hoffman. 2009. *Legalizing Identities: Becoming Black or Indian in Brazil's Northeast*. Chapel Hill: University of North Carolina Press.

French, John D. 2000. "The Missteps of Anti-imperialist Reason: Bourdieu, Wacquant, and Hanchard's *Orpheus and Power*." *Theory, Culture, and Society* 17, no. 1, 107–28.

Freyre, Gilberto. 1933. *Casa grande e senzala*. Rio de Janeiro: José Olimpio.

Gandolfo, Daniella. 2009. *The City at Its Limits: Taboo, Transgression, and Urban Renewal in Lima.* Chicago: University of Chicago Press.

Garcia, Antonia dos Santos. 2006. *Mulheres da cidade d'Oxum: Relações de gênero, raça e classe e organização espacial do movimento de bairros em Salvador.* Salvador: EDUFBA.

———. 2012. "Mulher negra e o direito à cidade: Relações raciais e de gênero." In *Questões urbanos e racismo,* edited by Renato Emerson dos Santos, 134–63. Brasília: ABPN.

Gay, Robert. 1993. *Popular Organization and Democracy in Rio de Janeiro: A Tale of Two Favelas.* Philadelphia: Temple University Press.

Gilliam, Angela. 1992. "From Roxbury to Rio—and Back in a Hurry." In *African-American Reflections on Brazil's Racial Paradise,* edited by David J. Hellwig. Philadelphia: Temple University Press.

———. 1998. "The Brazilian *Mulata*: Images in the Global Economy." *Race and Class* 40, no. 1, 57–69.

———. 2001. "A Black Feminist Perspective on the Sexual Commodification of Women in the New Global Culture." In *Black Feminist Anthropology: Theory, Politics, Praxis, and Poetics,* edited by Irma McClaurin, 150–86. New Brunswick, N.J.: Rutgers University Press.

Gilliam, Angela, and Onik'a Gilliam. 1999. "Odyssey: Negotiating the Subjectivity of Mulata Identity in Brazil." *Latin American Perspectives* 26, no. 3, 60–84.

Gilmore, Ruth Wilson. 2002. "Fatal Couplings of Power and Difference: Notes on Racism and Geography." *Professional Geographer* 54, no. 1, 15–24.

———. 2007. *Golden Gulag: Prisons, Surplus, Crisis, and Opposition in Globalizing California.* Berkeley: University of California Press.

Goldstein, Donna. 2003. *Laughter Out of Place: Race, Class, Violence, and Sexuality in a Rio Shantytown.* Berkeley: University of California Press.

Gomes, Nilma Lino. 1995. *A mulher negra que vi de perto: O processo de construção da identidade racial de professoras negras.* Belo Horizonte, Brazil: Maza Edições.

———. 2008. *Sem perder a raiz: Corpo e cabelo como símbolos da identidade negra.* Belo Horizonte, Brazil: Autêntica.

González, Roosebelinda Cárdenas. 2004. "Black Bodies, (in)Visible Hands: Black Domésticas' Struggle in Salvador, Bahia." Master's thesis. University of Texas–Austin.

Gore, Dayo F. 2011. *Radicalism at the Crossroads: African American Women Activists in the Cold War.* New York: NYU Press.

Graham, Sandra Lauderdale. 1992. *House and Street: The Domestic World of*

Servants and Masters in Nineteenth-Century Rio de Janeiro. Austin: University of Texas Press.

Greenfield, Gerald Michael. 1994. "Brazil." In *Latin American Urbanization: Historical Profiles of Major Cities,* edited by Gerald Michael Greenfield, 62–105. Westport, Conn.: Greenwood Press.

Gregory, Steven. 1999. *Black Corona: Race and the Politics of Place in an Urban Community.* Princeton, N.J.: Princeton University Press.

Gusmão, Neusa M. Mendes de. 1995. *Terra de pretos, terra de mulheres: Terra, mulher e raça num bairro rural negro.* Brasília: Fundação Cultural Palmares.

Hamer, Fannie Lou, and J. H. O'Dell. 1965. "Life in Mississippi: An Interview with Fannie Lou Hamer." *Freedomways: A Quarterly Review of the Negro Movement* 5, no. 2, 231–42.

Hamlin, Françoise. 2012. *Crossroads at Clarksdale: The Black Freedom Struggle in the Mississippi Delta after World War II.* Chapel Hill: University of North Carolina Press.

Hanchard, Michael. 1994. *Orpheus and Power: The Movimento Negro of Rio de Janeiro and São Paulo, 1945–1988.* Princeton, N.J.: Princeton University Press.

———. 2003. "Acts of Misrecognition: Transnational Black Politics, Antiimperialism, and the Ethnocentrisms of Pierre Bourdieu and Loïc Wacquant." *Theory, Culture, and Society* 20, no. 4, 5–29.

———. 2006. *Party/Politics: Horizons in Black Political Thought.* New York: Oxford University Press.

Harding, Rachel E. 2003. *A Refuge in Thunder: Candomble and Alternative Spaces of Blackness.* Bloomington: Indiana University Press.

Harrison, Faye V. 2005. *Resisting Racism and Xenophobia: Global Perspectives on Race, Gender, and Human Rights.* New York: Alta Mira Press.

———. 2008. *Outsider Within: Reworking Anthropology in the Global Age.* Champaign: University of Illinois Press.

Hautzinger, Sarah J. 2007. *Violence in the City of Women: Police and Batterers in Bahia, Brazil.* Berkeley: University of California Press.

Henery, Celeste S. 2011. "Where They Walk: What Aging Black Women's Geographies Tell of Race, Gender, Space, and Social Transformations in Brazil." *Cultural Dynamics* 23, no. 2, 85–106.

Holsaert, Faith, Martha Prescod Norman Noonan, Judy Richardson, Betty Garman Robinson, Jean Smith Young, and Dorothy M. Zellner, eds. 2012. *Hands on the Freedom Plow: Personal Accounts by Women in SNCC.* Champaign: University of Illinois Press.

Holston, James. 1991. "The Misrule of Law: Land and Usurpation in Brazil." *Comparative Studies in Society and History*, no. 33, 695–725.

———. 2008. *Insurgent Citizenship: Disjunctions of Democracy and Modernity in Brazil*. Princeton, N.J.: Princeton University Press.

hooks, bell. 1984. *Feminist Theory: From Margin to Center*. Cambridge, Mass.: South End Press.

———. 1990. *Yearning: Race, Gender, and Cultural Politics*. Cambridge, Mass.: South End Press.

Hunter, Tera W. 1997. *To 'Joy My Freedom: Southern Black Women's Lives and Labors after the Civil War*. Cambridge, Mass.: Harvard University Press.

Instituto Brasileiro de Geografia e Estatística. 2004. Diretoria de Pesquisas, Departamento de Emprego e Rendimento, Pesquisa Mensal de Emprego. Brasília: Instituto Brasileiro de Geografia e Estatística.

———. 2012. *Censo Demográfico 2010*. Brasilia: Instituto Brasileiro de Geografia e Estatística.

Imbassahy, Antônio. 2000. "Símbolo da Bahia." In *Notícias do patrimônio: Informativo do Instituto do Patrimônio Histórico e Artístico Nacional*. Salvador: IPHAN/Ministério da Cultura.

Jackson, John, Jr. 2003. *Harlemworld: Doing Race and Class in Contemporary Black America*. Chicago: University of Chicago Press.

Jesus, Carolina Maria de. 1997. *Bitita's Diary: The Childhood Memoirs of Carolina Maria de Jesus*. Translated by Emanuelle Oliveira and Beth Joan Vinkler. Armonk, N.Y.: M. E. Sharpe.

Jones, Claudia. 1974. "An End to the Neglect of the Problems of the Negro Woman." *Political Affairs*, no. 27, 151–68.

Johnson, Ollie A., III. 1998. "Racial Representation and Brazilian Politics: Black Members of the National Congress, 1983–1999." *Journal of Interamerican Studies and World Affairs* 40, no. 4, 97–118.

Kalili, Sérgio. 2003. "O relatório da vergonha nacional." *Revista Caros Amigos*, no. 78, 20–23.

Kelley, Robin D. G. 1993. "'We Are Not What We Seem': Rethinking Black Working-Class Opposition in the Jim Crow South." *Journal of American History* 80, no. 1, 75–112.

———. 2002. *Freedom Dreams: The Black Radical Imagination*. Boston: Beacon Press.

Kenyatta, Jomo. 1968. *Suffering without Bitterness*. Nairobi, Kenya: East African Publishing House.

Khagram, Sanjeev. 2004. *Dams and Development: Transnational Struggles for Water and Power*. Ithaca, N.Y.: Cornell University Press.

Koonings, Kees, and Dirk Kruijt. 1988. *Megacities: The Politics of Urban Exclusion and Violence in the Global South*. New York: Zed Books.

Kowarick, Lúcio. 1994. "One Hundred Years of Overcrowding: Slum Tenements in the City." In *Social Struggles and the City: The Case of São Paulo*, edited by Lúcio Kowarick, 60–76. New York: Monthly Review Press.

Kulick, Don. 1998. *Travesti: Sex, Gender, and Culture among Brazilian Transgendered Prostitutes*. Chicago: University of Chicago Press.

Lacarrieu, Monica. 2000. "'No caminho para o futuro, a meta e o passado': A questão do patrimônio e das identidades nas cidades contemporâneas." Paper presented at the V Congresso International da BRASA—Brasil 500 Anos, Recife, Brazil, June 18–21.

Lawrence, Bruce B., and Aisha Karim. 2007. "General Introduction: Theorizing Violence in the Twenty-First Century." In *On Violence: A Reader*, edited by Bruce B. Lawrence and Aisha Karim, 1–15. Durham, N.C.: Duke University Press.

Lefebvre, Henri, Eleonore Kofman, and Elizabeth Lebas. 1996. *Writings on Cities*. Cambridge, Mass.: Blackwell.

Leme, Maria Cristina da Silva, and Ana Fernandes. 1999. *Urbanismo no Brasil, 1895–1965*. São Paulo: Studio Nobel.

Lima, Ari. 2011. "Tradition, History, and Spirals of Time in the *Samba de Roda* of Bahia." In *(Re)Considering Blackness in Contemporary Afro-Brazilian (Con)Texts*, edited by Antonio D. Tillis, 27–43. New York: Peter Lang.

Lorde, Audre. 1998. *Sister Outsider*. Freedom, Calif.: Crossing Press.

Lovell, Peggy A. 1999. "Women and Racial Inequality at Work in Brazil." In *Racial Politics in Contemporary Brazil*, edited by Michael Hanchard, 138–53. Durham, N.C.: Duke University Press.

Luz, Ana Maria de Carvalho. 2002. *Quem faz Salvador?* Salvador: EDUFBA.

Machado, Eduardo Paes, and Ceci Vilar Noronha. 2002. "A polícia dos pobres: Violência policial em classes populares urbanas." *Sociologias* 4, no. 7, 188–221.

Marcuse, Peter, and Ronald Van Kempen. 2000. *Globalizing Cities: A New Spatial Order?* Malden, Mass.: Blackwell.

Matory, J. Lorand. 2005. *Black Atlantic Religion: Tradition, Transnationalism, and Matriarchy in the Afro-Brazilian Candomblé*. Princeton, N.J.: Princeton University Press.

McCallum, Cecilia. 1999. "Restraining Women: Gender, Sexuality, and Modernity in Salvador da Bahia." *Bulletin of Latin American Research* 18, no. 3, 275–93.

————. 2007. "Women out of Place? A Micro-historical Perspective on the Black Feminist Movement in Salvador da Bahia, Brazil." *Journal of Latin American Studies* 39, no. 1, 55–80.

McDuffie, Eric S. 2011. *Sojourning for Freedom: Black Women, American Communism, and the Making of Black Left Feminism*. Durham, N.C.: Duke University Press.

McKittrick, Katherine. 2006. *Demonic Grounds: Black Women and the Cartographies of Struggle*. Minneapolis: University of Minnesota Press.

McKittrick, Katherine, and Clyde Woods. 2007. *Black Geographies and the Politics of Place*. New York: South End Press.

Meade, Teresa A. 1997. *"Civilizing" Rio: Reform and Resistance in a Brazilian City, 1889–1930*. University Park: Penn State University Press.

Mitchell, Michael J. 2003. "Changing Racial Attitudes in Brazil: Retrospective and Prospective Views." *National Political Science Review*, no. 9, 31–51.

Mitchell, Michael J., and Charles H. Wood. 1998. "Ironies of Citizenship: Skin Color, Police Brutality, and the Challenge to Democracy in Brazil." *Social Forces* 77, no. 3, 1001–20.

Mohanty, Chandra. 2003. *Feminism without Borders: Decolonizing Theory, Practicing Solidarity*. Durham, N.C.: Duke University Press.

Mori, Natalia, Soraya Fleischer, Angela Figueiredo, Joaze Bernardino-Costa, and Tânia Cruz. 2011. *Tensões e experiências: Um retrato das trabalhadoras domésticas de Brasília e Salvador*. Brasília: Centro Feminista de Estudos e Assessoria.

Mullings, Leith. 2009. *New Social Movements in the African Diaspora: Challenging Global Apartheid*. New York: Palgrave Macmillan.

Murray, Martin J. 2008. *Taming the Disorderly City: The Spatial Landscape of Johannesburg after Apartheid*. Ithaca, N.Y.: Cornell University Press.

Nascimento, Abdias do. 1980. *O quilombismo: Documentos de uma militância pan-africanista*. Petrópolis, Brazil: Editora Vozes.

————. 1989. *Brazil: Mixture or Massacre? Essays in the Genocide of a Black People*. Dover, Md.: First Majority Press.

Nascimento, Elisa Larkin. 2008. *Guerreiras de natureza: Mulher negra, religiosidade e ambiente*. São Paulo: Selo Negro.

Nascimento, Maria Beatriz do. 1981. "Sistemas alternativos organizados pelos negros: Dos quilombos ás favelas." Master's thesis. Fluminense Federal University.

————. 1985. "O conceito de quilombo e a resistência cultural negra." *Afrodiáspora*, nos. 6–7, 41–49.

Ng'weno, Bettina. 2007. *Turf Wars: Territory and Citizenship in the Contemporary State*. Palo Alto, Calif.: Stanford University Press.

Nobles, Melissa. 2000. *Shades of Citizenship: Race and the Census in Modern Politics*. Palo Alto, Calif.: Stanford University Press.

Nobre, Maria Ivanilde Ferreira. 1995. *A dinâmica da população do Maciel/ Pelourinho no contexto das mudanças do Centro Histórico de Salvador*. Salvador: Universidade Federal da Bahia.

Odebrecht Organisation. 2004. *O Morada dos Cardeais*. Salvador: Odebrecht.

O'Dwyer, Eliane Cantarino. 2002. *Quilombos: Identidade, étnica e territorialidade*. Rio de Janeiro: Editora FGV.

Oliveira, Cloves Luiz Pereira. 1999. "Struggling for a Place: Race, Gender, and Class in Political Elections in Brazil." In *Race in Contemporary Brazil,* edited by Rebecca Reichman. University Park: Penn State University Press.

Oliveira, Nelson de, Lutz Mulert S. Ribeiro, and José Carlos Zanetti. 2000. *A outra face da moeda: Violência na Bahia*. Salvador: Comissão de Justiça e Paz da Arquidiocese de Salvador.

Paixão, Marcelo, and Luiz M. Carvano. 2008. *Relatório anual das desigualdades raciais no Brasil, 2007-2008*. Rio de Janeiro: Garamond.

Patillo, Mary. 2007. *Black on the Block: The Politics of Race and Class in the City*. Chicago: University of Chicago Press.

Pereira, Amauri Mendes, and Joselina da Silva. 2009. *O movimento negro brasileiro: Escritos sobre os sentidos de democracia e justiça social no Brasil*. Belo Horizonte, Brazil: Nandyala.

Perlman, Janice E. 2010. *Favela: Four Decades of Living on the Edge in Rio de Janeiro*. New York: Oxford University Press.

Perry, Elizabeth J. 2002. *Challenging the Mandate of Heaven: Social Protest and State Power in China*. Armonk, N.Y.: M. E. Sharpe.

Perry, Keisha-Khan Y. 2006. "Por uma pedagogia feminista negra no Brasil: O aprendizado das mulheres negras em movimentos comunitários." In *Educação, diferenças e desigualdades,* edited by Maria Lúcia Rodrigues Müller and Lea Pinheiro Paixão, 161–84. Cuiabá, Brazil: Conselho Editorial da EdUFMT.

———. 2008. "Politics is *uma Coisinha de Mulher* (a Woman's Thing): Black Women's Leadership in Neighborhood Movements in Brazil." In *Latin American Social Movements in the Twenty-First Century: Resistance, Power, and Democracy,* edited by Richard Stahler-Sholk, Harry E. Vanden, and Glen David Kuecker, 197–211. Lanham, Md.: Rowman and Littlefield.

———. 2009. "'If We Didn't Have Water': Black Women's Struggle for Urban Land Rights." *Environmental Justice* 2, no. 1, 9–13.

Perry, Keisha-Khan Y., and Ana Cristina da Silva Caminha. 2008. "'Daqui não saio, daqui ninguém me tira': Poder e política das mulheres negras da Gamboa de Baixo, Salvador." *Gênero* 9, no. 1, 127–53.

Perry, Keisha-Khan Y., and Joanne Rappaport. 2013. "The Case for Collaborative Research in Latin America: Brazil, Colombia, Ecuador, Mexico, Nicaragua, and Puerto Rico." In *Otros Saberes: Collaborative Research on Indigenous and Afro-Descendant Cultural Politics,* edited by Charlie R. Hale and Lynn Stephen. Santa Fe, N.Mex.: School for Advanced Research.

Pinheiro, Eloísa Petti. 2002. *Europa, França e Bahia: Difusão e adaptação de modelos urbanos (Paris, Rio e Salvador).* Salvador: Editora da UFBA.

Pinho, Osmundo de Araujo. 1999. "Espaço, poder e relações racias: O caso do Centro Histórico de Salvador." *Afro-Ásia,* nos. 21–22, 257–74.

———. 2011. "'Tradition as Adventure': Black Music, New Afro-Descendant Subjects, and Pluralization of Modernity in Salvador da Bahia." In *Brazilian Popular Music and Citizenship,* edited by Idelber Avelar and Christopher Dunn, 250–66. Durham, N.C.: Duke University Press.

Pinho, Patricia de Santana. 2010. *Mama Africa: Reinventing Blackness in Bahia.* Durham, N.C.: Duke University Press.

Ransby, Barbara. 2003. *Ella Baker and the Black Freedom Movement: A Radical Democratic Vision.* Chapel Hill: University of North Carolina Press.

———. 2012. *Eslanda: The Large and Unconventional Life of Mrs. Paul Robeson.* New Haven: Yale University Press.

Rappaport, Joanne. 2008. "Beyond Participant Observation: Collaborative Ethnography as Theoretical Innovation." *Collaborative Anthropologies,* no. 1, 1–31.

Ratts, Alex. 2007. *Eu sou atlântica: Sobre a trajetória de vida de Beatriz Nascimento.* São Paulo: Imprensa Oficial.

Ratts, Alex, and Flavia Rios. 2010. *Lélia Gonzalez.* São Paulo: Selo Negro.

Razack, Sherene H. 2002. *Race, Space, and the Law: Unmapping a White Settler Society.* Toronto: Between the Lines.

Rebouças, Diógenes, and Godofredo Filho. 1985. *Salvador da Bahia de Todos os Santos no século XIX.* Salvador: Odebrecht.

Reis, João José. 1995. *Slave Rebellion in Brazil: The Muslim Uprising of 1935.* Baltimore: Johns Hopkins University Press.

Reis, João José, and Flávio dos Santos Gomes. 1996. "Introdução: Uma história da liberdade." In *Liberdade por um fio: História dos quilombos no Brasil,* edited by João José Reis and Flavio dos Santos Gomes. São Paulo: Companhia das Letras.

Reis, Vilma. 2005. "Atocaiados pelo estado: As políticas de segurança pública implementadas nos bairros populares de Salvador e suas representacoes, 1991–2001." Master's thesis. Federal University of Bahia, Salvador.

———. 2008a. "Na mira do racismo institucional: Quebrando o silêncio diante da matança em Salvador." *Ìrohìn,* January 28, 10–11.

———. 2008b. "Uma pilha de cadáveres negros . . . Bom dia, direitos humanos! Bom dia, nova Bahia!" *Ìrohìn,* January 28.

———. "Quebrando naturalizações: Estratégias de enfrentamento ao trabalho doméstico de crianças e adolescentes e suas iniquidades de raça e gênero," CEAFRO website, http://www.ceafro.ufba.br/artigos/artigo01.asp.

Revista Caros Amigos. 2000. "Entrevista: Sueli Carneiro—uma guerreira contra o racismo." *Revista Caros Amigos,* no. 35, 24–29.

Rezende, Cláudia Barcellos, and Márcia Lima. 2004. "Linking Gender, Class, and Race in Brazil." *Social Identities* 10, no. 6, 757–73.

Robnett, Belinda. 1997. *How Long? How Long? African-American Women in the Struggle for Civil Rights.* New York: Oxford University Press.

Rocha, Luciane de Oliveira. 2012. "Black Mothers' Experiences of Violence in Rio de Janeiro." *Cultural Dynamics* 24, no. 1, 59–73.

Rolnik, Raquel. 1994. "São Paulo in the Early Days of Industrialization." In *Social Struggles and the City: The Case of São Paulo,* edited by Lúcio Kowarick, 77–93. New York: Monthly Review Press.

Romo, Anadelia A. 2010. *Brazil's Living Museum: Race, Reform, and Tradition in Bahia.* Durham, N.C.: University of North Carolina Press.

Samara, Tony Roshan. 2011. *Cape Town after Apartheid: Crime and Governance in the Divided City.* Minneapolis: University of Minnesota Press.

Sansi-Roca, Roger. 2007. *Fetishes and Monuments: Afro-Brazilian Art and Culture in the 20th Century.* Oxford: Berghahn Books.

Santos, Maria Stella de Azevedo. 1995. *Meu tempo é agora.* 2nd ed. Curitiba: Projeto CENTRHU.

Santos, Milton. 1959. *O centro da cidade de Salvador: Estudo de geografia urbana.* Salvador: Progresso, Universidade de Bahia.

———. 1987a. *O Espaço do cidadão.* São Paulo: Nobel.

———. 1987b. "Modernidade e memória" In *Milton Santos: O país distorcido,* edited by Wagner Costa Ribeiro, 24–26. São Paulo: PubliFolha.

———. 1996. *Território e sociedade: Entrevista com Milton Santos.* São Paulo: Editora Fundação Perseu Abramo.

Santos, Renato Emerson dos. 2012. *Questões urbanas e racismo.* Petrópolis, Brazil: Associação Brasileira de Pesquisadores Negros.

Santos, Sales Augusto dos. 2006. "Who Is Black in Brazil? A Timely or a False Question in Brazilian Race Relations in the Era of Affirmative Action." *Latin American Perspectives* 33, no. 4, 30–48.

Santos, Sales Augusto dos, and Nelson Olokofá Inocêncio. 2006. "Brazilian Indifference to Racial Inequality in the Labor Market." *Latin American Perspectives* 33, no. 4, 13–29.

Santos, Sônia Beatriz dos. 2006. "Feminismo negro diaspórico." *Gênero* 8, no. 1, 11–26.

————. 2008. "Brazilian Black Women's NGOs and Their Struggles in the Area of Sexual and Reproductive Health: Experiences, Resistance, and Politics." PhD diss. University of Texas–Austin.

————. 2009. "As ONGs de mulheres negras no Brasil." *Sociedade e Cultura* 12, no. 2, 275–88.

————. 2012. "Controlling Black Women's Reproductive Health Rights: An Impetus to Black Women's Collective Organizing." *Cultural Dynamics* 24, no 1, 13–30.

Scheper-Hughes, Nancy. 1992. *Death without Weeping: The Violence of Everyday Life in Brazil.* Berkeley: University of California Press.

Scheper-Hughes, Nancy, and Phillippe Bourgois. 2006. *Violence in War and Peace: An Anthology.* Malden, Mass.: Blackwell.

Seigel, Micol. 2009. *Uneven Encounters: Making Race and Nation in Brazil and the United States.* Durham, N.C.: Duke University Press.

Serra, Ordep. 2002. "Feições da cidade: Breve reflexão à margem do programa Quem Faz Salvador." In *Quem faz Salvador?,* edited by Ana Maria de Carvalho Luz, 21–34. Salvador: EDUFBA.

Shakur, Assata. 1987. "Affirmation." In *Assata: An Autobiography,* edited by Assata Shakur and Angela Davis, 1. Chicago: Lawrence Hill Books.

Sheriff, Robin E. 2001. *Dreaming Equality: Color, Race, and Racism in Urban Brazil.* New Brunswick, N.J.: Rutgers University Press.

Silva, Benedita da. 1999. "The Black Movement and Political Parties: A Challenging Alliance." In *Racial Politics in Contemporary Brazil,* edited by Michael Hanchard, 179–87. Durham, N.C.: Duke University Press.

Silva, Benedita da, Medea Benjamin, and Maisa Mendonça. 1997. *Benedita da Silva: An Afro-Brazilian Woman's Story of Politics and Love.* Oakland, Calif.: Institute for Food and Development Policy.

Silva, Cristiani Bereta Da. 2004. "Relações de gênero e subjetividades no devir MST." *Estudos Feministas* 12, no. 1, 269–87.

Silva, Denise Ferreira da, and Marcia Lima. 1992. "Raça, gênero e mercado de trabalho." *Estudos Afro-Asiáticos,* no. 23, 97–111.

Silva, Maria Nilza da. 2012. "Black Population: Segregation and Invisibility in Londrina." In *Questões urbanas e racismo,* edited by Renato Emerson dos Santos, 104–33. Brasília: ABPN.

Silveira, Oliveira. 1997. "o muro." In *Revista Continente Sul-Sur*. Rio Grande do Sul, Brazil: Editora Instituto Estadual do Livro.

Smith, Barbara. 2000. *The Truth That Never Hurts: Writings on Race, Gender, and Freedom*. New Brunswick, N.J.: Rutgers University Press.

Smith, Christen A. 2008. "Scenarios of Racial Contact: Police Violence and the Politics of Performance in Brazil." *E-misférica 5*, no. 2, http://www.hemisphericinstitute.org/hemi/es/e-misferica-52/smith.

———. 2009. "Strategies of Confinement: Environmental Racism, Police Terror, and the Built Environment in Brazil." In *Environmental Justice in the New Millennium: Global Perspectives on Race, Ethnicity, and Human Rights*, edited by Filomina Steady, 94–114. New York: Palgrave Macmillan.

Smith, Preston H., II. 2012. *Black Democracy and the Black Metropolis: Housing Policy in Postwar Chicago*. Minneapolis: University of Minnesota Press.

Sodré, Jaime. 2010. *Da diabolização à divinização: A criação do senso comum*. Salvador: EDUFBA.

Soja, Edward W. 2010. *Seeking Spatial Justice*. Minneapolis: University of Minnesota Press.

Souza, Marcelo Lopes de. 2008. *Fobópole: O medo generalizado e a militarização da questão urbana*. Rio de Janeiro: Bertrand Brasil.

Sterling, Cheryl. 2007. "Blackness Re-visited and Re-visioned in the Works of the Black Arts Movement and Quilomboje." In *The Afro-Brazilian Mind: Contemporary Afro-Brazilian Literary and Cultural Criticism*, edited by Niyi Afolabi, Marcio Barbosa, and Esmeralda Ribeiro, 51–72. Trenton, N.J.: Africa World Press.

———. 2010. "Women-Space, Power, and the Sacred in Afro-Brazilian Culture." *Global South 4*, no. 1, 71–93.

———. 2012. *African Roots, Brazilian Rites: Cultural and National Identity in Brazil*. New York: Palgrave Macmillan.

Stewart, Dianne M. 2005. *Three Eyes for the Journey: African Dimensions of the Jamaican Religious Experience*. New York: Oxford University Press.

Sudbury, Julia. 1998. *"Other Kinds of Dreams": Black Women's Organisations and the Politics of Transformation*. New York: Routledge.

Sugrue, Thomas. 1996. *The Origins of the Urban Crisis: Race and Inequality in Postwar Detroit*. Princeton, N.J.: Princeton University Press.

Telles, Edward E. 2006. *Race in Another America: The Significance of Skin Color in Brazil*. Princeton, N.J.: Princeton University Press.

Thomas, Miessha, Jerry Pennick, and Heather Gray. 2004. "What Is African-

American Land Ownership?," Federation of Southern Cooperatives Land Assistance Fund, http://www.federationsoutherncoop.com /aalandown04.htm.

Theoharis, Jeanne. 2013. *The Rebellious Life of Mrs. Rosa Parks.* New York: Beacon Press.

Trouillot, Michel-Rolph. 1995. *Silencing the Past: Power and the Production of History.* Boston: Beacon Press.

Twine, France Winddance. 1997. *Racism in a Racial Democracy: The Maintenance of White Supremacy in Brazil.* New Brunswick, N.J.: Rutgers University Press.

Ulysse, Gina A. 2008. *Downtown Ladies: Informal Commercial Importers, a Haitian Anthropologist, and Self-Making in Jamaica.* Chicago: University of Chicago Press.

United Nations General Assembly. 2012. "The Universal Declaration of Human Rights," Article 25, http://www.un.org/en/documents/udhr/index .shtml#a25.

U.S. Bureau of Democracy, Human Rights, and Labor. 2005. "Brazil." U.S. Department of State, http://www.state.gov/j/drl/rls/hrrpt/2004/41751 .htm.

Vargas, João H. Costa. 2004. "Hyperconsciousness of Race and Its Negation: The Dialectic of White Supremacy in Brazil." *Identities* 11, no. 4, 443–70.

———. 2006. "When a Favela Dared to Become a Gated Condominium: The Politics of Race and Urban Space in Rio de Janeiro " *Latin American Perspectives* 33, no. 4, 49–81.

———. 2008. "Activist Scholarship: Limits and Possibilities in Times of Black Genocide." In *Engaging Contradictions: Theory, Politics, and Methods of Activist Scholarship,* edited by Charles R. Hale, 164–82. Berkeley: University of California Press.

———. 2010. *Never Meant to Survive: Genocide and Utopias in Black Diaspora Communities.* Lanham, Md.: Rowman and Littlefield.

Vargas, João H. Costa, and Jaime Amparo Alves. 2009. "Geographies of Death: Intersectional Analysis of Police Lethality and the Racialized Regimes of Citizenship in São Paulo." *Racial and Ethnic Studies* 33, no. 4, 611–36.

Vine, David. 2009. *Island of Shame: The Secret History of the U.S. Military Base on Diego Garcia.* Princeton, N.J.: Princeton University Press.

Visweswaran, Kamala. 1994. *Fictions of Feminist Ethnography.* Minneapolis: University of Minnesota Press.

Vovô, Antonio Carlos. 2002. "No Ilê as coisas se modificam." In *Quem faz*

Salvador?, edited by Ana Maria de Carvalho Luz, 91–92. Salvador: EDUFBA.

Waiselfisz, Julio Jacobo. 2012. *Mapa da violência.* Rio de Janeiro: Centro Brasileiro de Estudos Latino-Americanos.

Wekker, Gloria. 2006. *The Politics of Passion: Women's Sexual Culture in the Afro-Surinamese Diaspora.* New York: Columbia University Press.

Werneck, Jurema. 2007. "Of Ialodês and Feminists: Reflections on Black Women's Political Action in Latin America and the Caribbean." *Cultural Dynamics* 19, no. 1, 99–113.

Wilding, Polly. 2012. *Negotiating Boundaries: Gender, Violence, and Transformation in Brazil.* New York: Palgrave Macmillan.

Williams, Erica Lorraine. 2013. *Sex Tourism in Bahia: Ambiguous Entanglements.* Champaign: University of Illinois Press.

Williams, Rhonda Y. 2005. *The Politics of Public Housing: Black Women's Struggles against Urban Inequality.* New York: Oxford University Press.

Williamson, Kenneth. 2012. "Night Becomes Day: Carnival, Contested Spaces, and the Black Movement in Bahia." *Journal of Latin American and Caribbean Anthropology* 17, no. 2, 257–78.

Winant, Howard. 2001. *The World Is a Ghetto: Race and Democracy since World War II.* New York: Basic Books.

Wright, Talmadge. 1997. *Out of Place: Homeless Mobilization, Subcities, and Contested Landscapes.* Albany: State University of New York Press.

INDEX

Page references in italics refer to illustrations.

activism, black: and Afro-Brazilian culture, 22, 24; gendered dimension of, xvii, 30, 75–81, 161–64; role of community in, 25; of Salvador, 35. *See also* antiracism resistance; grassroots organizations

activism, black women's: concerning land rights, 8, 148, 153, 163; effect on sexuality, 84, 85; family strategies in, 14; gendered dimension of, xvii, 30, 75–81; male perceptions of, 92; during military rule, 59; racial consciousness in, 26; relationship to black movement, 81–82, 85; spirituality in, 152–54, 156–61

activism, government-induced, 64

activists, black male, 161; political co-optation of, 163; sexism of, 164

activists, black women, xiv–xvii; in Brazilian urban communities, 151; challenges to hegemony, 160–66; defying of expectations, 168; in diaspora communities, 176–77; environmentalists, 158–59; ethics of, 160–61; invisibility of, 12–13, 166, 167; of Palestina, 14; personal transformations of, 165; public formations of, 58; racial identities of, 165; risks taken by, 161; spirituality of, 152–54, 156–61; strategies of, 150; struggle against police violence, 90; struggle for citizenship, 115; training for, 27; transformations of community, 165–66, 167; views of self, xvii

activists, black women (Gamboa de Baixo), xvi, 13, 55–56, 58–68, 70–86; as agents of change, 167; antiexpulsion publications, 65–55; on cholera outbreak, 60–61; civil disobedience by, 79; on collective rights, 166; CONDER protest by, 77–79; Contorno Avenue Protest of, 55–56, *57,* 121; on Contorno Revitalization Project, 62–63, 119; co-optation attempts toward, 163–64, 165; defying of expectations, 166–67; direct action by, 75–81; disruption of social order, 165–66; effect on community, 85, 165–66, 167–68; EMBASA protest, 76–77, 121–22, 160; financial freedom for, 84–85; gender identity of, 85–86; hostage taking by, 77–79; household responsibilities of, 146; housing activism of,

148, 162–63, 165; international resources of, 65; in land rights debates, 169–71; mobilization as residents, 152, 167–68; motivations of, 63; municipal government building protest, 57; personal life projects of, 148; political anthem of, 63, 170; political empowerment of, 64; political identities of, 40–41, 79–81; racial formation of, 85–86; radical formation of, 80; recruiting efforts of, 63; resistance to police violence, 118–19, 121, 138; security concerns of, 91–92, 94–97; self-esteem among, 80–81, 83, 85; self-identity among, 152; and state police action, 91; UFBA work of, 66. *See also* Associação Amigos de Gegê Dos Moradores da Gamboa de Baixo

Adriano (activist), 132, 133; flood damage problems, 98; meeting with Odebrecht, 145; participation in neighborhood association, 140–42; on police violence, 123

Africa: land expulsions in, 174–75; women landowners of, 156. *See also* diaspora, African

African American women: Brazilian studies by, xiii–xiv

agency, black Brazilian, xvii. *See also* black movements, Brazilian

Agnelo, Cardinal Dom Geraldo Majella, 105

Alexander, M. Jacqui, 157

Alto das Pombas neighborhood (Salvador), 28

Alto de Ondina neighborhood (Salvador), 29; state interventions in, 33, 34; topography of, 33–34

Amado, Jorge: *Sea of Death,* 153

Amnesty International on stresses of violence, 136, 137–38

Angela (activist), 71, 106

Annan, Kofi, 174–75

anthropology: solidarity work through, xix–xxi

antiracism resistance, xii, xiv–xvii, 21, 79; in black social movements, 157, 165; black women leaders of, xvi, 115; politics of, xvii. *See also* activism, black women's; grassroots organizations

Antônia (aunt of Telma dos Santos), 2, 4

Archdiocese of Bahia: Gamboa de Baixo's negotiations with, 101; property above Gamboa de Baixo, 99–101. *See also* Catholic Church

Articulação de Comunidades em Luta Por Moradia (grassroots organization), 11; *Como Salvador se faz,* 27; Gamboa de Baixo residents in, 20; housing forum of, 13–14, 27; tour of Salvador, 27–35

Assies, Willem, 64

Associação Amigos de Gegê Dos Moradores da Gamboa de Baixo: on cholera outbreak, 60–61; Contorno Avenue protest, 55–56; Council for the Defense of Gamboa de Baixo, 118–20; EMBASA protest, 76–77; general assemblies of, 142–44; Grupo de Mulheres in, 80–81, 86; meetings of, 139–46;

meetings with Odebrecht, 101, 106, 141, 144, 145; participation in Iemanjá celebrations, 154; as political space, 167; transfer of land titles to, 169; women's leadership of, 62–63. *See also* activists, black women (Gamboa de Baixo)

Avé-Lellement, Robert, 7

Bahia (Brazil): black diaspora in, 7; celebration of colonialism, 53; cultural preservation in, 49–50; culture of, 7; development agencies of, 104; domestic workers of, 146–52; gendered inequality in, 158; historical discourses of, 105; human rights abuses in, 124–25, 129–30; Ministério Público, 103; Navy, 48, 74, 169–71; police violence in, 124–25; poverty in, 5; racial inequality in, 158; urbanization programs of, 65, 171; Water and Sanitation Department, 60; white elites of, 89

Bahia Azul (sanitation company), 144

Bahia Marina Yacht Club (Salvador), 48, 105

Baiocchi, Gianpaolo, 64

Bairros, Luiza, xviii

Baixo das Quintas cemetery (Salvador), 132, 134

Banco dos Ingleses neighborhood (Salvador), 107; during COE raid, 111

Ban Ki-moon, 172–73

Bank of Brazil: profiling by, xi–xii

Bastide, Roger, 7

Bay of All Saints (Salvador), 5, 8, *18,* 37; ecological damage to, 105; neighborhoods facing, 40, 74; as spiritual resource, 160; tourism at, 50, 90

Belo Horizonte (Brazil): European model for, 43

black movements, Brazilian: effect on racial identity, 83; emergent needs for, 115; emphasis on racism, 165; neighborhood struggles in, xv–xvi, 58; scholarship on, 21–22; social programs for, 61; women activists' relationship to, 81–82, 85. *See also* activism, black

blackness: menacing meanings of, 50; as social category, xvii–xviii; visibility/invisibility of, 35–37

Black Panther Party for Self-Defense, 118

black politics, Brazilian: and cultural citizenship, 24; culture of, 20–26; identity formation in, 21, 79–81; invisibility of, 24; women in, 29, 79–81, 153. *See also* activism

blacks, Brazilian: criminalization of, 97, 107, 114–15; funeral rites of, 130–35; national heroes, 170; scholarship on, 24; social exclusion of, xviii, 36; socioeconomic barriers facing, 87–88

black women: global perceptions of, 166–67; marginalization of, 89; oppositional politics of, 153; political agency of, 166; racial profiling of, xi–xii; resistance by, 150; role in African diaspora, 153; stereotypes of, 16, 167

black women, African: ownership of land, 156

black women, Brazilian: access to resources, 9–10; collective memory of, 15, 52; as cultural producers, 157–58; cultural role of, 16, 157–58; education levels of, 165, 168; effect of urban restructuring on, 42; engagement with public policy, 15; experience of violence, xvi, 13–14, 120, 137; grassroots leadership by, xv–xvi, 11–16, 20, 23–34, 55–86, 160–61, 167–68; history of resistance, 13, 79; importance of streets for, 40–41; invisibility of, 166; marginalization of, 20; material resources of, 14, 85; morality of, 160–61; new freedoms for, 81–86; oppression of, 83; of Pelourinho, 45; police violence against, 120; political identities of, 25, 79–81; racial identities of, xviii; racial stereotypes of, 45; role in community building, 86, 146; socioeconomic barriers facing, 88; socioeconomic roles of, 15; spirituality of, 152–54, 156–61; stereotypes of, 171; unemployed, 88. *See also* activists, black women; domestic workers, Brazilian

Boa Morte, Valquíria, 60–61

Bomfim, Raiane, *69*

Bomfim, Simone, *69*

Bomfim family (Gamboa de Baixo), 68

Borges, Luciano, 51

Brandão, Ivan, 125

Brandão, Maria de Azevedo, 44

Brazil: black politics of, xvi–xvii, 20–26, 79–81, 153; black population of, 7; community–state relations in, 15; constitutional reform (1998), 10; cultural preservation in, 49–50; gender consciousness in, 167–68; homicide rate in, 125; ideology of streets in, 40–41; income levels in, 88–89; police violence in, 123–24; racial democracy ideology of, 21–22, 166; racial pluralism in, xviii; Secretariat for Politics of Promotion of Racial Equality, xviii; state–society relations in, 59; transition to democracy, 59; urbanization policies in, xx; white populations of, 9. *See also* Bahia

Brazilians: self-identification of, xviii–xix. *See also* blacks, Brazilian

Buenos Aires, modernist model of, 44

Caldeira, Teresa, 96, 113–14

Caldwell, Kia Lilly, 89

Camilo (activist), 112; experience of police violence, 125–26, 129–30; on women activists, 161

Caminha, Ana Cristina da Silva, xi–xii, xiv, 28, *69*, 113; on activism, 81–83; at Articulação de Comunidades forum, 14; on community change, 83–84; on community mobilization, 33; in CONDER protest, 78–79; on Contorno Avenue wall, 101, 102; domestic work of, 147–48, 150; in EMBASA protest, 76, *78*; on Gamboa de Baixo families, 68; home of, *96*; lecture at Brown University, 177; on male activists, 164; meeting with researchers,

166; participation in neighborhood association, 139–41, 143–45; police violence against, 109–12; security concerns of, 97; tribute to Dona Iraci, 131; university studies of, 135–36

Caminha family (Gamboa de Baixo), 68

Campo Grande neighborhood (Salvador): cholera threat to, 60

Campo Santo cemetery (Salvador), 131

Candomblé: as collectivizing force, 156; female deities of, 156; Iemanjá celebrations of, 144–45, 153–54, 154, 156–57; orixás of, 80, 81; as sociopolitical force, 168; suppression of, 41–43; women's leadership of, 41–43. See also spirituality; terreiros

Cardoso, Ruth Corrêa Leite, 59

Carneiro, Sueli, xviii–xix, 26, 165

Casa Branca terreiro: defacement of, 158

Catholic Church (Bahia): land owned by, 170; land usurpation by, 101. See also Archdiocese of Bahia

Center for Social Action Studies (CEAS, Salvador), 28, 64

Chicago School of Human Ecology, 44

children: police violence against, 120, 122

Chile: military regime of, 123–24

China: social protest in, 58

cholera: black women activists on, 60–61, 160

Cidade de Deus (film), 112–13

cities: consumption of history, 51; European models of, 43; fortress, 91–98; housing rights in, 172–73; modernist vision of, 44, 51; physical barriers in, 96–97

cities, Brazilian: Afro-Brazilian culture of, 9; black migrants to, 10, 72; class inequality in, 88; environmental justice in, 158–60; labor organizations of, 152; limitations of democracy in, 174; neighborhood segregation in, 43, 89, 91; physical barriers of, 95; race inequality in, 88; segregated neighborhoods of, 43, 89, 91; social transformation in, 157; spatial exclusion in, xv, 24, 26, 28, 40, 75

cities, U.S.: diasporic processes in, 176–77

citizenship, black: in communities, 81; cultural, 25; for Gamboa de Baixo residents, 120, 121; negation of, 9; rights of, 130; women activists' efforts for, 115

citizenship, Brazilian: for domestic workers, 153; ideology of, 22; land rights in, 170

class: in Brazilian slavery, 149; in Brazilian urban renewal, xix, 88; colonial legacy of, 15; divisions in Gamboa de Baixo, 67, 72; effect on material resources, 26; globalized processes of, 177; racism based in, 136; in sociospatial demarcation, 20; spatial distance dividing, 44; state-sponsored bias in, 9; in struggle over material resources, 26

Collins, Patricia Hill, 89, 150–51; on black feminist activism, 160–61; standpoint theory of, 152

colonialism, Brazilian: celebration

of, 47, 53; forts of, 47, 48–49; legacy of, 15; reinvention of, 52; in Salvador, 8, 43; spatial memories of, 50
colonialism, modern-day, 176
Comissão de Justiça e Paz da Arquidiocese de Salvador (CJP), 64
communities, black: access to natural resources, 158–60; citizenship rights in, 81; discourse of violence concerning, 107, 114; exclusion from planning process, 11–16; exploited women of, 151; grassroots politics of, 67–68, 70–75; human rights of, 176; internalization of violence, 136; in land rights movements, 11–16; marginalization of, 109, 115; material issues of, 85; police raids on, 108–9, 118, 137–38; policing of, 90; public erasure of, 105; relations with state, 15; resistance to violence, 138; role in black activism, 25; role in gender identity, 25; sanitation in, 159; stereotypes of, 171; women's building of, 86, 146. *See also* diaspora communities, African; neighborhoods, black urban
communities, fishing: of Gamboa de Baixo neighborhood, 33, 38, 70, *70,* 75, 84, 104, 123, 157; Iemanjá celebrations of, 153; of Salvador, 29, 74, 103; women of, 161
Companhia de Operações Especiais (COE), 114; raid on Gamboa de Baixo, 109–12. *See also* police, Brazilian

Conceição, Ana Célia Gomes, 1–3
CONDER (Companhia de Desenvolvimento Urbano do Estado da Bahia), 29, 34; meetings with Associação Amigos de Gegê Dos Moradores da Gamboa de Baixo, 141; protest against, 77–79
Contorno Avenue (Salvador), 18; construction of, xv, 37, 119; division of community, 37–39; impact on black population, 38; land appropriation for, 38; modernity of, 37; protest on (1997), 55–56, *57,* 121; revitalization along, 48; robberies on, 122; as socioeconomic barrier, 88; wall below, 94, *95,* 101–2, 108
Contorno Revitalization Project: Gamboa de Baixo activists on, 62–63, 119
Cordiviola, Chango, 36
Council for the Defense of Gamboa de Baixo, documentation of police violence, 118
Covin, David, 165
crime: in Gamboa de Baixo neighborhood, 127; homicide, 125; physical barriers to, 95–96. *See also* drug trafficking
criminality: elites' role in, 107; in perception of black neighborhoods, 16, 19, 91; perceptions concerning Gamboa de Baixo, 19, 38, 39, 67, 72, 90, 94–85, 107
Crispina (sister of Ana Cristina), 111
culture, Afro-Brazilian: attacks on, 24; of Bahia, 7; Bahian identity in, 35; and black activism, 22, 24; in black politics, xvi; commodification of, 50–51, 53; ethnographic study of, xiv; folkloric

aspects of, 22, 50; and grassroots movements, 152; of Salvador, 7–8; urban, 9; women's role in, 16, 157–58. *See also* spirituality

culture, Brazilian: house and street in, 40

culture, freedom to practice, 176

culture, Latin American: hypervisibility of, 24–25

Dávila, Jerry, 43

Davis, Mike, 91, 95–97

Declaration of Black Brazilian Women's Organizations, 148–49

Detinha, Dona, 74

diaspora, African: anthropology of, xix–xxi; futures for, 176–77; grassroots politics and, 152; human rights of, 130; land activism in, 175; racism in, xiv; religious traditions of, 160–61; in Salvador, 5, 7–8, 35; women's role in, 153

diaspora communities, African, xvii; anthropologists' role in, xxi; imagining of Africa, 156; liberation motif of, 157; participation in urban planning, 53; women's activism in, 176. *See also* communities, black

Dique do Cabrito neighborhood (Salvador): displacements from, 32; housing rights in, 31; waterway of, 32

displacement: everyday experience of, 24; global responses to, 174–75; grassroots activism against, 22; in Jamaica, 174, 176; threats to Gamboa de Baixo, xv, 17, 19, 65–67, 74, 83, 90, 97, 106, 137, 152; to urban periphery, 65;

violence of, 137–38, 172–73; in Zimbabwe, 174–75. *See also* land expulsion

domestic work: social movement theories of, 150–51

domestic workers: access to racial ideologies, 151–52; critique of racism, 151; observation of white elites, 151; "outsiders-within," 150, 167; racial exploitation of, 151–52; relationship with employers, 150, 167

domestic workers, Brazilian, 16, 19–20, 39, 146–52; access to education, 168; citizenship rights of, 153; cultural belonging for, 153; experience of gendered racism, 146; federal guarantees for, 149; invisibility of, 149, 168; leadership of terreiros, 152–54; resistance by, 149–50; unregistered, 149

domestic workers (Salvador), 16, 19–20, 39, 92; activism of, 146–47; exploitation of, 147, 148–49; of Gamboa de Baixo, 16, 19–20, 39, 92, 146–47; legal rights of, 147; unions of, 24, 147, 149; wages of, 147

drug trafficking: in Gamboa de Baixo, 92, 94–95, 126–28; violence in, 126, 128–30, 133–35, 138

elites, Brazilian: perception of police activities, 113; police protection of, 113–14; self-segregation of, 89, 91; urban space for, 36, 90

elites (Salvador): benefits of Operation Cleanup for, 47; role in criminalization, 107; spatial entitlement of, 102–6

EMBASA (Bahia Water and Sanitation Department), 60; construction of sewers, 144; meetings with Associação Amigos de Gegê Dos Moradores da Gamboa de Baixo, 141; protest against, 76–77, 121–22, 160
Espinheira, Gey: "Pelourinho," 45–46
ethnocentrism: in analysis of race, xiv

Federal University of Bahia (UFBA): study of Salvador, 35–36; work with Gamboa de Baixo activists, 66
Fishermen and Fisherwomen's Association (Gamboa de Baixo), 127
França, Geraldo (Gegê) Ferreira de, 60, 119, 143
Freyre, Gilberto, 20
funeral rites (Gamboa de Baixo): for Dona Iraci, 131–33, 135; for Dona Jacira, 132–33; for Raphael, 133–35

Gamboa de Baixo neighborhood (Salvador), 16–20, *49*; academics' reaction to, 82, 166–67; access to, 39, 122–23; access to material resources, 175; access to sea, 151; black males of, 135; burial practices of, 130–35; census of, 125; changes to, 83–84, 97; cholera outbreak in, 60–61; citizenship rights for, 120, 121; class divisions in, 67, 72; collective memory of, 70; community formation in, 72; community identity of, 68; crime in, 127; criminal discourse concerning,

19, 38, 39, 67, 72, 90, 94–95, 107; criminalization of, 127; cultural differences within, 74; demographics of, 16–17, 68, 70–75, 86; deteriorating perceptions of, 95; developers' misrepresentations of, 103–5; displacement threats to, xv, 17, 19, 65–67, 74, 83, 90, 97, 106, 137, 152; domestic workers from, 16, 19–20, 39, 92, 146–47; drug trafficking in, 92, 94–95, 126–28; effect of O Morada dos Cardeais on, 90, 98–99, 101–2, 106, 114; Elementary School and Community Center, 61, 142–43; environmental practices of, 152, 159; etymology of, 68; fear of police in, 122; Fishermen and Fisherwomen's Association, 127; fishing community of, 33, 38, 70, *70*, 75, 84, 104, 123; gay/lesbian members of, 85; gendered understandings of, 120–21; gender tensions in, 67; historical narratives of, 75; Iemanjá celebrations of, 144–45, 153–54, 156–57; impact of Contorno Avenue on, 38–39; inclusion in urbanization programs, 66–67; income levels in, 89; internal divisions within, 67, 72; kinship ties in, 68, 70, 72–74; land rights in, 68, 72, 79, 138, 157, 169–71; male activists of, 161; map of, *17, 73*; marginalization of, 19, 119, 128; media depictions of, 38–39, 67, 94; misrepresentations of, 107; in National Day of Black Consciousness, 58; negotiations with Archdiocese of Bahia, 101; newcomers to,

68, 70–71, 72–74, 162–63; as occupation, 68; occupations of, 70–71; panoramic view of, 17, *18*; police violence in, 94, *95*, 95–96, 97, 107, 108–14, 117–23, 127, 129–30; political autonomy of, 152; political identity within, 67–68, 72, 73, 79–81; political organizations of, xv, xvi, xvii, xix, 13–14, 23–24, 25–26, 54, 55–86; popular representations of, 18; positive image of, 138; in public imagination, 19; quality of life in, 66; racial consciousness in, 25–26; racialization of, 90, 120–21; racial tensions in, 67, 72; redevelopment plan for, 19; residential permanence for, 101, 138, 176; residents' stresses, 136–38; resistance in, 90, 121, 138; sanitation issues in, 60–61; security guards' harassment of, 105–6; security issues in, 91–92, 94–97, 98; self-containment in, 99; self-inclusion struggles of, 98; separation from Gamboa de Cima, 39; sexual freedom for, 84, 85; social abandonment of, 128; socioeconomic barriers in, 88; sociospatial character of, 19, 38; street protests in, 58; ties to Solar do Unhão, 162–63, 164; topography of, 17–18, 19–20; unemployment in, 71; violent deaths in, 97; visibility/ invisibility of, 37, 75; wall above, 99–100, *100*; walls in, 97, 99; water supply for, 60–61, 76–77; women leaders of, xvi, 16, 23–24, 28–29, 55–86, 143, 146, 161, 163; Women's Associa-

tion, 60, 86, 92. *See also* activists, black women (Gamboa de Baixo); Associação Amigos de Gegê Dos Moradores da Gamboa de Baixo

Gamboa de Cima neighborhood (Salvador), 18; during COE raid, 111; crime in, 107; separation from Gamboa de Baixo, 39; upper-class condominiums of, 107

gender: Brazilian concepts of, xiv, 167; colonial legacy of, 15; globalized processes of, 177; in grassroots organizations, 165–66; in neighborhood activism, 30, 35–81; role in black activism, xvii, 30, 75–81, 161–64; in sociospatial demarcation, 20; state-sponsored bias in, 9

gender identity: of Gamboa de Baixo activists, 85–86; role of community in, 25

Gilliam, Angela, 102

Gilmore, Ruth Wilson, 89

grassroots organizations: international solidarity among, 174

grassroots organizations, Brazilian: black women's leadership of, xv–xvi, 11–16, 20, 23–34, 55–86, 160–61, 168; community-based, 67–68, 70–75; and diaspora culture, 152; against displacement, 22; emergence of, 59; environmental, 158–60; gendered differences in, 165–66; international solidarity with, xx; neighborhood associations, 11–16, 22–23; resistance strategies of, 11–12; role of community in, 25. *See also* activism, black women's;

antiracism resistance; neighborhood organizations

Grupo de Mulheres (Gamboa de Baixo), 80–81, 86; discussions of racism, 81

Hanchard, Michael, 79; *Orpheus and Power*, 21–22

Harding, Rachel, 156

Harlem: gentrification of, 172

historical heritage: commodification of, 51–53; of Salvador, 43, 47–54

historical narratives: of Bahia, 105; construction of, 75; of Gamboa de Baixo, 75

Historic Center (Salvador). *See* Pelourinho

Holston, James, 11

hooks, bell, 89–90

housing rights: community struggles for, 176–77; United Nations on, 173

housing rights (Salvador), 30, 46, 66, 84, 90; black women's activism for, 148, 163, 165, 173–74

human rights: of African diaspora, 130; in black communities, 176; Brazilian abuses of, 123–25, 129–30; global issues, 172

identity, Brazilian: Bahian, 35; black women's, xviii, 165; Candomblé in, 41; gendered, 25; racial, xviii–xix, 21, 22, 83; racial politics of, xvii

Iemanjá (Candomblé goddess), 144; gifts to, 154

Iemanjá celebrations, 144–45, 153–54, *154*; activism in, 156–57; community formation in, 157;

women's leadership of, 153. *See also* Candomblé; terreiros

Ilê Aiyê (Afro-Brazilian cultural group), xix, 25, 35

Imbassahy, Antônio, 49

inclusion, politics of, 91–98

Institute of Applied Economic Research (IPEA), 124

Iraci Isabel da Silva Square (Salvador), 120

Itaparica Island (Salvador), 17

Ivana (activist), 73–74, 83

Jacira, Dona: funeral of, 132–33

Joelma (activist), 146

Juana, Dona (activist), 61

Karim, Aisha, 137

Kenyatta, Jomo, 158

Kingston (Jamaica): displacements in, 174, 176

Landes, Ruth: *The City of Women*, 41–42

land expulsion, 8–11; African, 174–75; by Catholic Church, 101; cultural politics of, 24; resistance against, xxi; in United States, 172. *See also* displacement

land expulsion (Salvador), 171; from inner city, 10, 46; from Pelourinho, 47, 48, 52, 62, 172; from Preguiça neighborhood, 48; from Rua Mangueira da Ribeira, 30

land rights: in African diaspora, 175; global, 171–72, 176–77; in United States, 177

land rights, Brazilian, 8–11; black women's activism for, 8, 148, 153,

163; black women's memory of, 15; in citizenship, 170; collective, 169–71; community movements for, 11–16; disputed, 2–3, 10–11; documentation of, 15, 72–73; environmental justice in, 160; legalization of, 20; racial struggles concerning, 25; role of spirituality in, 156–57; sociocultural aspects of, 156; socioeconomic freedom through, 10–11

land rights (Salvador), xv, 1–5, 169–71; in Gamboa de Baixo, 68, 72, 79, 138, 156, 169–71; media depiction of, xv, 1–5; transfer agreements for, 169–70

Lawrence, Bruce B., 137

Lefebvre, Henri: *The Production of Space*, 40

Lenilda, Dona (activist), 61; advocacy of unity, 72; political anthem of, 63, 170; recycling by, 71

Leo (activist), *119*; on Odebrecht, 104, 105

"Letter from the Black Youth of Salvador" (2003), 130

Los Angeles as fortress city, 91

Lueci (activist), *119*; advocacy of unity, 72; in CONDER protest, 78; in EMBASA protest, 76–77

Lula (activist), 141

Mãe Rosa (priestess), *159*

Marechal Rondon neighborhood (Salvador): development projects of, 31–32; housing rights in, 31; waterway of, 32

Maria, Dona (activist), 56, 76

Maria José (activist), 122, *155*; on Dona Iraci, 132; Iemanjá celebrations of, 144–45, 154; partici-

pation in neighborhood association, 140, 145

Marinalva, Dona (activist), 141, 142; meeting with Odebrecht, 145

martial arts, capoeira, 53, 139–40

material resources: access in Gamboa de Baixo, 175; black Brazilian women's, 14, 85; of black communities, 85; global struggle for, 157; role of class in, 26

McCallum, Cecilia, 16

McKittrick, Katherine, 89

Montevideo: modernist model of, 44

Movimento Negro Unificado (MNU), 22, 56, 64

Mugabe, Robert: urban reorganization under, 174–75

Museum of Modern Art Park of Sculptures (Salvador), 48

Nana (local resident), 85

Nanã (Candomblé goddess), 80, 81

National Day of Black Consciousness (Salvador, 2000), 56; Gamboa de Baixo in, 58

neighborhood organizations, black, xv–xvi, 11–16; effect on state practices, 58–59; emergence of, 59; gender in, 30; race in, 22–23

neighborhood organizations (Salvador), 11, 27, 56; of Gamboa de Baixo, xv, xvi, xvii, xix, 13–14, 23–26, 54, 55–86; relationship with NGOs, 64, 82. *See also* Associação Amigos de Gegê Dos Moradores da Gamboa de Baixo

neighborhoods, black urban: discourse of criminality for, 16, 19;

police destruction of, 91. *See also* communities, black
Neves, Edmilson, 2, 3
Nice, Dona (activist), 79, 80; participation in neighborhood association, 144, 145–46; on self-esteem, 81
Nicelia (sister of Ana Cristina), 110, 112, 136–37
nongovernmental organizations (NGOs), 11; of Salvador, 56, 64, 82
nuns, social work of, 61–62

Odebrecht company, 90, 98–99, 101; coastal development plans, 103; land purchases by, 142; meetings with Associação Amigos de Gegê Dos Moradores da Gamboa de Baixo, 101, 106, 141, 144, 145; misrepresentations by, 103–5, 106
Ogum (Candomblé god), 80, 81
Olodum (cultural organization), 25, 53
O Morada dos Cardeais (high rise, Salvador), 88, 90; during COE raid, 111; effect on Gamboa de Baixo, 90, 98–99, 101–2, 106, 114; impact of police action on, 109; landslide below, 98–99; marketing information for, 103; residents of, 102; security apparatuses of, 105, 108; wall below, 99–100, *100*
Operação Pente Fino (2008), 108–9
Operation Cleanup (Salvador), 46; benefits for elites, 47
Operation Murambatsvina (Zimbabwe), 174
Oxalá (Candomblé god), 80, 81

Oyá Onipó Neto terreiro, demolition of, 158, *159*

palafitas (wooden houses above water), 30–31
Palestina neighborhood (Salvador): family activism in, 14; media coverage of, 14; neighborhood association of, 3, 14; state-sponsored redevelopment of, 9; symbolism of, 14; urban renewal threat to, 1–5
Partido dos Trabalhadores (PT), 59
Pau da Lima neighborhood (Salvador): contaminated water in, 32–33
Pelourinho (Salvador): black women of, 45; changes to, 40–44; cleansing of, 44–47; de-Africanization of, 40–41; expulsions from, 47, 48, 52, 58, 62, 172; marketing of, 47; national patrimony status of, 47; prostitution in, 45–46; social abandonment of, 45, 53; social science research on, 46, 47; symbolic valorization of, 51, 52; tourism to, 46, 47, 53; as world heritage site, 47
Perry, Elizabeth, 58
Pinto, Makota Valdina, 158–59
police, Brazilian: abuse of power, 122; and black women activists, 91; cinema depictions of, 112–13; Companhia de Operações Especiais, 109–12, 114; extortion by, 122, 123; fear of, 122; formalization of equality, 90; helicopter use by, 109; Operação Pente Fino (2008), 108–9; politics of exclusion, 90; protec-

tion of elites, 113–14; raids on black communities, 108–9, 118, 137–38; repression of terreiros, 42; role in criminalization, 122; security for the poor, 98; state apparatus, 90, 107–14; use of technology, 109, 123; war against *marginais,* 109

police violence: activism against, 90, 118–19, 121–22; against children, 120, 122; daily, 90; documentation of, 118; against the elderly, 122; frequency of, 122; in Gamboa de Baixo, 94, 95, 95–96, 97, 107, 108–14, 117–23, 125–26, 127, 129–30; gendered nature of, 138; near holidays, 122; against males, 120, 125–26; statistics concerning, 123–24; in urban renewal, xv–xvi, 86, 90–91, 115; against women, 120

Ponta de Humaitá (Salvador), 50

poverty: feminization of, xvi

power relations, global, xiv

Preguiça neighborhood (Salvador): displacement of, 48

Projeto Habitar Brasil (urbanization program), 65

prostitution in Pelourinho, 45–46

quilombos (settlements of runaway enslaved Africans), legal recognition of, 10

race: Brazilian concepts of, xiv; in Brazilian urban renewal, xix; colonial legacy of, 15; within diasporic continuum, xiv; ethnocentric analyses of, xiv; globalized processes of, 177; in neighborhood movements, 22–23; in sociospatial demarcation, 20

racial consciousness, Brazilian, 21–22, 56, 58, 167–68; in Gamboa de Baixo community movement, 25–26, 67, 72

racial democracy, Brazilian: hegemonic values of, 22; ideology of, 21–22, 166

racism: class-based, 136; within diasporic continuum, xiv; ethnographic analysis of, xiii; gendered, 146; in majority-black countries, xii; in poverty, xvi; spatialized, 136; structural, 35, 58, 81; violent, 8

racism, Brazilian: ambiguity concerning, xviii; in cities, 88; complaint filed against, *xiii*; effect on terreiros, 41–42; gendered, xii, 23; institutional, 12, 20, 23, 43; mobilization against, 21; through profiling, xi–xii; in public sphere, 86; representational aspects of, 23; in Salvador, 35, 58, 81; scholarship on, 21; societal, 81; spatial exclusion in, 24; state-sponsored, xv, 9; systemic, 165, 168; in urbanization programs, 35, 58

Rama, Angel: *La ciudad letrada,* 36

Raphael (fisherman): funeral of, 133–35

Razack, Sherene, 138

Reis, Vilma, 114

Ribeira neighborhood (Salvador): beaches of, 29; revitalization of, 29–30

Rio de Janeiro: European model for, 43, 44; neighborhood activism in, 174; Olympic Games, 174, 177; urban periphery of, 174

Rio dos Macacos (Salvador): displacement from, 174

Rio Vermelho neighborhood (Salvador): Iemanjá celebrations of, 144, 153, *154*

Rita (activist), 77, *78,* 84, *93,* 111; burial of Dona Jacira, 132–33; domestic work by, 147, 148, 150, 151; experience of police violence, 117; participation in neighborhood association, 139, 141–43, 145–46; security problems of, 92, 94, 97

Rua Mangueira da Ribeira neighborhood (Salvador): apartheid in, 30; *palafitas* of, 30–31; relocation from, 30–31

sacizeiros (crack cocaine users), 92, 94

Salvador (Bahia): activists of, 35, 141; Afro-Brazilian culture of, 7–8; Articulação de Comunidades tour of, 27–35; Bahian identity of, 49; black diaspora in, 5, 7–8, 35; black laborers of, 7; cemeteries of, 131, 132; cholera outbreak in, 60–61, 160; Cidade Alta, 5, 37; Cidade Baixa, 5, 37; coastal population of, 88; colonial heritage of, 43; colonialism in, 8; commercial zone of, 37, 38; contrasts in, 35; de-Africanization of, 40–41, 43–44; demolition of beach cabanas in, *172;* economy of, 5; ecosystem of, 29; Europeanization of, 41; fishing communities of, 29, 74, 103; forts of, 47, 48–50; French urbanization in, 44; Gamboa de Cima, 18, 39, 107, 111; gated communities of, 89; historical heritage of, 43, 47–54; history of, 5; housing rights in, 30, 44, 66, 84, 90, 173–74; infrastructural changes in, 44; inner-city neighborhoods of, 9–10; intracommunity violence in, 92, 94, 96; LIMPURB agency, 139; map of, *6;* marginalized residents of, 19, 35; middle-class flight from, 45; migrants to, 72; murder rate in, 137; Museum of Modern Art Park of Sculptures, 48; neighborhood organizations of, 11, 27, 56; neighborhoods of, *28;* NGOs of, 56, 64, 82; Operation Cleanup, 46–47; Ponta de Humaitá, 50; protective services in, 98; public demonstrations in, 48, 56, *57;* racial divide in, 29, 36, 39, 81; radicalized feminization of, 42; sexism in, 81; slave trade in, 5, 8; socioeconomic barriers in, 88, 90; socioeconomic differences in, 29, 31; sociospatial order of, 66; structural racism in, 58; tenements of, 45; topography of, 5; tourism in, 29, 38, 46, 47, 50–52; UNESCO report on, 65; Urbanization Week (1935), 44; urban periphery of, 19, 65, 163, 174; Via Náutica initiative, 50; violent crime in, 97; "visible spectacle" of, 36; women environmentalists of, 158–60; women's social programs in, 60; world heritage sites of, 47; yacht clubs of, 48, 103, 105. *See also* Bay of All Saints; Contorno Avenue; domestic workers (Salvador);

Pelourinho; urban renewal (Salvador); *under names of specific neighborhoods*
Santa Rita, Rita (Ritinha) de Cassia Pereira, 28, 29–30, 165; in Grupo de Mulheres, 80; in land rights debate, 170; meeting with Odebrecht, 106, 145; participation in neighborhood association, 140, 143–44
Santos, Amilton dos: media coverage of, 12–13; during Palestina incident, 1, 3–5; residence of, 14
Santos, Cristiane Conceição: death of, 55–56
Santos, Luciana dos, xi–xii, xiv, 28, 29; tour of Alto de Ondina, 34
Santos, Milton, 52–53, 172
São Marcelo Fort (Salvador): restoration of, 47, 49, 50
São Marcos neighborhood (Salvador): flooding in, 32
São Paulo: police killings in, 124; poor residents of, 113; walls of, 96
São Paulo da Gamboa Fort (Salvador), 17, 140; ceremony at, 169–70; as national heritage site, 48; residents of, 48, *51,* 74; revitalization of, 48–49, 50
Sapucaia family (Gamboa de Baixo), 68
Scheper-Hughes, Nancy, 130
Scott, David, xx
Sena, Telma Sueli dos Santos: activism of, 1–3, *4,* 8, 10, 13; at Articulação de Comunidades forum, 13–14
Serra, Ordep, 7
sexism: ethnographic analysis of,

xiii; in public sphere, 86; in Salvador, 81. *See also* gender
Silva, Benedita da, 59
Silva, Iracema Isabel da (Dona Iraci), xvi, *119;* death of, 118, 120, 130–32; on expulsions, 63, 66–67; family of, 118; on fishing community, 75; funeral of, 131–33, 135; landmark commemorating, 120; on police violence, 121; resistance to police violence, 118, 120, 121–22
Silveira, Oliveira: "O muro," 87–88
Simone (local resident): home of, 95–96, *96;* during police violence, 109–12; security problems of, 95–96, 97
Sindicato das Lavadeiras, 147
Sindicato das Trabalhadoras Domésticas (Bahia), 147
slavery, Brazilian: hierarchies of, 149; violence of, 8
slaves, black women: sexual exploitation of, 45
slave trade in Salvador, 5, 8
Soares, Elza, 77
social justice: geographical aspects of, 89–90
social movements, Brazilian, 22; anthropologists' role in, xx–xxi; anticolonialism in, 157; antiracism in, 157; groups comprising, 22; issue-based, 24. *See also* activism; black movements, Brazilian
social movements, neighborhood-based. *See* neighborhood organizations
social science: U.S. blacks in, xiii–xiv
Solar do Unhão neighborhood

(Salvador), 104; activists of, 162–63; male leadership of, 162, 163, 164; ties to Gamboa de Baixo, 162–63, 164; urbanization projects in, 162, 163

space, urban, xv, 24, 26, 28; black women in, 40–41, 79; elites' claiming of, 90, 102–6; environmental reform of, 158–60; exclusion from, xv, 24, 26, 28, 40; loss of, 30; marginalized residents of, 9; public sociability of, 40, 41; racialized, 54, 86, 158–59; sexism in, 86; struggles for, 114–15

spatial consciousness, 40

spirituality, Afro-Brazilian: feminist ethics of, 160–61; role in land rights activism, 156–57; sea in, 156, 160; women's, 152–54, 156–61. *See also* Candomblé; terreiros

Stang, Sister Dorothy, 61–62

state–society relations, Brazilian: effect on national policies, 58–59

Stelmach, Adolfo, 2–3, 5

Stewart, Dianne M., 157

streets, in Brazilian culture, 40–41

subjectivity, black Brazilian: changing representations of, xiv

terra de mulheres negras (black women's land), 15

Terreiro do Cobre in Federação, 158

terreiros (Candomblé houses of worship), 30; effect of racism on, 41–42; gender solidarity in, 157; in neighborhood life, 42; police repression of, 42; racial solidarity in, 158; as sociopolitical spaces, 42, 156; women's leadership of, 41–43, 152–54, 156. *See also* Candomblé; spirituality

tourism (Salvador), 29, 38; at Bay of All Saints, 90; black culture in, 50–51, 53; historical, 52; to Pelourinho, 46, 47, 53; violence affecting, 107

Tropa de Elite (film), 113

Trouillot, Michel-Rolph, 74–75

Twine, France Winddance, 21

União de Negros pela Igualdade (UNEGRO), 22, 56, 64

United Nations: Habitat II Conference (1996), 64–65; Special Rapporteur on Torture, 124; Universal Declaration of Human Rights, 173

United Nations Educational, Scientific, and Cultural Organization (UNESCO) report on Salvador, 65

United States: Bureau of Democracy, Human Rights, and Labor, 124; land expulsions in, 173; land rights in, 177

Universal Declaration of Human Rights Article 25, 173

Urbanization Week (Salvador, 1935), 44

urban renewal: community participation in, 175–76; global, 8–9; production of knowledge concerning, 175; slash-and-burn approaches to, 177; social belonging during, 75; U.S. models of, 44; violent displacement in, 137–38, 172–73

urban renewal, Brazilian: activists' analysis of, xix; in Bahia, 65, 171; benefits for elites, 36; black participation in, 53; for capital accumulation, 47; class in, xix; col-

lective memory of, 58; colonial roots of, 171; dynamics of, 15; European models of, 43; exclusionary practices of, 24, 26, 28, 40, 75; forced relocations under, xv; hygienic considerations in, 46; institutional racism in, 43; knowledge production for, xx; police violence in, xv–xvi, 86, 115; racial patterns in, xix, 35, 58; in Rio de Janeiro, 174, 177; state-sponsored, 8–11; World Bank funding for, 47
urban renewal (Gamboa de Baixo): protests against, 58–86
urban renewal (Salvador), xv, 156; activists' challenges to, 66; coastal, 88, 103, 137, 171; community relations during, 90; exclusionary practices of, 75; of historical sites, 47–54; NGOs opposing, 64; nostalgia in, 51; in Palestina neighborhood, 1–5; police violence in, 90–91; racism in, 35, 90; stages of, 48; vertical construction in, 88, 98–102, 100
usucapião (adverse possession), 11

Via Náutica initiative (Salvador), 50
Vila Brandão neighborhood (Salvador): displacement from, 171
Vilela, Teotônio, 123–24
Vilma, Dona, 169
violence: affecting tourism, 107; against black women, xvi, 13–14, 120, 137; against Brazilian blacks, 114; community resistance to, 138; of displacement, 137–38, 172–73; drug-related, 126, 128–30, 133–35, 138; internaliza-tion of, 136; intracommunity, 92, 94, 96, 129, 130, 138; racial, 8; in Salvador, 97; state, 107–14; stresses of, 136, 137–38; structural, xvi, 13–14, 138. See also police violence
Visweswaran, Kamala, xx–xxi
Vitória neighborhood (Salvador), 39; cholera threat to, 60; residences of, 102–3; security guards of, 105–6; transportation from, 103
Viver Melhor (Better Living, program), 65
Voices for Communities Fighting for Housing Rights (Salvador), 141
Vovô, Antonio Carlos, 35

walls: barriers against crime, 95–96; below O Morada dos Cardeais, 99–100, 100; of Gamboa de Baixo, 97; social meaning of, 88, 89
water resources, 158, 160; community struggles for, 176; contaminated in, 32–33; for Gamboa de Baixo, 76–77
Women's Association (Gamboa de Baixo), 60, 86, 92
Woods, Clyde, 89
World Bank fund for Brazilian revitalization, 47
World Urban Forum (Naples, 2012), 173
Wright, Talmadge, 40

Zequinha (husband of Simone), 110, 111
Zimbabwe: displacements in, 174–75